Henry Veltmeyer is Professor of Sociology and International Development at St Mary's University in Halifax, Nova Scotia, Canada, and Visiting Professor of Political Science at the Autonomous University of Zacatecas, Mexico. He has published in the areas of sociological theory, Canadian political economy and issues of class and development in Latin America. He is the author of several books, including *The Canadian Class Structure*, *Canadian Corporate Power* and (with F. Leiva and J. Petras) *Poverty and Democracy in Chile*.

James Petras is Professor of Sociology and Latin American studies at Binghamton University, New York, USA. He is the author of over thirty books dealing primarily with Latin America, including *Neoliberalism and Class Conflict in Latin America*. He has published over 250 articles in professional journals, including the *British Journal of Sociology*, the *American Sociological Review* and the *Journal of Peasant Studies*. He has lectured at major universities in Europe, Latin America, the Caribbean, Australia, Asia and North America, and has contributed essays to *Le Monde Diplomatique*, *El Mundo*, the *Guardian* and *La Jornada*.

INTERNATIONAL POLITICAL ECONOMY SERIES

General Editor: Timothy M. Shaw, Professor of Political Science and International Development Studies, and Director of the Centre for Foreign Policy Studies, Dalhousie University, Halifax, Nova Scotia

Titles include:

Leslie Elliott Armijo (*editor*)
FINANCIAL GLOBALIZATION AND DEMOCRACY IN EMERGING MARKETS

Gabriel G. Casaburi
DYNAMIC AGROINDUSTRIAL CLUSTERS
The Political Economy of Competitive Sectors in Argentina and Chile

Matt Davies
INTERNATIONAL POLITICAL ECONOMY AND MASS COMMUNICATION IN CHILE
National Intellectuals and Transnational Hegemony

Yvon Grenier
THE EMERGENCE OF INSURGENCY IN EL SALVADOR
Ideology and Political Will

Jerry Haar and Anthony T. Bryan (*editors*)
CANADIAN–CARIBBEAN RELATIONS IN TRANSITION
Trade, Sustainable Development and Security

Tricia Juhn
NEGOTIATING PEACE IN EL SALVADOR: Civil–Military Relations and the Conspiracy to End the War

R. Lipsey and P. Meller (*editors*)
WESTERN HEMISPHERE TRADE INTEGRATION
A Canadian–Latin American Dialogue

Don Marshall
CARIBBEAN POLITICAL ECONOMY AT THE CROSSROADS
NAFTA and Regional Developmentalism

Juan Antonio Morales and Gary McMahon (*editors*)
ECONOMIC POLICY AND THE TRANSITION TO DEMOCRACY
The Latin American Experience

Henry Veltmeyer, James Petras and Steve Vieux
NEOLIBERALISM AND CLASS CONFLICT IN LATIN AMERICA
A Comparative Perspective on the Political Economy of Structural Adjustment

---

International Political Economy Series
Series Standing Order ISBN 0–333–71708–2 hardcover
Series Standing Order ISBN 0–333–71110–6 paperback
(*outside North America only*)

You can receive future titles in this series as they are published by placing a standing order. Please contact your bookseller or, in case of difficulty, write to us at the address below with your name and address, the title of the series and one or both of the ISBNs quoted above.

Customer Services Department, Macmillan Distribution Ltd
Houndmills, Basingstoke, Hampshire RG21 6XS, England

The Dynamics of Social Change in Latin America

Henry Veltmeyer
Professor of Sociology and International Development Studies
Department of Sociology
Saint Mary's University
Halifax

and

James Petras
Professor of Sociology and Latin American Studies
Binghamton University
New York

First published in Great Britain 2000 by
MACMILLAN PRESS LTD
Houndmills, Basingstoke, Hampshire RG21 6XS and London
Companies and representatives throughout the world

A catalogue record for this book is available from the British Library.

ISBN 0–333–74937–5

First published in the United States of America 2000 by
ST. MARTIN'S PRESS, INC.,
Scholarly and Reference Division,
175 Fifth Avenue, New York, N.Y. 10010

ISBN 0–312–22277–7

Library of Congress Cataloging-in-Publication Data
Veltmeyer, Henry.
The dynamics of social change in Latin America / Henry Veltmeyer, James Petras.
p. cm. — (International political economy series)
Includes bibliographical references and index.
ISBN 0–312–22277–7 (cloth)
1. Social change—Latin America. 2. Free enterprise—Latin America. 3. Latin America—Economic conditions—1982– 4. Latin America—Social conditions—1982– 5. Social movements—Latin America. I. Petras, James F., 1937– . II. Title. III. Series.
HN110.5.A8V42 1999
303.4'098—dc21 99–21890
CIP

© Henry Veltmeyer and James Petras 2000

All rights reserved. No reproduction, copy or transmission of this publication may be made without written permission.

No paragraph of this publication may be reproduced, copied or transmitted save with written permission or in accordance with the provisions of the Copyright, Designs and Patents Act 1988, or under the terms of any licence permitting limited copying issued by the Copyright Licensing Agency, 90 Tottenham Court Road, London W1P 0LP.

Any person who does any unauthorised act in relation to this publication may be liable to criminal prosecution and civil claims for damages.

The authors have asserted their rights to be identified as the authors of this work in accordance with the Copyright, Designs and Patents Act 1988.

This book is printed on paper suitable for recycling and made from fully managed and sustained forest sources.

10 9 8 7 6 5 4 3 2 1
09 08 07 06 05 04 03 02 01 00

Printed and bound in Great Britain by
Antony Rowe Ltd, Chippenham, Wiltshire

Contents

List of Tables	viii
List of Acronyms and Abbreviations	ix
Acknowledgements	xi

1 Development in the New Imperial Context of Globalization   1
    Critical Issues in the Globalization/Imperialism Debate   3
    The Dynamics of Change   3
    The Economic Benefits of Globalization and
      their Distribution   12
    The Political Dimension of Economic Restructuring and
      Globalization: the Question of Governance   15
    Labour in the World Economy   17
    Forces of Opposition and Resistance   18
    The Dynamics of Change in Latin America   19

2 Neoliberalism and the Search for Another Development   21
    Neoliberalism in Theory and Practice   21
    The Neoliberal Project   21
    Neoliberal Policy and Politics: Socioeconomic Impacts
      and Political Responses   24
    Structural Adjustment with a Human Face:
      The Model of Social Liberalism   28
    The War against Poverty: the NSP in Practice   31
    The Search for Alternative Development   36
    A New Paradigm?   36
    Forms of Alternative Development   37
    ECLAC and the Neostructuralist Model   41

3 The Restructuring of Labour   45
    Introduction   45
    Latin American Labour in a Global Context   46
    Labour Market Reform: A New Regime of Accumulation   48
    The Capital–Labour Relation in the Organization of
      Production   49
    Productive Transformation   49
    Production and Income Shares of Capital and Labour   50

	By Way of a Conclusion: Forms of Exploitation in the Production Process	55
4	**The Politics of Community-based Participatory Development**	**60**
	Introduction	60
	The Itinerary of a Concept	61
	The Latin American Experience of Decentralization: The Dynamics of a Democratization Process	65
	The Context of Decentralization	65
	Development 'from Above'	67
	Development 'from Below'	69
	The Limits of Community-based Participatory Development and Local Democracy	72
	Conclusions	75
5	**The Dynamics of Neoliberal Electoral Politics**	**77**
	The Neoliberal Political Cycle: First-Wave Regimes	77
	The Neoliberal Political Cycle: Second-Wave Regimes	80
	The Neoliberal Political Cycle: Third-Wave Regimes	85
	From Critics to Celebrants: Entrenching the Neoliberal Agenda	91
	Impoverishing Societies: The Crisis Multiplier in Neoliberalism	94
	Conclusion	98
6	**New Social Movements in Latin America: The Dynamics of Class and Identity**	**99**
	Introduction	99
	The Postmodern Agenda: A New Pivot of Social Analysis	101
	Postmodernism and New Social Movements in Latin America	105
	New Social Movements in Latin America: The Construction of Social Identity versus the Politics of Class	106
	Postmodernism in Perspective	110
	Counterpoints of Class: Fragments of an Alternative Form of Analysis	111
	The Latin American Peasantry: The Emergence of a New Force for Social Change	115
	Conclusions	119

7 Neoliberalism and the Latin American Left: The Search for a Socialist Project — **122**

Introduction — 122
The Itinerary of the Political Class: From
  the Barricades to the Ballot Box — 123
Social Organizations and Movements — 126
NGOs and Participatory Development:
  Solidarity from Below — 128
New Class Movements in the Countryside — 132
The Zapatista Challenge : The Dynamics of
  an Indigenous Movement — 134
The Formation of the EZLN and
  the Question of Ideology — 136
The 1 January 1994 Uprising: a People Under Arms — 138
Negotiations and the Appeal to Civil Society:
  The Transmutation of the EZLN into
  a Force for Democracy — 139
Transmutation of the EZLN and the Unity of
  Opposition Forces — 140
What is to be done in the Current Context?
  The Bases of a Socialist Alternative — 141
What are the Options Available to the Left? — 143

Notes — 145
Bibliography — 191
Index — 206

List of Tables

3.1	Levels of productive investment and capital formation, 1980–95, selected countries	50
3.2	Factor contributions to economic growth (percentages)	51
3.3	Wage income conditions in Latin America	53
3.4	Share of wages in GNP, selected Latin American countries	54
3.5	Employee earnings as a percentage of value added to manufacturing production	54
3.6	Dimensions of surplus labour and underdevelopment in Latin America, 1993–4	56

List of Acronyms and Abbreviations

AD	alternative development
ADC	Alianza Democratics de Campesinos [Democratic Peasant Alliance](El Salvador)
AMMAC	Mexican Association of Municipalities
CBO	community-based organizations
CDN	National Democratic Convention (Mexico)
CED	community economic development
CEO	chief executive officer
CEPAL	Economic Commission of Latin America (UN)
CBT	General Confederation of Workers (Argentina)
CNC	Nacional Confederation of Peasants (Mexico)
COB	Central de Obreros Boliviano (Confederation of Bolivian Unionized Workers)
CONAIE	National Confederation of Indigenous Peoples (Ecuador)
CTM	Confederación de Trabajadores Mexicana (Confederation of Mexican Workers)
EAP	economically active population
ECLAC	as CEPAL
EPI	industrialization by export promotion [export promotion industrialization]
EZLN	Zapatista Army of National Liberation (Mexico)
FDI	foreign direct investment
FHIS	Honduras Fund of Social Investment
FMLN	Military Forces of National Liberation (El Salvador)
FOSIS	Solidarity Social Investment Fund (Chile)
GATT	General Agreement on Tariffs and Trade
GNP	gross national product
GRO	as CBO
ICPF	International Commission on Peace and Food
IDB	Inter-American Development Bank
IFAD	International Fund for Agriculture and Development
IFIs	international financial institutions
ILO	International Labour Organisation
IMF	International Monetary Fund
LDC	least developed country

MAI	Multilateral Agreement on Investment
MDC	most developed country
NAFTA	North American Free Trade Agreement
NEM	neoliberal policy of adjustment
NGO	non-government organization
NIDL	new international division of labour
NPM	new peasant movement
NSM	new social movement
NSP	new social policy
OECD	Organization for Economic Cooperation and Development
OTB	Organizaciones Teritoriales de Base (Bolivia)
PT	Workers Party (Brazil)
RGC	rapidly growing country
SAP	structural adjustment programme
SIF	social investment fund
TC	Trilateral Commission
TNC	transnational corporation
WB	World Bank
WEF	World Economic Forum
WTO	World Trade Organization

Acknowledgements

The authors would like to gratefully acknowledge a generous grant from the Social Science and Humanities Research Council of Canada. It was a critical factor in the field research conducted in the preparation of this book.

The authors would like to dedicate this book to Annette and Robin, our companions in life, love and struggle, who have supported our efforts in steadfast good humour.

HENRY VELTMEYER
JAMES PETRAS

1 Development in the New Imperial Context of Globalization

Globalization is at the centre of diverse intellectual and political agendas, raising as it does crucial questions about what is widely considered to be the fundamental dynamic of our time – an epoch-defining set of changes that has radically transformed social and economic relations and institutions on the eve of the twenty-first millennium.

Globalization is both a description and a prescription. As description it refers to the widening and deepening of the international flows of trade, capital, technology and information in a single integrated global market. As with such terms as 'the global village' it serves to identify a complex of changes produced by the dynamics of capitalist development as well as the diffusion of values and cultural practices associated with this development.[1] In this context, reference is often made to changes in the capitalist organization of production and society, extensions of a process of capital accumulation hitherto played out largely at the national level, restricted to the confines (and the regulatory powers) of the nation-state. As prescription, globalization involves the liberalization of national and global markets in the belief that free flows of trade, capital and information will produce the best outcome for growth and human welfare.[2] At both levels (in the form of either description or prescription), globalization is presented with an air of inevitability and overwhelming conviction, betraying ideological roots.

How these epoch-defining developments and changes are interpreted depend in part on how globalization is conceived. Most do so as a process inscribed in the structures of the operating system based on the capitalist mode of global production. Others, however, conceive of it not in structural terms but as the outcome of a consciously pursued strategy, the political project of a transnational capitalist class formed on the basis of an institutional structure set up to serve and advance the interests of this class.

We have here a major divide in analysis. On the one hand, those who view globalization as a set of interrelated processes tend to see it as inevitable, something to which necessary adjustments can and should be made. This is even the case for analysts and theorists like Keith Griffin

(1995) on the left of the well-defined ideological divide within the field of development studies, a well-known proponent of Human Development as defined by the UNDP, and a declared advocate of radical change or social transformation. From this perspective (the inevitability of globalization), the issue is how a particular country, or group of countries, can adjust to changes in the world economy and insert themselves into the globalization process under favourable conditions. Griffin, for one, believes that such integration and adjustment is both necessary and possible. The issue, he argues, is how the forces driving the globalization process can be harnessed to serve the requirements of human development.[3]

On the other hand, those who view globalization as a project rather than as a process tend to see the developments and changes associated with it in different terms. In the first place, globalization is regarded as not a particularly useful term for describing the dynamics of the process. It is seen, rather, as an ideological tool, used for prescription rather than accurate description. In this context it is counterposed with a term accorded greater descriptive value and explanatory power: *imperialism*.[4] The network of institutions that define the structure of the new global economic system is viewed as intentional and contingent, subject to the control of individuals that represent and seek to advance the interests of a new capitalist class formed on the basis of institutions that include a complex of some 37 000 transnational corporations (TNCs), the operating units of global capitalism, bearers of capital and technology, and the major agents of imperialism. The World Bank, the International Monetary Fund (IMF) and other international financial institutions (IFIs) constitute the self-styled 'international financial community' or what Barnet and Cavanagh (1994) term 'the global financial network'. A host of global strategic planning and policy forums such as the G-7, the Trilateral Commission (TC) and the World Economic Forum (WEF); as well as the nation-state, restructured to serve and respond to the interests of global capital, form an integral part of the imperial system.

From this alternative perspective, globalization is neither inevitable nor necessary. Like the projects of capitalist development that preceded it – modernization, industrialization, colonialism, and development[5] – the new imperialism is fraught with contradictions which generate forces of opposition and resistance and which can, and under certain conditions will, undermine the capital accumulation process as well as the system on which it depends. The collapse of the Asian economies (Indonesia, South Korea, Thailand, Malaysia) is deeply rooted in their integration into the world's financial markets and the highly volatile movement of international capital. The globalists emphasize the constraints placed on government policy or the action of social groups, the strategies pursued by diverse social organizations, and the possibility of significant or substantial (systemic) change. The critics of globalism on the other hand, emphasize the opportunities and emergence of social forces for change provoked by the social contradictions of the imperialist system, developments that chronically disrupt all areas of life under capitalism. At issue in this controversy are the conflicting interests at play, the forces of opposition and resistance generated, and the practical political possibilities for mobilizing these social forces.

The inevitability of globalization as the context for the identifiable changes and developments *is a major issue*, although more often taken for granted than debated. However, it is by no means the only question that needs to be explored and settled. The aim and purpose of this book is to understand and explain some of the critical developments of our time, and to identify the fundamental issues involved in the current debate on globalization or imperialism, limited as it is.

To this end we focus on the critical issues which relate to the dynamics of social change in Latin America. The process or project of globalization (or imperialism) create conditions that provide the context within which this change occurs.

CRITICAL ISSUES IN THE GLOBALIZATION/IMPERIALISM DEBATE

The Dynamics of Change

There is little question about the profound changes undergone by capitalism in its national and global form of development in the post-World War II period. This is particularly true in the context of a deep systemic crisis that beset the system in the late 1960s. Nor is there much argument about the capitalist nature of the economic and social organization that has been put into place or that has emerged. That this organization has taken and is increasingly taking a global form also is not under dispute. In fact, this is the defining characteristic of the epochal shift that has occurred. What is disputed, however, is the significance and meaning of these changes, and the question as to whether globalization represents a qualitatively new phenomenon or, as argued by the authors, another phase of a long historical process of imperialist expansion.

Whatever view is taken on this point, and it is hotly disputed, it is possible to identify within the history of capitalist development a series of long waves, each of which is associated with a protracted period of crisis (in the conditions of capital accumulation) and a subsequent restructuring of the whole system. The last of these waves can be periodized roughly from the 1920s to the 1970s. By drawing on diverse perspectives on this development, we can identify some defining characteristics of the system put into place, the key elements of its structure:[6]

1. The concentration and centralization of capital that ensued in the last decades of the nineteenth-century, in the context of a system-wide crisis in the late 1870s, resulted in the merging of large industrial and financial forms of capital, the growth of corporate monopolies, the territorial division of the world into colonies, the export of capital, and the world-wide extension of the market based on a division of labour between countries specializing in the production of manufactured goods and those oriented towards the production of raw materials and commodities.[7]
2. The adoption of a Fordist regime of accumulation and mode of regulation resulted in a system of mass production and the scientific management of labour at the point of production within diverse formations of the nation state.
3. Under pressure from labour unions and Left parties a series of state-led economic and social reforms created the political conditions for a capital–labour accord on the share of labour in productivity gains, the social redistribution of market-generated income, and the legitimacy of a capitalist state based on the provision of social programmes (welfare, health and education) and the guarantee of full employment. In the pre-World War II context, these reforms were designed to save the capitalist system from its contradictory features and its propensity towards crisis. In addition, the representatives of the capitalist class accepted welfare reforms to compete with the new communist welfare states for the allegiance and loyalties of the working class in Europe, Asia and the rest of the Third World. These welfare reforms did not end the class struggle but did push it into reformist channels. These reforms, which in effect responded to some of the demands made by Marx in the Communist Manifesto, resulted in what Patel (1994) has termed 'the taming of capitalism'. In the post-war context, the deepening of social reforms temporarily instituted a social democratic form of state capitalism, a state-led capitalist development which served to expand production on both a national and a global scale.

4. In a post-World War II context of an East–West division of the world, the hegemony of the US within the world economic system, a decolonization process, and the resolve (at Bretton Woods) to impose a liberal world economic order created the framework for twenty-five to thirty years of continuous rates of rapid economic growth and capitalist development – the Golden Age of Capitalism.[8] Within the institutional framework and economic structure of this world order, and through the agency of the nation state, a large part of the developing world, countries organized as the Group of 77 within the United Nations system, were incorporated into the development process, initiating what Patel (1992) has termed the 'Golden Age of the South', characterized by high rates of economic growth and major advances in social development.
5. The nation-state in many instances was converted into an agency for development. Implementing an economic model based on nationalism, an industrialization and modernization strategy, the protection of domestic industry, and the deepening and extension of the domestic market to incorporate sectors of the working class and direct producers.

By the end of the 1960s this system experienced cracks in its foundation and began to fall apart under (structural and political) conditions of a system-wide crisis: stagnant production, declining productivity, and intensified class conflict over higher wages, greater social benefits and better working conditions. These conditions created a profit-crunch on invested capital.[9] In this context, two streams of political economy thinking emerged, one emphasizing the inherent tendency of capitalism towards crisis and the social contradictions that chronically disrupt all areas of capitalist life,[10] the other laying stress and focusing on various forms and levels of response to systemic crisis.

In these terms, it is possible to identify several responses:

1. *Diverse efforts of the US administration* to offset world market pressures on its production apparatus that were reflected in a rapidly deterioration in its trade balance and the loss of market shares to the economies of Germany and Japan. These efforts took a number of forms, including the unilateral abrogation of the Bretton Woods agreement on the value and thus the exchange rate of the US dollar (with a fixed gold standard) and the manipulation by the Federal Reserve Board of exchange and interest rates.[11]

6   Dynamics of Social Change in Latin America

2. *Relocation by the transnational corporations* (*TNCs*) of their labour-intensive industrial operations in the search for cheaper labour. In the process there emerged a new international division of labour (NIDL) characterized by the growth of a new global production system based on the operations of the TNCs and their affiliates, now estimated by UNCTAD to number some 206 000.[12] By 1980, the world's top 200 TNCs had an annual turnover exceeding three trillion dollars, equivalent to almost 30 per cent of gross world production and an estimated 70 per cent of international trade.[13] According to UNCTAD, 50 per cent of these operations, in terms of their market value, did not involve the world market but consisted of intra-firm transfers.

3. *The internationalization of capital* in both productive forms (investment to extend trade and expand production) and unproductive or speculative forms. The driving force behind this process was a policy of liberalization and deregulation. This strategy was designed and fostered by economists associated with the IFIs and adopted all over the world by governments that were either dominated by transnational capital or subject to its dictates. In this connection, the first form of capital to be internationalized and to escape the regulatory powers of the state involved the formation of offshore capital markets based on portfolio investments which speculated on foreign currency exchange rates. From the mid-1970s to the early 1990s the daily turnover of the foreign exchange markets climbed from 1 billion to 1.2 trillion dollars a day, close to 20 times the value of daily trade in goods and services.[14] Joel Kurtzman, editor of the *Harvard Business Review*, estimates that for every US dollar that circulates in the real economy 25–50 dollars circulates in the world of pure finance. Less than 5 per cent of circulating capital has any productive function whatsoever.[15] On the heels of these globalizing and ballooning money markets, which are defined by UNCTAD as 'less visible but infinitely more powerful' (in their effects than other capital flows),[16] a number of banks in the 1970s began to internationalize their operations, resulting in a large-scale debt financing of government operations and development projects in countries all over the developing world. This was particularly the case in Mexico, Argentina and Brazil, countries that collectively received by volume over 50 per cent of all such loans extended to countries in the developing world. In 1972 the estimated value of the overseas loans extended by these banks was two billion dollars.[17] The value of such loans peaked in 1981 at 90 billion dollars (58 billion for

Latin America), falling to 50 billion in 1995 in the wake of a major region-wide debt crisis.

In the late 1980s, these forms of capital, used to finance government operations or development projects, increasingly gave way to Foreign Direct Investment (FDI). This has become the capital of choice, representing, it is estimated, up to 60 per cent of the new capital extended in the 1990s to the developing world.[18] In 1990, the flow of FDI to Latin America and Asia, the two regions of this world that consumed the bulk of this development finance or investment capital, was valued at only 2.6 billion dollars, less than a twentieth of the international loans made that year. By 1995 the flow of FDI had increased to 20.9 billion dollars, more than 25 per cent of the loans extended to these two regions and close to one half of all official transfers. Though most FDI goes to the OECD countries the higher rates of return on productive as well as speculative investments in developing countries and areas, and the opening up privatization programmes to the TNCs, has resulted in a rapid expansion of FDI in this direction.[19] By 1993, according to UNCTAD, the developing countries as a whole attracted a record 80 billion dollars in FDI, double the flow of 1991 and equal to the total level of FDI in the world in 1986. As a result, the share of these countries in the global flow of FDI, the largest component of new resource transfers to the developing countries, from 20 per cent in the mid-1980s has reached 40 per cent.[20] One of the major consequences of dependence on foreign financing is the growing vulnerability and volatility of the economies and the financial markets as evidenced by the Mexican crash of 1994/1995 and the near collapse of the economies of South Korea, Indonesia and Thailand in 1997. Massive foreign financing provides an immediate spur of growth followed by a resounding economic crisis of over-accumulation, huge debt payments and collapse.

4. *The creation and growth of an integrated production system* based on a new international division of labour (NIDL), the global operations and strategy of the TNCs, as well as a new enabling policy framework and technologies that have dramatically shortened (and lowered the costs) of the transportation and communication circuits of capital in the production process and revolutionized the internal structure of production.[21]

By the end of the 1980s, entire lines of production and industries were technologically converted and transformed in the process, dramatically raising the productivity of labour as well as shedding large numbers of workers and employees. This trend (technological conversion and productive transformation) has been associated with a shift in the structure of production and generated profound changes in labour markets and class structures all over the world.

5. *The adoption of new flexible production methods* based on a post-fordist regime of accumulation and mode (or social structure) of regulation (of both capital and labour).These production methods were predicated on what has been termed a new 'social structure of accumulation', a structure that requires a radical change in the relation of capital to labour. The conditions for such a change have been generated in different contexts through the means of a protracted political process based on an on-going struggle between capital and labour which, according to Robinson (1996) has taken on the dimensions of another World War. The campaigns and battles in this war can be traced out at the national and the global level in both structural and political terms – structurally in the reduced share of labour (wages) in the benefits of economic growth (income).[22]

6. In the 1980s and 1990s capital launched *a direct assault on labour* in terms of its level of remuneration (wages), conditions and benefits, as well as its capacity to organize and negotiate contracts. This offensive has taken numerous forms reflected in empirical evidence of a reduced capacity and level of labour organization, the compression and polarized spread of wages,[23] the fall of wages as a share of national income, and widely observed changes in the structure of labour markets all over the world as well as associated conditions of employment and unemployment.

In this connection, the International Labour Organization (1996) argues that this system-wide decline in the value of wages, as well as the dramatic expansion of jobs at the low end of the wage spectrum, is due in part to changes in the structure of production (the shift towards services, and so on), the introduction of new technologies, and changes in the global economy. However, it adds, with reference to the USA, at least 20 per cent of the variance can be attributed directly to a weakening of labour's capacity to negotiate collective agreements, a weakening that is directly associated with the decline in organizational capacity, the level of unionization, and the decentralization of the negotiations (from the sectoral to the firm level), all consequences of a protracted political struggle with capital.

Chapter 3 elaborates on these conditions and their associated dynamics in Latin America. In terms of these conditions, it is evident that labour has borne the brunt of the restructuring and adjustment process. In the global context of this process it is estimated by UNCTAD[24] that up to 120 million workers are now officially unemployed (35 million in the European Community alone) and another 700 million are seriously underemployed, separated from their means of production and eking out a bare existence in what the ILO defines as the unstructured or informal sector, accounting for over 50 per cent of the developing world's labour force.[25] In addition to this reservoir of surplus labour it is further estimated that there has formed a mobile labour force of 80 million expatriate labourers that constitutes a new world labour market.[26]

7. *The institution of a New World Order* found expression in the founding of the IMF and the World Bank which laid the groundwork and established an institutional framework for a process of capitalist development and free international trade. Initially, in the 1940s, protectionist forces in the USA prevented the institution of a third element of this world economic order, namely the International Trade Organization. As a compromise solution, the institution of the General Agreement on Tariffs and Trade (GATT), a forum designed through various rounds of negotiation, cleared the way for a world market with low tariffs and the elimination of other barriers or impediments to a process of free trade in goods and services. It was not until 1994, fifty years later, that the original design was completed in the form of the World Trade Organization (WTO), instituted as part of an on-going effort to renovate the existing world economic order – to establish what ex-President Bush and the Heritage Foundation, a Washington-based right-wing policy forum, have termed the New World Order.[27]

The pursuit of the NWO and the widespread adoption of the Structural Adjustment Program (see Chapter 2) led to a new enabling policy framework for a global free trade regime and the constitution of a new imperial economy. Its one missing element was a general agreement governing the free flow of investment capital. It is to this end that the political representatives of imperial capital engage in designing behind the closed doors of the OECD, the club of the world's richest and most powerful nations, the Multilateral Agreement on Investment (MAI).[28]

The MAI and GATT have been criticized by the South Commission. It argues that the imperial arrangements pressed for by the GATT and to be facilitated by the MAI are not in the interest of the South. For one thing, 'a fully liberalized regime... would not necessarily promote widespread growth and development or take into account of developing countries' preoccupation',[29] On the contrary, the Commission notes, the world-wide implementation of liberalization, deregulation and privatization measures of the past 15 years have resulted in a significant deterioration of socioeconomic conditions for a large part of the world's population and a widening of the North–South gap as relates to market-generated wealth and income (see discussion below). In addition, these measures have seriously eroded the capacity of developing countries to pursue and advance their national interest, not to speak of controlling their destiny. In this connection, the South Commission echoes the conclusion of the UNDP that 'Globalization is proceeding largely for the benefit of the dynamic and powerful countries'.[30]

The UNDP's conclusion derives from its analysis of the anticipated results of the process unleashed by the implementation of the agreements negotiated by GATT in the Uruguay Round. The UNDP (1992) calculates that as the outcome of these agreements is an increase of 212 to 510 billion dollars in global income, the anticipated gains from the greater efficiency and higher rates of return on capital, as well as the expansion of trade. But the least developed countries are expected to lose up to 60 million dollars a year and sub-Sahara Africa, containing a group of countries that can least afford such a loss and its associated social costs, will lose 1.2 billion dollars.[31] The loss experienced by the developing countries from the GATT-induced growth in global incomes, from their unequal access to trade, labour and capital, was estimated by the UNDP at 500 billion dollars a year, ten times what they receive annually in the form of foreign assistance.[32] In this context, the UNDP adds, the notion or argument that the benefits of increased free trade on a global scale will necessarily trickle down to the poorest 'seem far-fetched' to say the least.

8. *The restructuring of the capitalist state* to serve the imperial project. For Aglietta (1979), among other regulationists, the world economy is theorized as a system of intersecting national social formations, which is to say the nation state has been able to resist what Petras and Brill (1985) have termed 'the tyranny of globalism'. As Lipietz, a companion-in-theory of Aglietta, has put it: 'a system must not be seen as an intentional structure or inevitable destiny [simply] because of its coherence...Its coherence is simply the effect of the interaction between several relatively autonomous processes, of the provisionally stabilized complementarity and ant-

agonism that exists between various national regimes of accumulation'.³³ These regimes, Lipietz notes, are identifiable at the level of the nation state and designed to secure 'the long term stabilization of the allocation of social production between consumption and accumulation'. The same applies to the corresponding 'mode of regulation' which 'describes a set of internalized rules and social procedures for ensuring the unity of a given regime of accumulation'.³⁴ In short, the nation state remains the major agency of the capital accumulation process even under conditions of its globalization, a point on which Petras and other class theorists are agreed.

However, notwithstanding the considerable evidence of the state's continued prominence and agency within the global development process it is just as clear that under given and widespread structural and political conditions, the powers of the nation-state have been significantly eroded, giving way to the influence of international institutions. A closer look at these IFIs (the World Bank, IMF, IDB, etc.) reveals, however, that in their internal composition, the mode of selection of their key policy makers (and the beneficiaries of their policies) a distinct set of nation states are dominant – namely the advanced capitalist or imperialist states of North America, Europe and Asia. This was already well-recognized in the 1970s when the sheer size and economic clout of the biggest TNCs, as well as their relative international mobility, was widely seen as a major pressure on national sovereignty – on the capacity of the state to either regulate the operations of capital or to make national policy. In the 1980s, under the conditions of a new world economic order, the powers of the state have been drastically reduced relative to TNCs and other global or international organizations. To political economists formed in an earlier mold such as Fred Bienefeld this fact is deplored in a search for conditions that might restore to the nation state its sovereign powers or policy-making capacity.³⁵ Others, Keith Griffin³⁶ among them, argue the inevitability of globalization and with it the reduced power of the state. From this perspective, the view or efforts of scholars like Bienefeld, oriented towards a Keynesian or welfare state, or a strong developmentalist state, able to determine national policy over vital areas of economic and social life, is somewhat quixotic and highly anachronistic.

Cutting across this debate is a view of the new role of the state in a context of globalization, where the issue is seen not as the reduction of the size and powers of the state, the loss of national sovereignty, or a hollowing out of its responsibilities and functions, but its realignment towards the interests of the transnational capitalist class.

The Economic Benefits of Globalization and their Distribution

Another major issue surrounds the question of whether world inequalities and the North–South gap in the distribution of economic resources and income is growing as the supporters of the imperialism thesis argue or whether, as globalization theorists argue, conditions are maturing for a reduction of these disparities and the closing of the North–South gap. This issue would seem to be easily enough settled on the basis of an examination of the relevant facts or available statistics. However, the question is by no means clear or settled. It has been widely recognized or conceded that the market-led or market-friendly developments associated with globalization have either exacerbated existing global inequalities as well as the level of the nation-state or have generated new inequalities. In other words, social inequalities in the distribution of economic or productive resources, and income, are widely assumed, or argued to be, increasing. There are many studies along these lines that have a critical approach towards capitalism in its neoliberal form and global development. However, even a number of studies by advocates of, or apologists for, globalization have come to the same position. The UNDP, for example, in its 1992 Human Development Report determined that from 1960 to 1989 those countries with the richest 20 per cent of the world's population saw their share of global output (income) rise from 70.2 to 82.7 per cent while the share of those with the poorest 20 per cent shrank from 2.3 to 1.4 per cent. UNIDO has argued the same point on the basis of more recent data.

Similarly, the World Bank and the International Monetary Fund have acknowledged that a large number of countries have regressed in the conditions of their development, in many cases to a level achieved in 1980 or even in 1970. These countries have clearly failed to participate in the fruits of recent development or to participate in what is seen as a 'trend towards prosperity'. In the case of sub-Saharan Africa it is estimated that per capita incomes since 1987 have fallen by 25 per cent. The Bank explains this failure in terms of wrong-headed or policy mistakes, an inability or unwillingness of the countries involved to draw the necessary lessons from the development record or consistently pursue prescribed policies and adopt the institutional changes required. The Bank assumes and takes the position that on the basis of correct policies that the gap in global incomes can be closed and that more and more countries could share in the 'trend towards prosperity'.[37]

Advocates of globalization have not been particularly or generally concerned about this identified increase in global social inequalities. With reference to a theory that has been converted into a doctrine increased inequality is generally taken to be the inevitable *short-term* effect of the market-led growth process based as it is on an increase in the national savings rate and the increased propensity to invest these savings, the necessary conditions for which include a larger share of capital in national income and ergo a decline in the share of income available for consumption, that is, distributed in the form of wages or salaries. A secular trend towards such a shift has been identified at the national level in diverse contexts, particularly in Latin America, but it is also taken to exist at the global level. Indeed, global disparities in income have reached such a point that some scholars are drawing attention to it as a problem that could reach crisis proportions. The political dimensions of these global social inequalities have been subject to considerable analysis, and, at the national level, to corrective policy.[38] The problem is that the social discontent generated by these inequalities is liable to be mobilized into movements of opposition and resistance, so underlying the adjustment process with the potential for destabilizing the political regimes committed to them.[39] On this point see Chapters 4 and 5.

Despite broad agreement among advocates and opponents of globalization that global inequalities in economic resources and income can be assumed or shown to be on the increase in the course of the past decade and a half, there are some who argue the contrary – that the North–South gap is closing. Interestingly (or oddly) enough, this point has been made inter alia by Keith Griffin, a recognized opponent of market-led development and an advocate of state regulation of the operations of capital on the market. As Griffin (1995) sees it, and argues in a heated debate with Manfred Bienefeld, the empirical evidence clearly suggests that the North–South income gap is closing rather than growing. As he sees it, global income inequality in recent years has begun to diminish. There has occurred, he notes, 'a remarkable change in the distribution of the world's income', with average global incomes rising, resulting in many of the poor becoming less poor.[40]

Is this an empirical or conceptual issue? How can Griffin's view be reconciled with the argument advanced by Bienefeld and many others that the North–South gap in wealth and income has been growing and has accelerated under conditions of structural adjustment and globalization?

The UNDP, for example, has documented a dramatic worsening of the disparity in income distribution between the richest and poorest segments of the world's population identified along North–South lines. According to the UNDP (1992), over the past two decades the disparity between the poorest and richest 20 per cent of the population has increased from 11/1 to 17/1. UNIDO, which makes reference to an earlier study by Griffin and Khan (1992), makes the same point in different terms, noting the obvious fact (also noted by the UNDP) that globalization has clear winners and losers, and the developing countries are the clear losers. A part of the discrepancy in viewpoint and analysis lies in the assumption made by Griffin and others that in the rise in average global incomes the poor are relatively better off. However, as Bienefeld points out, most of the world's poor do not have access to any or income-generating productive resources. And with the explosive growth of the world's informal sectors, and low-income activities or forms of employment, as well as the sharp decline of real wages and wage incomes in many parts of the world, a significant part of the world's population is worse off today than fifteen years ago. Quite apart from the growth of average incomes aggregated at the global level, this deterioration in socioeconomic conditions is reflected in the persistent growth of those in poverty whether measured in terms of absolute numbers or as a percentage of the population.

As to the dynamics of this process they might take the form of structural forces (or that is how they appear to many economists), but they relate to actions by organizations and capitalist enterprises that are clearly and very much taken in their own interests. This is the point, one that is not well understood or is ignored by many economists, made by the prime minister of Malaysia in his critical remarks on a global economic system that allows 'traders [to] take billions of dollars of profits and pay absolutely no taxes to the countries they impoverish'.[41] Michel Chossudovsky (1997) documents the working of this process on a global scale.

The 'globalist view' that describes the world market as made up of integrated, interdependent national economies was totally demolished by the events leading to and following the collapse of the Asian economies. The flight of overseas capital and the accumulation of unpayable foreign loans led to the massive bankruptcy of banks and enterprises. The Asian regimes putting out the begging cup to the big banks of Europe, North America and Japan highlighted the power of imperial relations in the so-called internationalized economy. US and European TNC buyouts of large Asian corporations for a fraction of their previous value, the dictates by US and European leaders of the terms of refinancing further highlights the imperial nature of these inter-state relations in the world economy: the differential outcome of the Asian and Latin American crises in which the latter lose and the imperial financiers win describe not 'integration' and inter-dependence but subordination and imperialism. The inequalities and exploitation that define the inter-state system illustrate the utility of the imperial over the globalist conceptual framework

The Political Dimension of Economic Restructuring and Globalization: The Question of Governance

On the political level, one of the arguments of globalization theorists has been that the diffusion of democratic institutions or the democratization of existing institutions accompanies the growth of 'free markets'. This process has unfolded at various levels. One has been a widespread trend towards decentralization of government that for the most part can be traced back to initiatives 'from above and within' the state apparatus. Chapter 6 analyses the dynamics of this trend. In theory, if not in practice, this process has created some of the mechanisms and conditions (local power) for popular participation in public decision-making. However, the critics of 'decentralization' point to the lack of control by local authorities over the allocation of funds, the design of macro-economic policy and the undemocratic nature of the selection of local officials. Another dimension of the '(re)-democratization' process has been a shift away from military regimes and unconstitutional governments towards civilian regimes formed within the institutional framework of liberal democracy. Chapter 5 expands on this theme and identifies the associated or lack of dynamics of change.

These trends have been so pervasive, and concomitant with the institution of market-friendly economic reforms and the SAP, that they have revived notions of a necessary link between economic and political forms of liberalization. Whereas the orthodox view of liberal scholars and politicians has been that authoritarian regimes are more likely to institute free market neoliberal reforms and to create the political conditions for rapid economic growth, the 'new' theory or ideology is that political liberalization (the institution of liberal democracy) either is the necessary precondition for or the inevitable result of the prescribed market oriented reforms. In this context, the USA administration and international institutions such as the World Bank have turned against the dictatorships and authoritarian regimes that they once nurtured or supported. In the name of democracy and as its self-appointed guardians they now promote the institutionality of liberal democracy, and even require it as a condition of access to aid, loan or investment capital. On this point see the World Bank's 1997 World Development Report.

Needless to say, this issue remains unsettled. What is nevertheless clear is that the democracy now called for by the USA involves what Dahl, Robinson and others have termed 'polyarchy', an elite-led form of liberal democracy. Not only is there no effective form of popular participation or substantive democracy in this institution, but under conditions of globalization effective decision making on key policy issues, including the regulation of capital, have been shifting towards international institutions such as the IMF, the World Bank, and the G-7 Forum that are notoriously undemocratic in their political processes.

At issue here is the capture of the state by global capital, or its reorientation towards the interests vested in the globalization process. In this context, the role of the new neoliberal state can be defined in terms of three critical functions: (i) facilitation of the global capital accumulation process; (ii) the creation and maintenance of the infrastructure for this process; and (iii) maintenance of public order and the conditions of public security.

The role of the neoliberal state that is prescribed by these functions has been primarily to facilitate the accumulation process on a global scale and, it would seem, to regulate labour, which for some reason is less mobile today than it was in an earlier era of globalization from 1870 to the first World War. To assume this role, the state has been generally downsized, decentralized, and modernized, as well as hollowed out in terms of its regulatory and policy-making capacities.

Another matter of particular concern to global capital is the question of governance or the capacity to govern. The problem is posed by Robert Kapstein, Director of the US Council on Foreign Relations, precisely in terms of the growing social inequalities in the global distribution of incomes which, he argues, exceed the level at which the forced opposition and resistance can be contained.[42] At issue is an emerging and potentially explosive level of social discontent which could all too easily be mobilized politically into movements of opposition and resistance. The forces generated and mobilized by these movements, Kapstein fears, are likely to undermine and destabilize those newly formed democratic regimes committed to market-oriented or friendly economic reforms. As a result these regimes are unlikely to stay the course,

Development in the Context of Globalization 17

underlying the political will needed to implement fully and consistently the prescribed and needed medicine of structural adjustment. The governability of the whole process, he concludes, is at risk, threatened by mounting forces of opposition and resistance.

Labour in the World Economy

As argued in Chapter 2 labour has borne the brunt of the capitalist globalization process and its mechanisms of adjustment. This process has two major dimensions *vis-à-vis* labour. On the one hand, the capitalist development process has separated large numbers of direct producers from their means of production, converting them into a proletariat and creating a labour force which at the global level is estimated to encompass 1.9 billion workers and employees in 1980, 2.3 billion in 1990, and close to three billion by 1995.[43] On the other hand, the demand for labour has grown more slowly than its supply. The process of technological change and economic reconversion endemic to capitalist development has generated an enormous and growing pool of surplus labour, an industrial reserve army that is estimated at one third of the total global labour force. In addition, the forces generated by the process of capitalist development have separated many producers from their means of production, creating an enormous proletariat, an estimated 50 per cent of which is either unemployed or underemployed, eking out a bare existence in the growing informal sector of the third world's burgeoning cities and urban centres or on the margins of the capitalist economy. Chapter 2 examines the underlying dynamics and the effects of this process.

Our prognosis for the next decade is that the deepening crisis in Asia and the continuing crisis in Latin America will lead to the enormous growth of informal workers with incomes at or below the level of subsistence; large-scale movements of impoverished workers and peasants back and forth between urban and rural economies; the cheapening of industrial production and a decline in well-paid jobs in the advanced capitalist countries; the growth of poorly-paid service jobs; and a worldwide crisis of living standards for labour.

Technological innovations, largely related to the processing of information, will lead to the growth of a small elite of well-paid engineers in software design and executives and a mass of poorly-paid 'information processors' – the new proletariat. The outsourcing of labour-intensive computer work to low wage areas is already a growing social phenomenon. Thus, the centrality of wage labour, contrary to the prognosis of the globalization theorists who argue the 'disappearance of wage labour', will actually greatly increase even as it is impoverished. Insofar as the new information systems are linked to the vast movement of speculative capital, it can be seen as an integral technical instrument in the assault on productive capital and the living standards of wage workers.

The social – and political – implications of this change are momentous. For one thing, it will generate a radically different social structure and system of class relations. For another, it highlights the strategic position of labour. Combined with the growth of a huge industrial reserve army (mainly informal and contingent in form), and its depressant effect on the wages of the employed, the change wrought in the labour force and the social structure of society will undermine and weaken the capacity of capital to discipline labour and to stimulate the accumulation process.

Forces of Opposition and Resistance

For the sake of analysis, economy and society are often portrayed as a system, which is to say a set of interconnected structures, the conditions of which are objective in their effects and whose operation (on people, classes, nations) can be theorized by reference to 'laws of development'. The problem with this systems perspective is that it is all too easy to confuse an analytical tool, in this case a theoretical model, with reality. In this confusion structures are reified and their conditions are attributed an objectivity that they do not have. As a result the structure of economic and social relations that people enter into is viewed as a mould into which they must pour their behaviour. And the institutionalized practices that make up the structure of the system appear as a prison from which there is no escape, subjecting individuals, and entire nations, to forces that are beyond their ability to control let alone understand. Needless to say, this view breeds complacence and resignation – and notions of inevitability. Globalization appears as an immanent and intelligible process to which adjustments must needs be made.

The reality, however, is otherwise. In fact, the system, if it exists (and for the sake of analysis we too assume that it does), is fraught with contradictions that generate forces of opposition and resistance – of social change. The dynamics of these forces are described and analyzed in several chapters. However, as a matter of principle, for the sake of both analysis (the interpretation of the observed and documented developments) and political action, we argue that there is nothing inevitable about globalization viewed either as a process or a project. Like the logic of the underlying system, it is instituted by an identifiable class of individuals – transnational capitalists – and advanced in their collective or individual interest related to the accumulation of capital.

THE DYNAMICS OF CHANGE IN LATIN AMERICA

This book is about the dynamics of social change in Latin America. First of all, Chapter 2 brings into focus the neoliberal project which is generating the major forces of change. The internal contradictions and problems associated with this project and the theoretical model of the economy associated with it are so glaring that they have led to an ubiquitous search for a viable alternative. The major efforts in this regard are reviewed in this chapter, with particular reference to the solution provided by the United Nations Commission for Latin America. Then in Chapter 3 we turn towards an examination of the conditions that impact in particular on the Latin American working class. It is argued here that labour is the primary mechanism of internal adjustment to the so-called globalization process and the construction of a New Economic Order. The politics of this adjustment is examined in terms of a strategy to make labour more 'flexible', that is, more amenable to the dictates of capital.

In Chapter 4 our attention turns towards a related strategy to decentralise government decision-making as the institutional basis of a community-based form of participatory development. We identify two sets of dynamics with respect to this decentralization process, one associated with an agenda pursued by forces that operate within the state apparatus, the other with forces generated within the popular sector of an emerging civil society and mobilized by social organizations formed in this sector. Our argument is that despite appearances to the contrary, and the beliefs shared by many in the popular movement, that decentralization is an initiative 'from above' rather than 'from below' and responds to a political agenda pursued by the economically dominant and political classes.

In Chapter 5 we elaborate on the dynamics that relate to the electoral processes within the neoliberal economies of Latin America. We argue here that the electoral process has served to buttress the status quo and is highly susceptible to elite manipulations. We further argue that the political dynamics of change, with particular reference to the electoral process, favours the deepening of neoliberal policies. We establish the limits of the electoral process insofar as any substantial social change favouring the popular sectors is concerned.

In Chapter 6 we turn towards an examination of the dynamics associated with the emergence of new social movements in the region, particularly those that are peasant-based and led. We review the intellectual debate that surrounds this question and establish the class basis and nature of these movements. In doing so we take issue with the postmodernist perspective to which many intellectuals have turned in the current context in an effort to demobilise the dynamic forces of change generated by these movements.

In Chapter 7 our attention turns towards a political analysis of these dynamics associated with the emergence of new social movements in the countryside. As we see it, these movements provide an important base for the reconstruction of the socialist project in the region. We discuss the dynamics of the forces mobilized by the political and the social left in the context of the electoral process and a development project approach based on the agency of community-based social organizations. In this connection we draw particular attention to the social forces for change mobilized by the uprising of Mayan peasants in Chiapas.

The Zapatista uprising allows us to reflect on some of the difficulties encountered by movements of opposition and resistance to neoliberalism and imperialism – to capitalism in its present form. Unfortunately, neither this nor any of the social movements that we identify and profile provide a solution to this problem. Nevertheless, we argue that it is in the social forces generated by the dynamics of these movements that we must ground the search for the reconstruction of a socialist project. We establish here the major challenge faced by the Left in the present conjuncture.

2 Neoliberalism and the Search for Another Development

NEOLIBERALISM IN THEORY AND PRACTICE

The Neoliberal Project

Development as a political and intellectual project has its roots in the eighteenth century project of modernising the economy and creating economic progress, but to all intents and purposes it was born in the post-war period of the 1940s and 1950s. The historical context of this process includes (i) a cold war between the socialist and capitalist blocs; (ii) anti-colonial wars that resulted in the national independence of countries in sub-Saharan Africa and in Asia; and (iii) the institution of a liberal world economic order.[1]

In this context, at the intellectual level were constituted two paradigms, one of which ('orthodoxy') presumes the institutionality of the capitalist system, and the other, based on an analysis of political economy, is oriented towards an alternative system (socialism to be precise). Most of the political and theoretical postulates in the field of development were elaborated within the limits of the first paradigm, one that allowed two lines of thought (liberal and structural) and the construction of two economic models: one, based on classical and neoclassical theory of an untrammelled unregulated laissez faire form of free market capitalism; and the other, based on an approach that emphasized the need for state intervention in the market and the importance and role of the state in planning for development.[2]

In the 1950 and 1960s what dominated in the theory and the practice of development were structuralist forms of thinking about the obstacles to and the dynamic forces of economic growth.[3] The central proposition of this theory had to with how to increase the level of capital accumulation on the basis of the domestic saving rate and assuring the effective investment of these savings. The structuralist theoreticians advanced several ideas and models in this respect. The major one was the specification of a mechanism for increasing the saving rate by means of the extraction of surplus value from the traditional sector of agriculture to finance modernization (and the technological reconversion) of the industrial productive apparatus in the modern capitalist sector.[4]

The state, conceived as promoter of the modernization and development process, availed itself of several economic and extra-economic mechanisms put in practice in the 1960 and 1970s (particularly in the Newly Industrializing Countries of Asia):

(i) the compression of wages, by political means (as in South Korea) of repressing demands of the working class, converting in the process savings into capital;
(ii) less transparent methods such as inflation and what we might call 'financial repression' that reduces and prevents the advance in and potential gains of wages; or/ and
(iii) transferring and appropriating the productive capital accumulated in other regions of the world on the basis of higher rates of profit and lower rates of labour remuneration.[5]

From 1965 to 1980, Latin America experienced rate of growth superior to the world average – close to 6 per cent per annum. But this growth, by virtue of its dependency on external financing, had a high economic cost manifest in conditions of a debt that reached crisis proportions in 1982 (from $28 billion in the 1970s to $239 billion).

In the context of this crisis the political regimes and the economies in the region were subjected to a neoliberal programme of stabilization and structural adjustment measures that introduced far-reaching reforms into the institutionalized structure of the economy and society. Elements of this structural adjustment programme (SAP) were introduced in the 1970s in Chile, Argentina and Uruguay in the context of a military regime and a first round of neoliberal experiments, but it reached its apotheosis at the beginning of the 1980s, and from then it has been consolidated throughout the region. By the end of the decade only four countries had not introduced a sweeping programme of economic and political reforms and these did so with a vengeance in the early 1990s.

The central idea behind the SAP formulated and pushed (imposed, to be exact) by the IMF, the World Bank and its regional satellites such as the Inter-American Development Bank (ADB), was elaborated by Adam Smith in the seventeenth century: an invisible hand of the market whose operations, under competitive conditions, would result in an optimum (that is, efficient) distribution of society's productive resources and the benefits of economic growth.

Neoliberalism and the Search for Another Development

The theoreticians of neoclassical economics extended this idea with several postulates such as the following

(i) the dynamics of the system derive from the utilitarian decisions (rational calculus of personal interest) made by each individual;
(ii) the motor of the economic expansion process is the international division of labour (production) based on the principle (the law) of comparative advantage;
(iii) private enterprise is the best conductor of this motor;
(iv) prices in their totality create and maintain a balance among demand and the supply of any commodities; and
(v) the free market produces the maximum social welfare on condition of 'getting prices right'.[6]

Within the framework of these ideas, the economists of the World Bank and the IMF elaborated a policy programme of stabilization and structural adjustment measures. The basic elements of this policy package (SAP) are as follows:

(i) a 'realistic' rate of currency exchange (that is, a devaluation);
(ii) anti-inflationary measures and cuts in the public expenditures (a policy of austerity measures, elimination of subsidies, and so on);
(iii) an economic opening, via a liberalization policy with respect to trade and capital flows;
(iv) the deregulation of private sector activity and markets;
(v) privatization of the means of production; and
(vi) downsizing and the modernization of the state.[7]

In the 1970s this stabilization and structural adjustment programme was implemented by the military regime of Pinochet in Chile, involving, according to McKinnon, a World Bank (WB) economist and a principal architect of the SAP, the most radical and sweeping changes in history. In the same context but in a very different conjuncture, the SAP was imposed by the IMF and the WB in a number of countries in sub-Saharan Africa. And in the 1980s, in a context of a region-wide debt crisis, a shortage and haemorrhage of capital, economic stagnation, and a process of political democratization,[8] the SAP was implemented to various degrees in nearly all countries in Latin America. At the end of the decade just four regimes in Latin America had not liberalized their economies and disciplined their working classes, but these too took the same road in the 1990s, leaving no exception to the world of neoliberalism.

Neoliberal Policy and Politics: Socioeconomic Impacts and Political Responses

The impacts of the SAP can be seen at a structural level and at level of the socioeconomic conditions that correspond to this structure. At the structural level these impacts are associated with the class structure formed by the objectively given relations of production. In the capitalist societies this structure is formed by and revolves around the labour-capital relationship, which defines the capitalist class, composed of the large, medium and small bourgeoisie; and the working class, that assumes different shapes and has many divisions and strata but whose members share a wage relationship. In the interstices of this structure, can be found what Marxists term a petite-bourgeoisie, a middle class traditionally formed by independent producers and the operators of businesses – the small and medium entrepreneurs.[9] And this middle class also has several strata and sectors that include among others the professionals, intellectuals and those who manage capitalist and public enterprises and that provide several other services to capital.[10]

With respect to the SAP's structural impacts, in relationship to the capitalist class, the operating process is that of the concentration and of the centralization of capital, resulting in the fusion of many and for the remaining a struggle to survive. Looking at just 1988 there were innumerable fusions of the largest capitals organized in form of what the UN Center for the Study of Transnational Corporations terms 'the Billionaire Club' – 300 or so of the biggest transnationals that by themselves and their affiliates control 25 per cent of world production and in total (an estimated 35 000 in the late 1980s) control world trade, half of it by means of transfers among affiliated companies without recourse to the market.[11]

With respect to the middle class, the authors have estimated that at the world level its productive and entrepreneurial sectors constitutes around 15 per cent of the EAP but generate the bulk of all productive enterprises and net new employment.

The size and the weight of this class vary considerably: up to 25 per cent of the EAP in developed countries or in some developing countries like Argentina, but less than 10 per cent in many of the less and least developed countries. There is a lack of systematic comparative studies in this respect, but all the case studies available reveal or suggest that the general impact of the SAP on this class has been significant,[12] in terms of a trend towards bankruptcies, bank indebtedness and other conditions of proletarianization – and, in some contexts, of impoverishment.[13] In many cases, in the countryside, in rural society, this class has been heavily hit by neoliberal policies (economic opening, liberalization of imports, drop in prices, credit restrictions, elimination of subsidies, decrease in purchasing power capacity, and so on) as in Mexico, where bank indebtedness affects close to 60 per cent of producers and entrepreneurs, forcing hundreds of thousands, according to El Barzon (a social movement of close to a million independent producers and entrepreneurs) to the point and beyond of bankruptcy.[14]

In Argentina, where, it has been argued, the middle class has been the most heavily hit by neoliberal policies, thousands of small and medium-sized rural producers in the month of October and the first days of November 1996 realized a series of struggles (a week of resistance), with mobilizations in Rosario, Vila and other localities of the Santa Fe, Chaco and Cordoba.[15] In Santa Fe, these mobilizations were coordinated with the Movement of Women in Struggle formed by the wives and daughters of small and medium producers. This movement, formed in June of 1995, in a desperate attempt to prevent the auctioning of the house and land of a Lucia Cornelis, is typical of the anti-neoliberal movements of the middle class being formed in several contexts (see El Barzon, in Mexico, for example) in the region.

Without a doubt the working class in its various sectors has borne the brunt of neoliberal policies, having absorbed most of their heavy social costs (discussed below). As to the structure of this class, in many countries the working class has been transformed in terms of its relation to capital, its forms and conditions of employment and work (and social existence) and organization. At the beginning of the 1980s, the working class in many places had as its central component the industrial proletariat, wage-workers in heavy and basic industries (in construction and manufacturing) as well the public sector. After years of hard struggle and organization it had won the right to decent work conditions, with wages adjusted to productivity gains.

In many contexts workers had acquired if not political and economic power at least an organized social force. In the 1980s all this changed in the wake of an offensive launched on several fronts by the capitalist class.[16] Towards the end of the decade and into the 1990s neoliberal policies had changed radically the working class, dividing it and reducing its 'traditional' sector to but an echo of what it once was, creating the base of a very different class, in the streets rather than the factories and offices; located in the informal sector of the urban economies, subject to conditions of economic and social insecurity, disorganization, and low pay, with labour remunerated at levels well below its value;

subject to precarious and irregular occupational conditions and forms of employment – short contract and temporary or part-time work; and characterized by the formation of a huge reserve army of surplus labour, under conditions of unemployment and underemployment. The conditions of this transformation, as well as its forms, vary from country to country, but they can be identified in the countries to the North as well as those in the South.[17]

At the level of economic and social conditions associated with and derived from this structural transformation, the impacts of the SAP are equally extensive, having produced what has been called a silent revolution (without the noise of the social revolutions of the previous decade).

The impact of neoliberal policies, in place in many countries of the third world for over ten years, in terms of productive capacity and economic growth has been heavily debated and discussed. Although there is no consensus in this respect, most studies – including some commissioned or prepared by the IMF – has found no systematic relationship between structural adjustment and economic growth. What is clear is that in many cases, thanks to neoliberal policies, macroeconomic balance has been achieved, particularly relative to Latin America's galloping inflation.

As for economic growth the issue is not so clear, although it would seem that the countries in East and Southeast Asia that have grown so rapidly over the past two decades have done so without a neoliberal policy regime and its associated reforms, while many (the majority) of countries in Latin America and sub-Saharan Africa have seen their growth rates dramatically reduced under the SAP.[18]

According to the World Bank, the average per capita income in the world of 1994 was $4470, considerably more than in 1980. But the disparities in the distribution of this income is such as to strip this statistic of any meaning. 20 per cent of the world's richest population appropriate 78.7 per cent of the total income, while the poorest 20 per cent receive only 1.4 per cent. Seen in another way, 63 of the least developed countries (LDCs), representing 56.2 per cent of the world population, receive but 4.2 per cent of world income while the most developed countries (MDCs), those of the OECD, representing 14.8 per cent of world population, receive 79 per cent of world income. The degree of income concentration is such that today just 385 individuals (the Forbes 400) receive – that is, appropriate – a total combined income equivalent to that received by the poorest 40 per cent.[19] In less than 30 years the degree of disparity in the distribution of world income, aggregated and calculated at the national level, has changed from 30/1 to 60/1, a dispersion that reaches 100/1 at the extremes, and this disparity and gap has deepened in the 1980s period of structural adjustments.[20] In recent years this issue has been heavily debated and subject to analysis at the national level where the same disparities can be traced out.[21] The consensus, we can say, among all the serious researchers of this issue is that inequalities have increased significantly in the last decade and a half, resulting in an extension (and deepening) of poverty and its conditions, creating furthermore new forms of it; and that there is an unquestionable connection between neoliberal policy of adjustment (the NEM) and these results.[22]

The connection (between neoliberal policies and the distribution of income – and wealth, which is even more concentrated) is derived in large part from the compression of wages produced by a variety of extra and economic and extra-economic mechanisms. The operations and impacts of these mechanisms can be traced out in a shift in the distribution of national income between labour and capital[23] and in the dramatic fall – severe in many cases – of real wages (in its purchasing capacity) for the working class.[24]

More than anything, neoliberal policies have produced a broad and deep division in society at all levels, polarising it into two, procuring the benefits in the form of wealth for 'the winners', subjecting 'the losers' to conditions of exploitation and social exclusion: social and economic insecurity, low remuneration and returns on their labour and, and, for many (2.4 billion, 40 per cent of the world population, it is estimated) conditions of abject poverty. In other words, the benefits of neoliberal policies are very concentrated in one group and very reduced social strata, excluding the vast majority. It is estimated that at least a third of the world population is almost totally excluded from the system and its fruits, deprived not only their basic needs but of their economic human rights, of employment, and so on. In the words of Ignacy Sachs, they constitute a 'fourth world' that, for the most part live in the countries of South Asia, sub-Saharan Africa and parts of Latin America, but that can also be found in the underclass and (to use a phrase of Marcos) the 'forgotten hollows' (huecos perdidos) of the first world. Just as the privileged minorities of the third world constitute the presence of the North in the South, the excluded and poor being formed in the first world of the USA and other countries of the OECD constitute the presence of the South in the North. The North and the South thus have penetrated each other.[25]

The impacts of neoliberal policy can also be identified at the political level. They have led to a political reaction on the part of various classes.

It is not for nothing that in the 1980s so many countries, particularly in Latin America, experienced waves of protest to this policy and that several forms of resistance are continuing to rise.[26]

In theory, the high social costs of this policy can be seen as a bitter medicine to be swallowed so as to assure in time an eventual improvement in the health of the patient. The problem is that these patients have not been content with their treatment nor willing to swallow the bitter pill of SAP at all costs, particularly with reference to its unjust distribution. In the wake of this disillusionment, discontent and protest, those who have prescribed the neoliberal medicine and monitored its effects, the 'witch doctors of the IMF', to use an expression of Lopes Portillo, ex-President of Mexico, have clearly become concerned, even frightened. The threat and danger contained in the acts of resistance, and refusal to accept the medicine doled out to them, consists in the possibility that this discontent might be mobilised not only against the medicine and its providers but against the underlying system itself. Expressions of this concern and fear can be found at the global level[27] and, in many contexts, at the domestic level, where this concern has produced a critical response from the same institutions that had elaborated the SAP in the first place: the World Bank, the IMF, and the other regional and international financial institutions such as the IDB. This internal reaction[28] has resulted in the elaboration of a new development paradigm – and a new economic model. To this we now turn.

Structural Adjustment with a Human Face: The Model of Social Liberalism

The new paradigm (and the corresponding model), elaborated at the end of 1980s, has five components:[29]

(i) an emphasis on popular participation, that is, the incorporation of the identified beneficiaries of public policy and associated projects, particularly the poor and women;[30]
(ii) decentralization of decision-making and the implementation and administration of public policy, sharing it with institutions of local (municipal and regional governments) and other partners (NGOs);
(iii) prioritizing the problems and the conditions of extreme poverty, alleviating their effects with projects financed by a special social investment fund set up to this purpose;[31]

(iv) specific policies with relation to health, education and employment – and, in some versions, the promotion of micro-enterprise) – and in order to incorporate women into the development process, empowering them/assuring their active participation; and
(v) structural reforms designed to create a favourable environment for a new social policy (NSP) and a social development process.

The axis of the new model is a social policy elaborated to give adjustment a human face, a social dimension. The new social policy (NSP) has its origins in an experiment conducted in Bolivia in 1985, but its mode or paradigm case is FOSIS in Chile, and, to a certain point, Solidarity in Mexico (see discussion below). In either case, the NSP (social liberalism) took the place of the traditional social policy that was part of a welfare state oriented towards universality (benefiting the middle and working classes). In contrast, the NSP, supported by more limited funding, was directed towards ('targeted') the problems of extreme poverty found in marginal communities. At least such is the theory, given that in the exemplary case of this policy (Chile) it has been found that up to 25 per cent of benefits under the NSP are received by the richest social stratum in the country. In any event (see the discussion below), the evaluations that have been made of the programmes based on this new social policy has demonstrated a mild positive impact in the case of Chile, with some identifiable alleviation of the conditions of extreme poverty,[32] But in no other case has poverty been alleviated let alone reduced, and not even in Chile has the NSP affected the underlying structure of poverty, a structure that continues to reproduce the conditions of this poverty.

According to the International Monetary Fund (IMF), the economic policy and the development model proposed by the IMF is not derived from neoliberalism. The reason is that the IMF's policies do not depend on only the invisible hand of the market, but also on the visible hand of the state and, furthermore, on the third hand of solidarity between the rich and the poor. As for the market and the state, the critical institutions of the process are conceived in more balanced terms, granting more importance to the state than assigned it in the neoliberal model. In this context, as discussed below, is formed the base of a political and theoretical convergence and synthesis of the structuralist postulates of ECLAC (neostructuralism) and those of neoliberalism.[33]

In any event, despite the closing of the space between the two models (neoliberalism, neostructuralism), enough remains as to permit and support a continuing debate on the respective roles and limits of the state and the market.

However, the critical point of the social liberalism model is the underlying if unspecified relationship of solidarity between the rich, the intended and effective beneficiaries of the process (because of their supposedly higher propensity to invest their savings) and the poor (the bearer of their social costs). In this respect, there is resort to a strategy and policy of decentralization, popular participation, and solidarity – based, in some contexts (Mexico), on a new social pact between the entrepreneurs and the workers.

As for 'participation' and 'decentralization', two principles and the pillars of social liberalism (structural adjustment with a human face), relevant policies and reforms have been implemented in various contexts.[34] This policy of social liberalism is based in an expanded concept of development: not only with respect to an increase in per capita production but an advance in 'human development' that can be defined and measured in terms of an increase in the capacity of society to provide their members choice and freedom (and opportunity) to realize their potential.[35]

To give institutional form to this concept, and thus to create the necessary conditions for realizing it, the multilateral financial institutions (mainly, the World Bank) and the operating agencies of the United Nations such as UNDP, UNIDO and UNICEF not only have promoted a national policy of structural adjustment (to release the economic and social forces of the society) but a strategy of decentralization. The forms of this strategy have been, and are, variable, but it basically consists of collaboration with local institutions, in particular municipal governments and the NGOs, that operate as intermediaries between the central government and community-based grassroots organizations.[36]

In Bolivia, for example, this concept of development was institutionalized in the Law of Popular Participation. This law responds in part to the demands of the country's indigenous peoples over the years for autonomy and access to and control over land and other productive resources, and of the Left for popular participation.

This has been a central claim of the left in the recent years at municipal level, where its political class has had a considerable quota of success (see discussion down). The problem for the left, and in many cases for the communities involved, is that the policy of decentralization, of municipalization of resources and decision-making, has had (and continues to have) a double intentionality – and impact.[37] On the one hand, this policy has opened some spaces at local level for political action and for the participation of grassroots social organizations in decisions that relate to development projects and social development in the community. In this context, as in Bolivia, it is very difficult for the Left to oppose the policy of decentralization and popular participation. On the other hand, this policy has not resulted in any case in empowerment of the people. In the case of Bolivia, the institutionalization of the Popular Participation Law has operated, in practice at least, in the weakening of community- or class-based organizations such as unions that had had or might have some capacity to address issues that go beyond the community, challenge the structure of economic and political power, and effect change in class-based structures that operate nationally. The point is that the decentralization of government responsibility and decision-making has generally been an initiative 'from above' (on the agenda of the government itself) and the outside (primarily the World Bank).

In the same context, the NGOs in their mediating role between the central government and community-based social organizations have also tended to weaken the latter.

The War against Poverty: The NSP in Practice

In the 1990s, after a decade and more of structural adjustment, some 200 million people in Latin America are forced to live in conditions of poverty, almost half the population (and in Central America this per cent increases to 70 per cent). Nearly everyone, with the exception of those closest to the accumulated wealth of society, see in this poverty the principal problem to be addressed if not solved, be it from a social justice perspective (a question of principle) or with reference to concerns about what the conditions of poverty can bring about. Neoliberals see it as a pathology that has nothing or little to do with their policies or with the structure created by them. Poverty is, in the words of Ernesto Zedillo, President of Mexico, 'the legacy of many decades of statism and authoritarianism'.[38] When poverty is analysed in terms of its 'structural'[39] conditions, or, as Zedillo, are referred to for political reasons, it is blamed on the old policies of yesteryear's interventionist regimes in spite of the fact that they have not been seen in practice from at least ten to fifteen years in most cases. For sure, there exists an ambiguity or contradiction within neoliberal thought on the matter, given that poverty is also seen (and accepted) as a transitory condition of the adjustment process that disappears or is reduced as the result of the economic growth generated. Be it as it may, neoliberal politicians do not see in poverty the possibility of attacking its root causes, for which reason its policy is not to eradicate it, nor even to reduce its incidence, but rather to alleviate or attenuate its effects.

As already explained, the principal approach of the advocates of adjustment with a human face is to dismantle traditional social programmes with a universal orientation and that benefits largely the middle and the formal working classes, and to more effectively target the social investment funds on the problems of extreme poverty. Within the institutional framework of neoliberal policies, the strategy, elaborated by the economists of the World Bank, the UNDP and ECLAC, consists of three critical elements:

(i) an attack on extreme poverty, directing the social investment funds towards communities of greatest need and social marginality;
(ii) to the degree possible, privatization of the social welfare programme – of social security, health, and education (and, in all cases, the reduction of state expenditures in the area); and
(iii) decentralization of decision-making, implemented with the participation of community-based organizations and of the local governments (Solidarity).

We briefly summarize the implementation of this policy in some revealing and typical cases.

The case of Honduras

From its beginnings in 1990 until 1994 the FHIS (Honduran Fund of Social Investment) has financed and impelled 5,454 projects, 70 per cent of them short term in the area of infrastructure, 19 per cent in the area of social assistance, and seven per cent classified as 'productive'.[40] It is very unlikely that the FHIS benefited mainly or significantly the poor and the most vulnerable, given that only 10 per cent of all completed projects have been located in the six most marginalized areas of the country and 58 per cent of them are concentrated in the five richest areas. The distribution of FHIS projects has also favoured the urban areas, with lower rates of marginality and generalized poverty than the rural areas. In her 1992 evaluation Fuentes explained this failure of FHIS to hit its target in the government's 'war against poverty' in political terms (with eyes on the 1993 elections and the concentration of the electors in the urban areas) and, in part, in terms of lack of experience.

The case of Peru

Foncodes was initiated mid-1991 on the basis of pressures from the IDB, which was concerned about the viability of the government's shock policy, the most radical adjustment programme seen in the region, implemented by Fujimori soon after his election in 1990 as the country's President. From January to May, 1993, Foncodes was put into high gear with an investment of 125 million dollars in 7100 projects, more than all of 1992. An analyst of this investment spurt, Jo-Marie Burt (1996), also saw in this a political and not a technical logic – in this case the November 1993 referendum with respect to the new constitution proposed by Fujimori (to allow his re-election). In this context, Fujimori could be seen virtually each night by television viewers inaugurating one project or another (new schools, sewers, etc.) in the *villas de miseria* in the cities and the countryside. Thus Foncodes became a political instrument for Fujimori in his bid for re-election.

The case of Mexico

Several evaluations of Solidarity, initiated by Carlos Salinas de Gortieri at the beginning of his Presidency and ended in June of 1995 for some reason or other, have drawn the same conclusion as was drawn in the cases of Honduras and Peru, namely that it was more of a political instrument (a means of securing votes) than a social policy.[41] To be sure, the government had to pay dearly for these votes, although total expenses in the social sector were less than social expenditures in years prior to the 1983 inception of the structural adjustment programme. As with FHIS, the programming of Solidarity, lacked a productive orientation, with the majority of projects directed towards the building of infrastructure and short-term in nature; and, contributing next to nothing to the technological reconversion of the productive apparatus and by no means able to replace the wages lost in the process.

To see in more detail how Solidarity operated it is necessary to view it from the perspective and within the institutional framework of the policy of the central government's social policy. A revealing case of this is the role of Solidarity in the government's efforts to modernize the agricultural sector, that is to say, of transforming the structure of production and its corresponding social relations (restructuring its inefficient and non-profitable small producer/peasant sector consisting of less than half of the agricultural area but some four million ejiditarios, comuneros, minifundistas, and labourers, and their families – that is to say, three-quarters of the rural population).[42]

The process has been traced out by Enrique Atorga Lira.[43] He sees it as a conspiratorial process advanced in five phases:

The first phase (i) began with the dismantling of various forms of state support. Under the rubric of cutting expenditures, deregulating the economy, and correcting market distortions, credit (in the form of Banrural) was cut back, as was insurance support (Anaxa); the government programme of technical assistance (SARH) was eliminated as was the provision of seeds (PRONOSE), subsidized credit for inputs (FERTMEX) and support for coffee growers who in their majority are very small producers and 60 per cent indigenous; the price of electricity was allowed to rise as were the cost of water for irrigation and other inputs; support for marketing and price stabilization (Conasupo) was terminated; and, the banks were reprivatized, eliminating dozens of support programs.[44] In the context of this restructuring the peasants were forced to turn towards the commercial banks with credit at high interest rates and difficult terms, placing them in the hands of exploitative intermediaries, rapacious caciques and usurers.

The second phase (ii) involves a counter-agrarian reform, labelled by the government 'land for the peasants:', a constitutional change designed to commodify communally-owned productive land and incorporate it into the market, permitting peasants to freely sell or rent their property which had been protected by the Constitution in its collective form (as *ejidos*). Constitutional reform, of article 27, served the purpose of creating better conditions of productivity and profitability by making possible the formation of large-scale commercial enterprises, with the capacity to compete on the world market, and the expulsion of marginal producers – that is, the peasants, making up an estimated 50 per cent of all producers, and, in effect, treated as surplus.

The third link (iii) in the chain of events put into motion by the government was Solidarity, a program which, contrary to government rhetoric (and neoliberal theory) had the overall effect of increasing the level of indebtedness and the incidence of poverty among small producers, and benefiting directly the class of powerful and rich landowners and capitalist producers.[45] The limits of the process (and the depths of the government's duplicity)[46] were reached in the government's efforts to secure the participation of the peasants in the process of their own destruction.

The fourth phase (iv) of the government's modernization of agriculture began with the institution of Procampo, a capital incentive programme in the sector designed to speed up the construction of capitalism in the countryside. To sum up in few words Procampo's impact in the sector it has been to lower the price of corn and beans, the two basic staples of the peasant social and household economy, their basic means of subsistence. The underlying aim of the pressures placed on these prices was to encourage if not force the peasants to sell or rent their land or to shift production towards a more commercially viable or lucrative crop.[47] Procampo gave a subsidy of 350 dollars to the producer, some relief relative to their extreme poverty but a lot less than the decrease in the price of their products provoked by the programme. It also led to an increase in the cost of consumption items, expenses incurred in the collection of this 'subsidy', and the loss of purchasing power of wages in the market (over 50 per cent of all peasant produces, it has been estimated, are partially dependent on wages for household income).

The final phase of the restructuring process (v) – not to speak of the Alliance for the Countryside, a modernization programme designed to the benefit of the medium and large growers in the sector – was constituted by the US government in its closing of the border to the mass of peasants seeking their only remaining solution to the problem of their survival.

The case of Chile

FOSIS (the Solidarity Social Investment Fund) has been presented (at the Social Development Summit sponsored by the United Nations in 1995) as the model of the new social policy, a programme designed by the government as a major means of reducing the incidence of extreme poverty, alleviating its conditions. It was initiated in 1990 as an instrument of combating the poverty which, in spite of the plaudits given to the Chilean model by the international financial community, still afflicts two of every five persons in the country (in comparison to 1970 when only 17 per cent of the population suffered from poverty).[48]

In some respects FOSIS differs from other social investment funds (SIFs). First, it is institutionalized within the government' social policy. Thus it is subordinated to the Planning and Co-operation Ministry instead of controlled directly by the Presidency as it is in Mexico, Peru, and other places. But, at the same time it was designed as a complement to other social programmes instead of substituting for them. There are also differences as to priorities. Most programmes based on the NSP emphasize short term emergency projects relating to the creation of employment and social assistance. FOSIS, on the other hand, is oriented toward long term projects and uniquely directed towards the goal of attacking the root causes and not just the symptoms of extreme poverty.

Thus, FOSIS has prioritized the financing of projects related to training and marketing, providing credit and technical support to small companies (33 per cent), of self-capacitation of the bas organizations in marginal communities (33 per cent), small producers and indigenous communities (16 per cent), and training and youth training programmes (18 per cent).[49]

FOSIS is also seen by many as an efficient model of a social policy to combat poverty. For example, it is an integral part of an amalgam of government anti-poverty measures directed to 71 communities identified by their high rates of marginality and extreme poverty. Almost 40 per cent of projects financed by FOSIS have been located in these communities.[50]

However, FOSIS has not been free from criticism. In the first place, it is responsible to a significant degree for the demobilization of the base social organizations in many poor communities. It is probable that this was – and is – also an integral part of government policy, and in the context of this policy NGOs for the most part have been converted into policy instruments of the government, mediating agencies that in practice have resulted not in the capacitation and empowerment of community-based organizations, many of which had emerged in the 1980s struggle against the military regime. On the contrary, NGOs have generally contributed to the demobilization of these organizations, a weakening and dispersal. In this sense, perhaps FOSIS might be seen as a success. It is a question of perspective. What is also questionable is the claim of FOSIS to efficiency in the war against extreme poverty. An investigation and report to the senate in 1994 revealed that up to 25 per cent of all programme benefits were received by the non-targeted richest social stratum in the country.[51]

THE SEARCH FOR ALTERNATIVE DEVELOPMENT

A New Paradigm?

The process of development is multi-dimensional. Its critical or major dimensions are:

(i) *economic*, with reference to the process of increasing productive capacity and the output of goods and services, a process that traditionally has depended on industrialization;[52]
(ii) *social*, with reference to the process of improving the quality of life of the population and a more equitable or just distribution of society's productive resources and the benefits of the process;[53]

(iii) *political*, with reference to the process of releasing and freeing individuals (and oppressed peoples) from structures and conditions that inhibit or limit their capacity to develop their human potential;[54]

(iv) *cultural and ethnic*, with reference to the process of assuring the respect for autonomy, human rights, cultural identity, and indigenous forms of organization particularly of the indigenous peoples that for centuries have been marginalized and oppressed – lost in the interstices of the dominant society and culture;[55] and

(v) *ecological*, with reference to the need to protect the environment and not to exceed the limits of the ecological systems on which human life and the development process depends.[56]

Up to the 1970s analysis of the development process – its theory and practices – was advanced within the limits of two paradigms: one that is defined by a spectrum of proposals that ranges from orthodox liberalism (*laissez faire* capitalism) to a heterodox structuralism (of a regulated form of capitalism and planned development); and another (Political Economy) that is defined by a range of theoretical and political positions and proposals (Marxism, Dependency Theory) that are predicated on the belief in the need for more radical change – social transformation (revolution) rather than reform of the operative capitalist system, and that are therefore oriented an alternative socio-economic system (socialism).[57]

In this context, there was founded a movement guided toward the construction of a third worldview, an alternative paradigm that escapes the identified limits and basic domain assumptions of existing approaches and models, and that conceives of development in a different way. This search for an alternative form of development (AD) can be traced back to the foundation in 1974 of the Dag Hammarskjöld Foundation for Alternative Development and its publication outlet *Development Dialogue*.[58]

From its beginnings this search for an alternative development has crystallized in a movement of global scope and impact, with hundreds of centres for the design and propagation of proposals consonant with an alternative conception of development.

Forms of Alternative Development

The spread of the movement for AD is impressive. It has diversified and takes multitudinous form (its proponents do not believe in one single path towards development). Forms include conceptions of development on a human scale (Max-Neef, Elizonda and Hopenhayn); that is participatory (Rahman, UNRISD), equitable and sustainable (Wolfgang Sachs), human (Max-Neef, UNDP, ICPF), liberating (Goulet) self-centred and self-reliant (Schuldt, Amin), from the inside (Sunkel), from below, people-centred (Korten), community-based and directed (UNICEF), and equitable (ECLAC).[59]

The postulates and theoretical and political propositions (and some models) of this alternative development are diverse and wide-ranging – and the search continues – but it is possible to identify some domain assumptions, common elements, and guiding principles – the heart, we might say, of these alternative proposals, the pillars of the various models constructed within this alternative conception of development. They can be summarized in the following terms:

1. *The community as the base of development.* Forms of AD are not based on the protagonistic forces or dynamism of either the state or of the market, the two central institutions of the liberal-structuralist (orthodox-heterodox) approaches and models. These are distinguished by their alternative ideas and propositions with respect to these two institutions – viz. the role and weight accorded to each in the process of the development. For the exponents of AD the process of development is based rather in community-based organizations; it is defined at the level of the community, an entity characterized by an awareness of collective identity (what sociologists call 'community spirit', something that tends to be lost in the processes of development – modernization, industrialization, urbanization). The community appears as the social base and the beneficiary of development, both object and subject of the process.[60]

2. *Popular participation as an essential condition (of solidarity).* It is essential that the beneficiaries, the object of the process, are at the same time the self-constituted social subject or agent of the development process, the principal protagonist in the development of the community in all of its dimensions – economic, social, political, cultural and ecological. Both neoliberalism (modified as social liberalism) and neostructuralism (a constituted by ECLAC) identifies and projects 'participation' as an essential condition of the process of the development, the 'missing link' between the process of productive transformation and the achievement of equity or social justice in the distribution of productive resources. How-

ever, participation takes the form of incorporating the intended beneficiary into a process initiated at the centre of the system (from above and outside). It has been discovered that without participation of the targeted beneficiaries of the process development as a general rule does not work and associated projects or programmes fail to achieve their strategic objectives.[61]

The incorporation of women, the poor, indigenous people, and respect for the environment, have been converted into basic principles and essential components of both (neo)liberal and (neo) structuralist models and proposals for development. It is the corollary of the widespread proposal to decentralize decision-making and government administration – to delegate responsibility and transfer it to regional and local governments; and to implement public policy, deliver programmes, and execute projects with the support of NGOs.

However, 'participation' in these models has as its basic purpose the incorporation of the intended beneficiaries into the development process and not their constitution as a collective social subject, with the objective of empowering people directly.[62] This is the goal and strategic objective of an alternative development.[63]

The problem is to specify and create the necessary conditions for this form of participation – of an alternative process. This is also the biggest challenge for exponents and agents of Another Development.

3. *Local action and control.* Related to the question of popular participation is the idea of the need to privilege local action. The strategy and the models for national development advanced by neoliberals and neostructuralists (see the following section) share a global context. In this context, those models and proposals contain ideas as to the conditions created by the structure of international relations and of the global economy, and of the need to adjust to developments in this economy (for the insertion of national economies and their enterprises into the globalization process) to the purpose of creating better opportunities and conditions for national development. The propositions (there are no well defined models as yet) of AD, on the other hand, presuppose the need for a selective delinking from this world economy (to pursue a path of national self-reliance), or, at least, an alternative focus on conditions that directly affect the local community. In this context, for example, proposals for AD focus on the need for (a) using locally available resources, both natural and human;

(b) designing technologies appropriate to the human scale of small enterprises and the use of local resources (versus more capital intensive and imports that are monopolized by TNCs), expensive and not locally available);[64] (c) to encourage the formation of local and regional centres of technological research and development, with respect to both appropriate technology and enterprise development management;[65] (d) the creation of industry in or close to the rural communities in the countryside; (e) strengthening local – and regional – markets and reorienting the institutional framework for a cooperative form of production organization; (f) with eyes on these markets, to capitalize and to encourage the formation of small and co-operative enterprises with a high capacity for generating employment and income growth, raising thereby the level of mass consumption as well as promoting community development; and (g) developing local financial institutions with the capacity to capitalize local companies and providing credit to local producers.[66]

4. *An integrated approach.* Aside from these three principles or pillars (a community basis, popular participation, local action) the propositions and proposals of AD (it is difficult to speak of models) are characterized by their emphasis on the multidimensionality and an integral form of development.

If one were to establish a hierarchy among the several dimensions of the development process, then, according to Ignacy Sachs, the emphasis must be on the social aspect, accepting the ecology as a finite and definite limit, and the economic as a means of achieving an integrated form of social and human development.[67] In any event, what has to be underlined is the integrity of the process, viz. the integral connection of the social and the economic with nature and the environment (to be in a symbiotic relation of communion with her rather than one of absolute dominance, respecting its limits and integrity), equity or social justice in the distribution of productive resources, and the human scale of the forms of organization and development

To conclude, the weak point in the search for an alternative development has to with its limited scale and connection with the national development process. A motto of alternative development is: to think in global terms but to act locally. This formulation points towards the problem of connecting the multiplicity of community development projects with processes that reach well beyond these communities and that generate at other levels (national, global) structural conditions of local development. The challenge (and difficulty) is to take these structural conditions into account in that they create an inevitable context which community development practitioners too often ignore or are ignorant of. The problem, in short, is to connect the processes of national development and those that operate at the community level – the global and the local. In this regard, the AD movement provides very few ideas aside from:

(i) the proposal of forming connections and links between public policy and the actions of social organizations and citizens;[68]
(ii) democratizing the structures and the institutions of the state, creating thereby political spaces for the actions of these organizations at the national level – and ditto at the global level;[69] and
(iii) seeking and forming organizations and forms of mediation (and networking) that can assure the effective participation of civil society in national institutions such as education, health, banking, and other indispensable state institutions.

What these proposals generally avoid is a discussion (and perhaps understanding) of the institutions of the global and national market, and of the relationships of class that sustain both these institutions and those of the state. And in this failure can be found the theoretical and political limits of the movement formed by the search for an alternative development.

ECLAC and the Neostructuralist Model

The UN Economic Commission for Latin America (ECLAC, or CEPAL in its better known Spanish acronym), with its headquarters in Santiago, Chile, is one of the few political and intellectual fortresses formed to contain the wave of neoliberalism that swept over so much of Latin America in the 1980s. At the turn of the 1990s the limits and contradictions of neoliberalism had been clearly exposed, leading its exponents and apologists towards a search for a series of reforms that would give it a Human Face and thus to salvage it from the forces that threatened it.

However, although the resulting facade could, and did, soften the system's worst effects it could not obviate its negative impacts, nor contain the forces of resistance and opposition. Even the defenders of the system and the ideologues of neoliberalism had recourse to a search for an alternative model, one that would at the very least control and channel the protests generated by neoliberal policies. In this context, ECLAC responded with the design of a model that opened up the possibility of putting the continent of Latin America on a new and more viable road, one that would leave intact the basic pillars of the capitalist system. At least, this is how ECLAC viewed the challenge confronting it.[70]

In Latin America, the debate as to the possible alternatives to neoliberalism has travelled the extremes of the political spectrum: from technocratic proposals to make it more efficient and viable (reducing its social costs), calls for a new utopia and rejection of the doctrine, to the construction of an alternative more popular model. In this context, ECLAC occupies the centre. In the 1960s, ECLAC had been the principal promoter of the import substitution industrialization (ISI) policy. But with the apparent exhaustion or failure of this policy and the apparent success of the alternative policy of industrialization by export promotion (EPI), advocated by neoliberal economists on the basis of neoclassical theory and with reference to the high growth rates of the East Asian economies, ECLAC lost much of its considerable influence. At the end of 1980s, ECLAC sought to escape its intellectual – and political – isolation and to recover this influence together with its pioneering role in the field of development by the construction of an alternative model based on neostructuralist assumptions. Although it is aligned to several assumptions that are antithetical to neoliberalism, the neostructuralist model constructed by ECLAC exhibits a curious amalgam of neoliberal and alternative propositions. First, it is evident that ECLAC theoreticians are now in agreement with neoliberals as to the need for a structural adjustment to changes in the world economy and that one must pursue such adjustment in a context of macroeconomic equilibrium, that is, fiscal discipline, balanced accounts, and control of inflationary tendencies, whether these be attributed to monetary causes (excess money supply), as argued by the monetarists aligned with neoliberalism, or the structure of the economy, as long argued by ECLAC economists. Thus ECLAC now accepts the neoliberal argument of the need to avoid a substantial deficit in the national and fiscal accounts of trade (and of capital). However, it is not in agreement with other elements of the neoliberal recipe.

The essence of the neostructural model can be found in its redefinition of the goal of the development process. Instead of pursuing the goal of economic reactivation, the growth of production, at any – and considerable – social cost (under conditions of macroeconomic stability and a more efficient restructuring of the production apparatus), ECLAC argues the need to combine 'productive transformation', the engine of growth, with 'equity', a more just distribution of society's productive resources. In this regard, ECLAC essentially returned to the 'growth with equity' approach (no specific model had been formulated) advocated by the proponents of liberal and social reform within the dominant paradigm in the 1970s.[71] Like the 'growth with equity' approach of the liberal and social reformers in the 1970s, ECLAC's proposal for productive transformation with equity was predicated on a series of economic and political reforms of the dominant capitalist system – to give it a social dimension and a human face.

The neoliberal model is based on the idea that the benefits of growth, which initially are necessarily concentrated, sooner or later trickle down to other social sectors including the poor, absolving politicians and technocrats of the responsibility for assuring their equitable distribution. ECLAC economists do not subscribe to this 'theory', which is to say, they do not believe that it will happen. Nor do they believe it to be economically necessary. Rather, they postulate equity both as a necessary precondition for and a requirement of a process of development that is sustainable (in social and political terms); and that require specific measures that go beyond mitigation of the conditions of poverty: improved access to productive resources of a broader range of diverse economic agents, radical reform in the tax regime, and the redistribution of income and other resources. Such reforms imply a much more active role for the state than that proposed by neoliberals.

In essence, ECLAC proposes an effective developmentalist state on the East Asia model, one with relative autonomy (*vis-à-vis* diverse social classes, including the dominant capitalist class); that assigns the private sector primary responsibility for production, but, in alliance with this sector, assumes the responsibility for regulating capital and intervening in the economy as required to assure productive investment in infrastructure and social capital, technological reconversion of the productive apparatus, the industrialisation process, and social welfare.

In practice, the policy of the current *concertacion* regime in Chile is seen by many, including its own protagonists, as an example of the ECLAC model. Others see in this regime nothing but neoliberalism with a human face, which, it could be argued, is all that ECLAC offers.[72] In any event, in its theoretical formulation of public policy ECLAC can be said to go further than Chile's social democrats in proposals as to the need for a redistribution of productive resources, agrarian reform, and a progressive tax regime.

The theoretical model constructed by ECLAC constitutes a set of postulates and proposals that to some extent, as indicated, are grounded in an analysis of various lessons drawn from the experience of the rapidly growing countries (RGCs) of East Asia and that discards key elements of neoliberal dogma.[73] The problem with the model, and its weak point, as with so many, is how to put it into practice? This problem in good part is political. On this point, at the global level the ECLAC model has received strong endorsement from UN operational agencies such as the UNDP, but financial institutions as the world Bank, the IMF, and the Organization of World Trade, are much less enthusiastic, even politely hostile. These institutions are tied and have a vital commitment to the neoliberal model, and they are in a position to block implementation of the ECLAC model.

At the domestic level problems of implementation can be even greater. How to convert an ineffectual state, servile to the interests of the dominant class into an efficient and effective state that is relatively autonomous, and capable of strategic planning, of regulating capital, and of promoting development? How to impose the redistribution of the society's productive resources without provoking a capital flight and an economic crisis? How to attract the foreign investment on which the model remains dependent (in its *rapprochement* with neoliberalism ECLAC has rejected its earlier position of independence *vis-à-vis* foreign capital), or to prevent its decamping once it is subjected to some restriction? With the resumption of some protection to strategic industries, how does the government prevent or answer to the retaliatory responses of the USA and the World Bank?

Is the state capable of negotiating a reduction or cancellation of an external debt of over 500 billion dollars that continues to severely constrain or strangle many economies in the region – a debt that has in any case been paid many times over and widely regarded as illegitimate? How to assure its relative autonomy from the operative social forces – of the pressures and demands of 'civil society'? In the Asian countries this 'autonomy' was achieved as the result (and severe political costs) of political repression of the working class as well as strong arm tactics used against recalcitrant sections or groups within the capitalist class. But ECLAC proposes democratic mechanisms – a policy of participation and decentralization (of public policy decision-making and administration), seen as 'the missing link' between 'productive transformation' and 'equity', the institutional means of securing popular participation.[74] In this context, how to reconcile immediate demands to pay back the large social debt contracted by neoliberal regimes with the technocratic plans for development in the medium or long term?[75]

In these questions we not only locate the challenge faced by ECLAC in the implementation of its neostructuralist model but its political – and theoretical – limits.

3 The Restructuring of Labour

INTRODUCTION

In recent years the World Bank, the OECD, and PREALC among other international organizations, policy-makers and academics have identified and addressed head-on the perceived need for labour to adjust to the requirements of the new economic order and to become more flexible.[1] The rationale presented for this research and policy agenda is that labour either adjusts to these requirements or it confronts a worsening of the problems that afflict it – unemployment, economic insecurity, bad jobs and low income. In this context these and many other organizations have taken up the banner of labour and labour-market reform – of a mandated or legislated restructuring of 'industrial relations', associated labour markets, and the organization of labour in production.

It is the thesis of this chapter that this entire process of labour reform, together with the political process of convincing labour to go along with it – to adjust to it, is part of an offensive waged by capital against labour, and as such is based on an agenda that reflects the interests of capital, to be opposed and resisted at all costs. However, labour cannot do so without understanding what is at issue. To this end (to provide a few elements of such understanding) this chapter is organised as follows. In section one we deconstruct the agenda of the World Bank and other such organizations, with reference to conditions confronted by workers in Latin America. In sections two and three we explore key dimensions of these conditions as they relate to the organization of labour in the production process and associated labour markets. Our main focus here is on the issue of wages and their connection to productivity gains in the organization of production and in the process of capital accumulation. We also bring into focus the issue of productive investment as it relates to a process of technological conversion and productive transformation underway in Latin America and elsewhere. In the concluding section we draw together the threads of our analysis, providing a brief theoretical discourse on the problems of Latin American labour.

Latin American Labour in a Global Context

According to the World Bank, about 99 per cent of the workers projected to join the world's labour market over the next 30 years will live and work in what it labels the 'low- and middle-income' countries of Africa, Asia, the Caribbean and Latin America (the latter currently constituting about 8.4 per cent of the world's Economically Active Population; 6.1 of production; and 3.9 per cent of exports and 3.2 per cent of imports, down from 12 and 10.1 per cent in 1950).[2] As the Bank sees or constructs it, there is, with the support of a concerted programme of structural adjustment policies, a global trend towards increasing integration into and the interdependence of countries within a global economy, but there is no discernible trend towards convergence – towards equality in the form and conditions of such integration among countries or between the small number of the rich, the larger number of relatively well-off workers, and the much larger number of poor workers across the world. Indeed, the Bank argues, there are serious 'risks that the workers in {the} poorer countries will fall further behind' and that some national groups of workers, especially in sub-Saharan Africa, could become increasingly marginalized in a global process of 'the general prosperity in countries that are enjoying growth'.[3]

The only preventative remedy for avoiding this trend and for participating in a perceived (and partially projected) dynamic of rising incomes, better working conditions and enhanced job security is for all countries to systematically pursue the right domestic policies, sound labour policies that promote labour-demanding growth. Such policies, the Bank notes, fundamentally involves 'the use of markets to create opportunities', and specifically include legislation designed to create more flexible forms of labour and labour markets. Conditions of such flexibility include, on the part of workers, greater mobility – the capacity to relocate if necessary – and a willingness to accept whatever jobs are on offer, with possibly lower levels of remuneration; and, on the part of employers, increased capacity to participate in the production process, able to hire, fire, locate, and use workers as required at the point of production, and to pay them on the basis of market conditions.

It is with explicit reference to this idea[4] – of a labour market in which the forces of supply and demand can and do reach equilibrium, providing an optimum allocation of resources (returns to factors of production) – that the World Bank has virtually stalked the corridors of power all over Latin America in the search of policy-makers with the political will, and the institutional capacity, to introduce a programme of legislative (and, if necessary, constitutional) labour reforms. Associated with this idea is the notion that in general wages are too high,[5] the result not only of government interference with the labour market (particularly in the legislation of minimum wages) but of the excessive monopoly power of the unions.[6] As the Bank sees it – and it is argued (or asserted rather) vociferously with as much technical support and data it can muster (and interpret on the basis of the formulae constructed for this purpose) – the high wage rates, excessive benefits accorded to workers in the social programmes introduced by earlier populist governments, and the general inflexibility of workers, lead private sector entrepreneurs to withdraw from the production process, thus contributing towards the problems of high unemployment, informalization, and poverty (see Tables 3.3 and 3.6 for glimpses into the scope and depth of these problems).[7]

How have Latin American policy-makers responded to such advice and to the associated pressures to adopt it? First of all, virtually every country in the region in the 1980s instituted a programme of structural adjustment that created the preconditions and an institutional framework for the proposed new labour policy, the material conditions of which were being formed on the basis of an on-going process of technological conversion and productive transformation.[8] Those governments that had not done so have all come around in the 1990s, including Argentina, Peru and Venezuela, and even Brazil which, for the most part, had not participated in the liberalization, privatization, and dimensions of the adjustment. On the institutional basis of this structural adjustment and its associated reforms, the entrepreneurs and employers of labour everywhere (or, in many cases) have joined the financiers – and the World Bank – in demanding reforms of labour legislation, and where required (as In Brazil) the constitutional amendments required to allow and secure greater flexibility of labour markets. In some cases, as in Mexico and El Salvador, the new labour regime has been established within the export enclave of an expanding maquilladora industry.[9] In other situations, as in Chile, the new labour regime was introduced on a national basis as a critical component of a process of industrial conversion and productive transformation.[10] In each and every case, the process of structural adjustment and productive transformation has been accompanied by a political struggle to introduce through legislative reform, administrative fiat, or, increasingly, by executive decree, a more flexible form of production and a corresponding labour regime.

Labour Market Reform: A New Regime of Accumulation

The basic idea, advanced in the World Bank's 1995 World Development Report, widely diffused in various publications and numerous conferences staged and sponsored by the Bank and its sister institutions, and underlying the series of Plans for Economic and Social Development introduced by country after country in the region as of around 1989, is that the solution to the region's problems, particularly that of unemployment, requires a new and more flexible mode of organizing production, as well as legislative (and perhaps constitutional) reform leading to the increased flexibility of labour. In Latin America as elsewhere, the Bank argues, government regulation of labour was designed primarily as an instrument of social policy, above all to secure and protect the right to full employment, adequate and minimum wages, and secure tenure. In practice, such legislation, particularly as relates to minimum wages, rather than serving as it should, as a means of achieving an efficient allocation of resources, has produced a most inefficient and inflexible labour market in which the demand for labour has not been able to keep up with its supply, resulting in, among other things, an unmanageable and costly problem (in economic and social – as well as political – terms) of high unemployment and the increasing informalization of work arrangements and conditions.[11]

The response of the Bank, reflecting its concern that 'at the world level [as well as in the region] there exists a serious [problem] with unemployment and informality', and without even any abstracted reference to the underlying process of industrial conversion and productive transformation. Is that governments need to reform their labour codes, to ensure a greater flexibility of labour – and thereby the reduction of labour costs in production and the generation of more and better employment.[12]

The problem, as the Bank sees it, is twofold. On the one hand, minimum wage legislation distorts the proper functioning of the labour market, leading to the withdrawal of capital from the production process and thus unemployment as well as informalization. On the other hand, it is necessary to reduce or suppress the monopolistic bargaining power acquired by labour through its sector-wide 'representative unions' so that entrepreneurs and workers can arrive at and arrange independent agreements in accord with market conditions and requirements.[13] And one of the key requirements, the Bank makes clear, is the lowering of excessively high wages in the productive (and public) sectors of the economy, and of the associated benefits legislated by government,

which effectively reduce and inhibit the participation of entrepreneurs in the production process.[14]
The effective response to these requirements, and the solution to the underlying and associated problems is labour market reform designed to make labour more flexible. Since 1989, such reform has been placed on the political agenda of most countries in the region, together with a programme of technological conversion and productive transformation, a new social policy designed by the World Bank to soften the blow of the SAP on the poor,[15] the decentralization of government (to create a more participatory form of community-based development),[16] and the modernization of the state apparatus (to create a more efficient and democratic system of public service and administration).[17]

The Capital–Labour Relation in the Organization of Production

The change in the relation of capital to labour wrought by the structural adjustment and reform process of the 1980s and 1990s can be traced out on both a structural and a political level. In structural terms, the change relates to (i) the organization of labour within a process of technological conversion and what CEPAL terms 'productive transformation';[18] (ii) the contribution of labour to production as measured by its productivity; (iii) the rate of exploitation (extraction of surplus value) as measured by the return to capital and labour of their respective contribution to production – the share of profit and wages in national income and in value added; and (iv) the evolution of real wages relative to growth in the gross national product (GNP).

Productive Transformation

With respect to the process of productive transformation, determined or regulated essentially by the rate of investment and the pace of technological conversion, significant advances have been made in key production sectors and industries in a number of countries, particularly Argentina, Brazil, Chile, Colombia and Mexico.[19] The pace of advance in this transformation has been both conditioned and limited by the generally low levels of productive investment reflected in Table 3.1.[20] In this respect, Chile is the only country in the region that has had in recent years what would appear to be an adequate level of productive investment compared to levels found in the expanding economies of East and Southeast Asia.[21] Another critical factor in the regional process of productive transformation is the relative contribution of capital and labour

Table 3.1 Levels of productive investment and capital formation, 1980–95, selected countries(% of GNP)

	1980–1	1984–5	1990	1994–5
Argentina	25.3	17.6	14.0	19.9
Brazil	23.3	19.7	21.9	24.5
Chile	16.6	12.3	23.3	29.3
Mexico	27.2	21.2	21.9	24.5
Peru	29.0	18.4	15.5	22.2
Bolivia	14.2	7.0	13.2	15.5
El Salvador		12.6	13.7	18.5
Latin America	**24.8**	**19.2**	**19.7**	**19.6**
Developing Countries	25.7	23.4	24.7	25.8
Least Developed Countries	17.3	14.6	16.1	15.5
East Asian NICs	34.4	26.2	31.3	32.1
South Korea	32.0	29.6	36.9	38.4
China	30.1	38.6	33.2	42.6

Source: UN (1996): 143, 156, 193, 196, 305; World Bank (1995).

and the impact of what is termed in the modern theory of growth as 'total factor productivity'.[22]

With regard to this factor, it would appear that the relative contributions to production of capital and labour has been and remain relatively low and generally less than the increase in 'total factor productivity' (see Table 3.2).[23] Although this point needs a closer look and more detailed and systematic analysis, we can postulate that to some extent the relative increase in total productivity is associated with a change in the organization of production, viz. increased flexibility, as well as the incorporation of new information-rich technologies and an increased orientation towards export markets, which has allowed for a greater realization of the surplus value embodied in the social product.

Production and Income Shares of Capital and Labour

As for the distribution of the social product or national income between capital and labour, governments in the region generally have not established any specific policy. The operating theory behind this do-nothing policy is the same as that used to justify the proposed policy of labour flexibility and the elimination of minimum-wage legislation: that the free market is the most efficient mechanism for allocating resources on the basis of equitable returns to productive factors.[24] On

Table 3.2 Factor contributions to economic growth (%)

		GNP	Capital	Labour	TFP
Chile	1986–90	6.58	2.85	0.08	3.92
	1991–3	8.12	4.08	0.07	3.98
Colombia	1986–90	4.63	1.94	0.10	2.59
	1991–3	3.77	2.41	0.09	1.27
Peru	1986–90	–1.70	0.95	0.11	–2.80
	1991–3	2.26	0.69	0.11	1.46
Brazil	1986–90	1.94	1.60	0.08	0.26
	1991–3	1.48	0.84	0.08	0.56
Mexico	1986–90	1.38	1.47	0.13	–0.20
	1991–3	2.35	2.28	0.12	0.00

Source: FUSADES (1966: 6), calculated on the basis of World Bank data.

this basis the World Bank has pushed for the elimination of minimum-wage legislation as an obstacle to the proper functioning of the labour market and indirectly to an efficient and equitable distribution of the social product (national income) or the economic surplus. On the same basis, the World Bank has designed a Plan for Economic and Social Development, subsequently adopted with variations by virtually every country in the region,[25] that did not include an explicit wages policy, it being understood that the advocated liberalization of prices, together with the proposed labour market reforms, by itself would lead to an optimum level of wages and employment; and that, therefore, minimum wages, like that of wages in general, should be negotiated directly by the parties involved under market conditions. Thus has the Bank put into motion its proposal to abolish minimum wage legislation, supported with the assertion that such legislation interferes with the working of the market forces of supply and demand and leads to the withdrawal of capital from the production process, so bringing about unemployment as well as increased informality and impoverishment.

Another proposition of the theory underlying the Plan for Economic and Social Development implemented in the region[26] is that when liberalized (freed from government interference), the labour market would automatically regulate the level of wages according to the marginal productivity of labour, at which point the supply of labour would be equal to its demand.[27] So what has been the dynamic of this relationship between wages and the marginal productivity of labour?

With reference to 'research' conducted by and reported on by the Bank at its Second Annual Conference on Latin American and Caribbean Development in Bogota,[28] the experience of Chile, Colombia, and Peru with labour market reform (flexibilization) has been demonstrably positive: a decrease in the official rate of open unemployment with an adjustment of wage levels towards the marginal productivity of labour. As for the employment issue there would appear to be no factual basis to the Bank's assertion, although serious questions about the explanation given.

However, on the issue of the marginal productivity of labour there is not even a basis in fact.[29] If the Bank were correct in its assertion one would expect to find a long-term empirical trend towards the growth of average productivity at a rate below that of real wages, which, in turn, would have tended to reduce the participation of capital in the production process. Is there any evidence of such a trend? First, it is clear enough that real wages have generally declined, a trend that can be traced out in every country in the region since at least 1982. On average, real wages have dropped from 15 to 25 per cent since 1985, but in a number of cases they have dropped by as much as 50 to 86 per cent (Table 3.3,).[30] In the case of Argentina, Peru, and Venezuela real wages in 1995 had not yet recovered levels achieved in 1970, while in Mexico, according to the Bank of Mexico, they had lost 71.4 per cent of their 1976 value, reaching their lowest point in thirty years.[31] Given this trend, coupled with an actual decrease in the number of workers in the formal sector,[32] it is hard to imagine that the rate of growth in labour productivity would be negative as supposed by the Bank. Given the lack of data and comparative systematic analysis it is, in fact, not so easy to calculate the precise connection between wage levels and productivity gains, but the studies that have been done suggest a gradual but persistent increase in productivity throughout the 1980s and 1990s.[33]

Given the apparently low levels in the contribution of capital and labour to the production process (see Table 3.2),[34] this increase in productivity has to be explained in terms of factors other than labour and capital, factors such as the reorganization of production for greater flexibility. At one level, the decline in real wages could reflect a reduced level of labour productivity associated with the destruction of productive capacity brought about by the cut in social programmes and an investment in 'human capital' (the education and health of workers). But given the divergence between rates of productivity growth and wage rates,[35] it is clear enough that real wages, both on average and at minimum levels, are neither adjusted to or determined by the marginal productivity of

Table 3.3 Wage income conditions in Latin America, selected indicators and countries (accumulated % change)

		Real average wages	Real minimum wages	Index minimum wages	Per capita income
Argentina	1980–6	7	47		–23
	1986–90	–22	–64		–15
	1990–1	–7	39		5
Brazil	1979–87	19	–27		3
	1987–90	–29	–26		–6
	1990–4			47–49	
Chile	1980–7	–5			–3
	1987–90	11	27		18
	1990–4			73–93	
Mexico	1970–84	–15	–20		31
	1981–4	–30	–32		–12
	1984–7	–16	–17		
	1987–9	–2	–16		2
	1990–4			42–38	
Peru	1979–86	–5	–15		–7
	1990–4			21–14	
Venezuela	1981–86	–19	6		–31
	1980–90				

Sources: Alimir (1994: 7–32); Rosenbluth (1994: 170, 175); FUSADES (1996: 5).

labour. More generally, the brutal compression of wages can better be connected to (and explained in terms of) structurally or politically determined conditions of unemployment and inflation as well as the direct repression of working class organizations.[36] In any case, over the long term real wages in the region have tended to evolve to levels well below the marginal productivity of labour, in the process creating an essential requirement and condition for a process of renewed capital accumulation: the extraction of surplus value from its direct producer, the working class.

In structural terms, the contribution of labour to a process of capital accumulation (the extraction of surplus value) is reflected in the share of wages in the income derived from the social product – and in its share of the value added in the process. In each and every case, these ratios have tended to decrease over the course of ten to fifteen years of neoliberal reforms, in some cases dramatically – by as much as 25 per cent (see Tables 3.4 and 3.5). And, by the same token, the share of capital in national income and the value added increased correspondingly, anywhere from around 60 to 75 per cent. However, the significant increase in the rate of exploitation (estimated by Montesino and Gochez to be in the order of 190 per cent in the case of El Salvador), and in the transfer of income from labour to capital, did not translate into a process of renewed and sustained capital accumulation, raising a number of critical questions.

First, it would seem that (i) the sharp compression of wages and reduction in the share of wages in national income has been used in a major way as a mechanism of internal adjustment,[37] but that (ii) the extraordinarily high social costs of this adjustment, borne largely by workers, cannot even be justified in terms of the imperative of renewed accumulation and sustaining the process of national capitalist development. Productive investments in the region have been and remain at levels well below the level of surplus value extracted and the income

Table 3.4 Share of wages in GNP, selected Latin American countries

	1970	1980	1985	1988	1990
Argentina	40.9	31.5	31.9	24.9	-
Bolivia	36.8	39.6	26.9	-	-
Brazil	34.2	35.1	36.3	-	-
Chile	47.7	43.4	37.8	-	-
Ecuador	34.4	34.8	23.6	16.0	15.8
Mexico	37.5	39.0	31.6	28.4	27.3
Peru	40.0	32.8	30.5	25.5	16.8
Uruguay	52.9	35.7	36.3	39.7	-
Venezuela	40.3	42.7	37.6	34.6	31.1

Source: CEPAL, *Anuario Estadistico*, selected years.

Table 3.5 Employee earnings as a percentage of value added to manufacturing production

	1967	1971	1975	1979	1983	1987	1989	1992
Brazil	17.3	23.6	18.9	20.7	19.7	15.1	15.0	23
Chile	25.1	22.8	12.3	18.2	17.1	16.8	16.6	18
Mexico	44.0	42.7	39.1	34.7	23.8	19.8	19.8	22
Venezuela	30.1	30.0	27.3	28.5	31.6	26.8	24.2	19
Colombia	28.2	24.0	20.6	19.7	20.9	18.9	16.1	15

Source: World Bank, *World Development Reports*, various years.

transferred from labour.[38] Only in Chile has a substantial part of the income transferred from labour been converted into capital, generating a comparatively high level of productive investment in physical and social capital.[39] In most other countries, a substantial part of the economic surplus generated by, and extracted from, the workers and the direct producers has been dedicated to the servicing of the external debt[40] unproductive or speculative 'investments', the purchase of the shares of privatized companies (which accounts for well over 50 per cent of the wave of new investments in the 1990s, and the consumption of the wealth and income generated in the process.[41]

BY WAY OF A CONCLUSION: FORMS OF EXPLOITATION IN THE PRODUCTION PROCESS

At issue in the World Bank's approach to labour market reform in Latin America are the policies required to reduce the high levels of un- and under-employment in the region as well as the trend towards informalization and its associated conditions of low productivity and income. Table 3.6 provides a brief glimpse into the actual distribution of some of these conditions.[42] The evident tendency for an extension of these conditions, and a deepening of their social effects, underscores the seriousness of the issue – of confronting the World Bank's conception of the problem and its remedy of labour market reform which, we have argued, is at best designed to address and solve quite a different problem (to create the conditions for a renewed and sustained process of capital accumulation). And, as we see it, the Bank's proposed remedy does not correctly identify the structural sources of the problem – of the problem as experienced by labour or as perceived by capital. Thus it might be useful to review some points of our analysis and to briefly identify the key dimensions of the problem as we see it, to contribute thereby towards a better understanding of it as well as a more appropriate political response.

The aim of the World Bank's approach to labour market reform in Latin America as elsewhere is to promote the restructuring of the relation of capital to labour in the production process. And it is well understood by the Bank and other agents and apologists of capitalism that the essence of this capital–labour relation is the extraction of surplus value from its direct producer, the worker, in the form of the wage, which represents the value of the labour expended in the process. The facts and nature of this productive relationship are well known, although it fell upon Marx over a hundred years ago to unveil its then hidden secret in a very different context. As Marx emphasized, the key to a sustainable process of capital accumulation is the extraction of relative surplus value on the basis of an exchange of equivalents, wages for labourpower, the value of which, as with every other commodity, is determined by the socially necessary labour-time needed to produce it. The production of relative surplus value is, as Marx argued, the truly revolutionary path towards capitalist development, as opposed to the production of absolute surplus value – increasing the productivity of labour on the basis of technological conversion as opposed to the lengthening of the work day or, as we will argue, reducing wages without a change in the technological and social conditions of production. The production and extraction of relative surplus is predicated on the substitution of capital for labour, the incorporation of new technology which (i) will raise the organic composition of capital, (ii) slough off labour, and (iii) increase the productivity of labour.

In this process of technological conversion and productive transformation, to use contemporary language, labour is exchanged for wages at its value, which, given that this value is determined by and reflects the latest technological advances, implies that it is has some connection to the resulting increases in productivity. In this process, the value of labour power is essentially a function of technology although, as Marx

Table 3.6 Surplus labour and underdevelopment in Latin America, 1993–4: countries ranked by *per capita* income (percentage distribution of EAP, population and GNP)

	Unemployment (1)	Informal sector (2)	Rural agric. society (3)	Rural prod. (4)	Poverty (5)
Argentina	17.5	45.4	13	6.5	20
Bolivia	4.6	48.1	41	16.4	97
Brazil	5.1	48.8	29	10.5	73
Chile	7.4	37.6	16	9.1	56
Colombia	8.5		28	14.9	45
Mexico	6.3	41.0	26	7.6	51
Peru	8.8		29	6.9	75
Uruguay	10.8	34.4	10	10.7	-
Venezuela	10.9	44.3	8	4.7	-

Sources: (1) CEPAL (1996): 14; (2) CEPAL (1995): 179; (3)–(4) World Bank (1995); (5) Jazairy, *et al.* (1992).

emphasized, the rate of exploitation, which is conditioned by the capacity of workers to participate in any productivity gains, is by and large determined by political conditions of the class struggle – the correlation of class forces. In this context, and with reference to developments in the region but that have unfolded worldwide as of the mid-1970s, it would seem that the balance of class forces has turned against labour, resulting in among other things a decreased capacity of workers to participate in the productivity gains of new technology – to adjust wages to productivity.[43] Although this development is worldwide, the situation of workers in Latin America and elsewhere on the margins of the globalized capitalist economy is worse than that of those at the centre of the system in that the conditions of relative surplus value extraction, at the heart of the accumulation process, are often and generally combined with those of absolute surplus value[44] as well as of what has been conceptualized as 'super-exploitation' – the extraction of surplus value on the basis of a reduction of wages below the value of labour-power.[45]

The conditions of this super-exploitation are complex and variable but its basic mechanism is easy enough to identify: the formation and operation of what Marx regarded as an industrial reserve army', a large reservoir of surplus labour – surplus to the requirements of capital. The existence of such a reservoir of surplus labour can be identified at the global level – in, for example, the large mass (28 million or so) of unemployed workers in Europe, as well as the interstices of an emerging global labour market – but its most substantial and significant formation is found in the economies of Latin America and other countries and regions that are, as it were, 'in the process' of development. A characteristic feature of this process is the formation of what in the urban economies of these societies has been identified as the 'informal sector' and in the rural economies a mass (and at times a class) of small producers, a subsistent and local economy of basic grain peasant producers. Table 3.6 indicates for Latin America the scope of these economic activities and their associated problems, which are the major objects of the World Bank's professed concern – the chief target of its policy programmes.

Although it applies equally well to the large and growing informal sector, the conditions of a surplus population have been documented and to some extent analyzed in the context of the region's peasant economies of small grain producers. In this context, what has been emphasized has been the classic working of a surplus population as a lever of capital accumulation – allowing capitalist entrepreneurs to depress the wages of their workers and, in the process, to increase profits and maintain the competitivity of their enterprises. However, several additional dimensions of this economic function have been identified for the subsistence and commercial operations of the small scale producers linked to the peasant economy: as with the informal sector they provide wage goods at low prices, even at below the cost of production, as well as a source of employment and additional income for family members. In this regard they provide to some extent a subsidy to the capitalist operations in the area. Evidence of this can be found in the basic grain component of the food basket on the basis of which the Ministry of Planning and policy-makers in every Latin American country estimate the minimum income requirements and the incidence of poverty within the urban population. Generally speaking, what is found is that the cost of basic grains over time tends to rise more slowly than the other components of the food basket.[46]

Analysts also tend to agree that the small producers of these basic grains, the social base and a principal target of the Bank's – and governments' – ubiquitous anti-poverty programmes, often serve as a refuge (source of employment) for an over-abundant surplus population. In this regard, the small-producer sector of Latin America's rural society, like the urban informal sector, can be seen to function as a reservoir of surplus labour, holding in reserve the labour of the semi-proletarianized *temporeros,* the landless producer-workers who migrate annually for wage-work on a seasonal basis in the agro-export industries that continue to dominate the rural economies of so many Latin American societies.[47] In addition, in the border and northern and central states of Mexico, such as Zacatecas, the small producer sector provides a source of cheap surplus labour for the low wage service industries and the agricultural sector of the US economy. In both cases, the rural society of small producers underwrites some of the reproductive costs of the labour subsumed directly or indirectly by the capitalist enterprises both in the free trade zones and in the industries that have been subject to the process technological conversion and productive transformation. We regard this as super-exploitation.

These developments and conditions can be found all across Latin America. Not only do they underlie the problems targeted by the World Bank (un- and under-employment and poverty), but they are connected to the identified problem of a relatively limited unsustainable process of capitalist development in the region.[48] The major problem in this regard is the failure of the region's capitalists and policy-makers, often one and the same, to convert the surplus value extracted from the workers (and the disproportionate share of national income which they have appropriated through various means) into capital – productive investment in physical and social capital. This problem, as we have seen, is largely a question of these capitalists pursuing and relying on a strategy of cheap labour for enterprises and industries oriented towards exports on the world market.[49] In this regard, in many cases the cost of labour in the process of production has been lowered to a level of 20 per cent and lower – as low as 10 per cent in the case of Mexico.[50]

On the basis of this strategy capital has little to no interest in maintaining the purchasing power of wages and dynamizing the local and regional markets on which the process of capitalist development generally has to depend.[51] Nor does it have much interest in taking what Marx regarded as the revolutionary path towards capitalist development – productive investment and capital accumulation on the basis of relative surplus value.[52] In this context, the World Bank's proposed labour market reforms, even when designed to facilitate the process of technological conversion and productive transformation, is condemned to failure. They will not prevent either capital or labour, which in any case will (have to) bear the social costs of adjustment, from being marginalized in the global process identified by the Bank – 'the general prosperity of countries that are enjoying growth'.

4 The Politics of Community-based Participatory Development

INTRODUCTION

No concept is as central in the study of development, or as problematic in its application, as 'participation', viewed from the most diverse theoretical perspectives as a critically important precondition and condition of the development process. Over the years this concept has had diverse points of reference and has been subject to a numerous twists both in its conception and various efforts to institutionalize it – to put it into practice. These twists not only reflect various shifts in conception, but changes in the context of real conditions that underlie and to some extent induce these shifts. In the context of conditions given in the 1980s, the concept of participation or participatory development has been closely linked to a widespread process of government decentralization and local community-based development.

Underlying and associated with this trend, providing for it a context of socio-economic and political conditions, can be found (i) the emergence of a neoconservative anti-state ideology (expressed *inter alia* in the idea of a minimalist state and a trend towards the downsizing and privatization of government operations and services); (ii) a counter-revolution in development thinking and practice; and with it (iii) the institution of a neoliberal model of structural adjustment. Under these conditions, the concept of 'participation' also has been linked to a widespread global trend towards the decentralization of government services and powers in the 1980s and an associated search for a local community-based and-directed form of development.

The purpose of this chapter is to reconstruct and analyze the dynamics of this decentralization process in the context of conditions that define the Latin American experience. To this purpose, the chapter is organized into three parts. The first traces the major twists and turns in the concept of participatory development. In the second part we examine the trend towards decentralization of government services in the Latin American context. In this context we argue that the impetus for the process relates to both initiatives from above (from within government itself) and from below (from pressures to democratize the political institutions of society and the relations between the state and civil society). In the third part we examine several dynamics of this twofold process, highlighting a number of findings that are summarized in the conclusion.

THE ITINERARY OF A CONCEPT

The concept of popular participation is deeply embedded in the theory of democracy but in the contemporary post-World War II context of development studies, one of the earliest formulations of the concept can be found in a 1964 study by the UN Economic Commission of Latin America (CEPAL, in its better known Spanish acronym). CEPAL's concept of participation as a necessary condition of development at the time was somewhat anachronistic in that it did not have the slightest resonance or intellectual force, formulated as it was in the context of (i) capitalism's 'Golden Age', an extended period of unprecedented continuously high annual rates of growth in total output,[1] and (ii) the intellectual adjunct to this Golden Age – the grandiose optimistic prognosis and formulae for successful development advanced by the 'grand theorists of the new discipline'.[2] It would be twenty-five years before ECLAC, the founder and principal expositor of the structuralist thinking that dominated the study of development,[3] would come back to this concept of participation. In the meantime the concept would be given a systematic reformulation by exponents of a search for Another Development, a form of development that depended on neither the functioning of the free market nor the agency of the state in regulating it.

This search for Another Development, announced publicly at a conference organized in 1974 by the Dag Hammarskjold Foundation,[4] was initiated in a very different and changed historical context. The world economic order installed at Bretton Woods in the wake of the second World War, and the associated Golden Age of capitalist development, had exhausted their limits and the entire global capitalist system had gone into a deep structural crisis manifest in (i) a general tendency towards declining productivity; (ii) stagnant rates of growth in output; (iii) an underlying 'profitability crunch' (a declining rate of profit on invested capital); (iv) the discovery (by the World Bank) that at least 800 million people in the 'Third World' of sub-Saharan Africa, Asia and Latin America were unable to meet even their basic needs; (v) the simultaneous emergence of mass unemployment and runaway inflation; and (vi) the inability of the developmentalist (interventionist) state to deal with the problem of underdevelopment and poverty or of the actually existing state to cope and deal with the problems of unemployment and inflation.[5]

The conditions of this changed context were reflected in development thinking – and practice – at a number of levels. First, the central concept of development was broadened and extended to include a specific and distinctly social dimension – health, education, social security and welfare (meeting basic needs). In these terms, the concern for and goal of development, the object of the development process, was no longer just a matter of economic (GNP per capita) growth but included the creation of social conditions, the meeting of the population's basic needs, the amelioration if not the reduction or eradication of world poverty, and a more equitable distribution of the world's productive and economic resources – and the benefits of economic growth.[6]

In this changed context, various formulations of 'participation' or 'participatory development' had two major centres of reference. On the one hand, the reform-oriented liberal intellectuals that dominated the field as development consultants and planners, as well as the national governments and international organizations that employed them or contracted their services, generally took 'participation' to mean the incorporation of the intended beneficiaries into the development process. Thus it was recognised that in terms of education and health women were generally central agents in the development process but excluded from most of its benefits; and that in terms of both improved access to society's productive resources and increased wage employment the participation of women was both liberating (from the shackles of tradition) and a necessary condition of their social development – a means of social capital formation. In this intellectual context, 'development' was (and is) predicated on changing not the system that produces its socioeconomic conditions but changing the position of women – or of agricultural producers, the urban poor, or other intended beneficiaries of the development process – within the system; to remove any barriers to their equal access or opportunity.

On the other hand, participation was conceived of within the diverse frameworks of various alternative approaches to development that emerged in the 1970s as a source of empowerment – constituting and capacitating the objects of the development process as active subjects, involving them in each and every phase including initial diagnosis and the determination of the community's problems and needs.[7]

Subsequently, in the 1980s and 1990s, these alternative approaches coalesced into an intellectual movement with certain identifiable features and basic principles: (i) development as empowerment, the expansion of choice, the realization of a potential given to every human being in equal measure;[8] (ii) the need to go beyond the state and the market, the development agencies identified in the dominant development discourse, towards the community, the locus and key agency of the development process;[9] (iii) popular participation as the *sine qua non* of the development process, its goal, means, and agency;[10] (iv) the necessary conditions of participatory development are that it be human in-scale (small), local or community-based, and people-led;[11] and (v) that it requires both equity (a more equitable distribution of society's resources, that is, social transformation) and democracy, predicated on a fundamental change in the nature of the state and its relation to civil society.[12]

Probably the most systematic formulation given to this concept of participatory development was by UNRISD which organized and sponsored a series of international forums and conferences on its various dimensions (and the principles and possible conditions of its implementation) from 1979 to 1982.[13] This formulation by UNRISD constituted a touchstone of various reformulations and experiences in the 1980s, in a radically changed context. The social base of these formulations and experiences was constituted by a vast and growing complex of grassroots community-based organizations (GROs or CBOs) and an international network of non-government organizations (NGOs).

The 1980s provided another critical conjuncture of conditions that produced or led to what amounts to a counter-revolution in development thinking and practice[14] and an associated neoliberal model of structural adjustment and free-market reforms in national economic policies: *liberalization* (of trade and the flow of capital), *deregulation* (of private activity), *privatization* (of the means of production and state enterprises), and *downsizing/modernization* of the State.[15] The ideas behind this structural adjustment programme (SAP) had been around for some time, indeed since at least the 1960s, and in the 1970s they were introduced by Chile and several other military regimes in the Southern cone of South America, and imposed by the IMF in Jamaica and several countries in sub-Sahara Africa, but it was not until the economic and debt crisis of 1982–3 in the South, and the coincident ascent to state power of a series of neoconservative regimes in the North, that the political conditions for its implementation became widely available. In this context, regime after regime in Latin America and elsewhere in the South implemented the SAP. By 1990, only four countries in Latin America had not done so, and these (Argentina, Brazil, Peru, Venezuela) would do so in the space of a few years – Peru in 1993, Argentina in 1994, and Venezuela and Brazil from 1994 to 1996.

The 1980s in Latin America and elsewhere in the South were characterized by the contradictory dual context of (i) a debt crisis, the conditions of which included an excessive dependence on external financing, a haemorrhage of internal financial resources, and a decline in the rate of domestic capital formation and investment; and (ii) a redemocratization process, the major conditions of which were the reinstitution of an elected civilian constitutional regime and the opening up of a space for the action of political parties at the national level and community-based organizations (CBOs) and non-government organizations (NGOs) at the local and regional level. Within this context, SAPs were implemented with social, economic and political impacts that have been extensively studied and documented.[16] As for their economic impacts, the general pattern has been for the restoration of macro-economic equilibrium (control of inflation, balanced accounts) without the economic reactivation, the restoration of sustainable economic growth, predicted by the theorists of structural adjustment.[17] At the social level, the most striking impact of SAPs has been the extension and deepening of social inequalities (and inequities) in access to productive resources and the distribution of income. The conditions of this inequality include (i) a dramatic deterioration in the share of labour in national income and a corresponding increase in that of capital;[18] (ii) a dramatic fall in the real value (purchasing power) of wages;[19] (iii) the polarization of household income, with a dramatic increase in the number of low income households and a decreasing share in total national income;[20] (iv) the concentration of income in the form of capital and the private fortunes of a small number of super-rich billionaires; and (v) the growth and deepening of poverty, extending from 40 per cent of the population in Latin America to 44 in 1989 and over 50 per cent by 1993.[21] Politically the major impact of the SAP has been the generation of latent and manifest forms of social discontent which have exploded in various waves of semi-spontaneous riots and protests, and the proliferation of diverse forms of resistance and opposition.[22]

By 1989, after at least four to six years of SAP experience in most cases, the neoliberal programme of structural (free market) reforms reached its limits and entered into a form of crisis. For one thing, as indicated the anticipated economic recovery and reactivation had not occurred. For another, the social inequalities generated by the SAP in turn generated a level and forms of social discontent that undermined the stability of the political regimes in the region and their neoliberal policies.[23] And the redemocratization process expanded the political space for the mobilization of this discontent. Under these conditions (and based on a new understanding as to the requirements of structural adjustment),[24] the IMF, the World Bank, and the IDB among other financial institutions and the operating agencies of the UN system (including ECLAC), overhauled and redesigned the SAP, giving it a social dimension (a new social policy) and a 'human face'.

The new development strategy – 'social liberalism' as it is referred to in the region – formulated in this context[25] and widely implemented in Latin America after 1989 with various permutations provided by ECLAC,[26] has five basic characteristics, each a pillar of an associated theoretical model : (i) an emphasis on *participation*, that is, the incorporation of the targeted beneficiaries, in particular women and the poor;[27] (ii) *decentralization* of decision-making related to the design and the financing of development programmes and projects, sharing the authority and power of vital decisions with local governments and community-based institutions (*partnership*); (iii) targeting the poor – prioritizing the problems and conditions of extreme poverty, alleviating and mitigating them with policies and projects financed with a special social investment fund;[28] (iv) specific policies related to health, education and productive employment – and, in a number of versions, small - and micro-enterprise development – with the aim of incorporating women and the poor into the development process, *empowering* them and securing their active participation;[29] and (v) *structural reforms* (including the privatization of social services) that will provide an appropriate institutional framework for the new social policy and the process of social development involved.

THE LATIN AMERICAN EXPERIENCE OF DECENTRALIZATION: THE DYNAMICS OF A DEMOCRATIZATION PROCESS

The Context of Decentralization

If one were to sum up what the 1980s meant for Latin America in terms of objective conditions for its development one could do so in terms of four assertions: (i) debt crisis, economic stagnation, and the decline of economic conditions for the majority of the population (in some cases deterioration to a level achieved in 1970);[30] (ii) the retrenchment of military and authoritarian regimes and their replacement with constitutional democratically elected civilian regimes;[31] (iii) the widespread implementation of the structural adjustment programme (SAP), an amalgam of stabilization and austerity measures (currency devaluation, anti-inflation) and 'structural' economic reforms (outward orientation, liberalization, deregulation, privatization, downsizing) designed by the IMF and the World Bank;[32] and (iv) the refoundation of the capital accumulation process based on a radical change in the capital–labour relationship and the associated class structure.[33]

Within the context of these objectively given conditions, one of the most notable developments in many Latin American countries was the formation – and proliferation – of a variety of highly participatory strategies: self-help projects, independence and reciprocity in production and exchange of products between the urban poor, as well as the organization of communal soup kitchens and dining halls, and the provision of community housing and services.[34] The development of this popular economy in the so-called (and burgeoning) informal sector, which functioned without the mechanisms of the formal market and the state and was responsible for virtually all the enterprise and employment generated in the 1980s,[35] was a response, on the one hand, of the urban poor to the economic and political conditions of the economic crisis (the inability of the formal economy to absorb them) and political dictatorship (the closing of a political space for the operation of their traditional political organizations), and, on the other, of specific strategies pursued by governments seeking in the context of a generalized fiscal crisis to reduce the level of demand for their services and subsidies.[36]

Whatever the connection, the growth and relative success of this popular economy coincided with government efforts to reduce and downsize the state and to privatize social services, as well as a neoconservative ideology that celebrated the resourcefulness and creative energies of individuals viewed as superior agencies to governments. The end result, as much a coincidence of interest and objective necessity as the effect of any consciously pursued strategy, was, as we have seen, a new social policy (NSP) implemented by virtually every government in the region. And behind this policy was a new institutionality that included a decentralization of government services and powers in partnership with local governments and intermediary non-government organizations, designed in theory so as to increase the level of popular participation and local powers of decision-making.

It had become a widely-accepted matter of principle that the success of development projects and programmes depended on increasing the level of popular participation, the empowerment of the beneficiaries to help them take a more active role in the process of their own development.[37] And quite apart from this stated and widely-accepted principle (and even before the onset of a fiscal crisis), a number of governments in Latin America sought to increase the level and forms of local participation, viewing it not so much (or at all) as a means of empowering the people but as (i) a functional resource, a means of meeting social demands with limited and declining government resources and capacity and as (ii) a means of shoring up or establishing its legitimacy. In this context, various economic and social development strategies to decentralize government, to change thereby the relation between the state and civil society, were designed and experimented with across the world and in most countries of Latin America. The Latin American experience will be briefly summed up and evaluated here, with particular emphasis given to developments in Bolivia, Ecuador, and Mexico.

The political context for the movement to decentralize government in Latin America was constituted by a redemocratization process which can be traced back to the retreat in Ecuador of the armed forces to their barracks and the approval of a new constitution in 1979, and that culminated in the victory of the *Concertacion Democratico* en Chile in 1989.[38] In this context, the dynamics of the broad-based movement to decentralize the government operations of the nation-state were based, on the one hand, on initiatives taken by the central government (and what in Latin America is termed 'the political class') and, on the other hand, pressures and demands 'from below' – from groups organized within civil society.

Development 'from Above'

As for the initiatives 'from above' the first by far (well in advance of the conditions that generally gave rise to the movement towards decentralization) was taken by the government of Colombia, which decentralized a number of government departments and transferred (or shared) a wide range of administrative responsibilities (from urban planning, housing, and education to utilities and some infrastructure) as early as the 1960s. By 1978, the process of administrative decentralization had advanced to the point of seriously undermining and weakening the working of local municipal governments, which had more or less been displaced by the decentralized agencies of the central government. As a result, the central government in 1978, for reasons that are not clear (in most cases, it is a question of either maintaining control, seeking efficiency or reduced costs, or securing legitimacy),[39] instituted a number of measures designed to reduce the 'excessive centralism' of its decentralized agencies and to strengthen and capacitate responsible local governments. These measures included the transfer of a greater share of total public revenues towards local governments, resulting in what amounted to the most effectively decentralized system of government in the entire region, with up to 24 per cent of public funds in control of local governments (versus 5 per cent in Ecuador, three to 4 per cent in Mexico, and a regional average today of below 10 per cent).

In Ecuador, decentralization in the same form (administrative transfer, devolution of responsibility) was instituted in 1979 in the context of a newly approved democratic constitution and demands for autonomy and local self-government by a number of indigenous communities and regional organizations. In this context, the announced objectives of decentralization were the strengthening of democracy and the creation of an institutional framework appropriate to the implementation of a new social policy targeted at the extreme social inequalities and high level of social exclusion (marginality) that characterized the economy and society.[40] However, in attempting to implement its planned measures, the government encountered a series of obstacles, particularly in relation to the active participation of both local administrators and the targeted or intended beneficiaries. Although the issue needs further and closer study a likely reason for this lack of participation was that the transfer of administrative responsibility and authority was not matched by the transfer of financial resources needed to exercise this authority and assume the transferred responsibilities. It was not until 1990, in the context of a major indigenous uprising and widespread push for local control over the extraction and exploitation of natural resources, and with the direct and active support of both the World Bank and the IDB (seeking to implement its new social policy and partnership strategy), that the government took steps in the direction of strengthening local governments by the transfer of financial resources. However, as in other such World Bank supported and funded programmes, the end-results were meagre, with little to no institutional strengthening which (in retrospect) can be attributed to the fact that very few financial resources were in effect transferred to local governments (in 1992 only 5 per cent of total government revenues) and that the vast bulk of project funds (90 per cent) were channelled into urban infrastructure, with little concern for institutional strengthening. Even the formation, in 1996, of a decentralizing committee, and the preparation of a Decentralization and Deconcentration Law that involved the active participation of over a 1000 institutional representatives, and backed up by another indigenous uprising and its demand for 'national' (ethnic) and regional autonomy, has done little to change the situation, despite a provision in the law for increasing the municipal share of public funds to around 8 per cent.[41]

In Mexico, decentralization has been on and off the political agenda for years, indeed since 1970, but it only came to occupy a critical part of government policy in the 1980s, with the advent of an administration committed to a neoliberal model of capitalist development. Under these conditions, decentralization took three forms: (i) the strengthening of federalism via the sharing of responsibilities between the central and local governments;[42] (ii) strengthening the institutional capacity (and political independence) of local governments via municipal reform in the form of transferring a larger share of financial resources to local and state governments (for local governments a tripling of its current share of 5 per cent); and (iii) promoting regional development via the incorporation of state and local governments in decisions relating to federal public investments within each locality; the institutional mechanisms of los Convenios Unicos de Desarrollo and the Strategic Programme of Regional Integration (to address regional imbalances, and prioritizing medium-size cities).[43]

As of 1989, with the advent of a new government by (the then-darling of the international financiers but now-disgraced) Carlos Salinas de Gortieri, the strategy of administrative decentralization was supported and supplemented with Pronasol, an institutionalized form of the World Bank's New Social Policy designed so as to incorporate into the development process the large number of the country's marginalized communities and poor municipalities.[44] However, despite this flurry of institutional measures and no end of political debate and discussions with representatives of local and state governments, as well as a host of initiatives and innovative experiments from these circles,[45] Mexico today remains one of the most highly centralized governments in the region, attested to by the fact that only 3 to 4 per cent of public funds are allocated to local municipal governments.

Development 'From Below'

No country in the region illustrates as well as Bolivia the social dynamics of development from below with regards to the process of government decentralization. Bolivia provides a clear case of both the role played by civil society in the process and of the difficulties and problems involved in the effort to institute local democracy in various forms.

Formal democracy was instituted at the national level in 1982, as the result of an intense long struggle waged by a wide variety of civil and class organizations grouped within the powerful Bolivian Workers Centre (COB), indigenous peasant organizations and social movement, and regional civic corporate bodies (*Comites Civicos Departmentales*) that grouped together community-based organizations of civil society as well as provincial and municipal government authorities. Like the class-based organizations ranged within the COB, these civic committees, organized around the demands for regional control and autonomy, had been revitalized as a result of their struggle against the dictatorship of the central government and its internecine political conflicts. One of the major demands of these *Comites* was precisely political-administrative decentralization, which was understood unambiguously as a means by marginal regions and communities of securing regional control over their resources – and a measure of autonomy. As a result, in Bolivia decentralization became the central axis of the redemocratization process – of the movement in the 1980s of changing the relationship of the state to its civil society.

In this context, as of 1982 there was opened up an intense political debate, resulting in among other developments the preparation of up to 22 legislative projects. However, for want of consensus among the diverse factions of what in Bolivia is termed 'the political class' none of these projects were translated into law until 1992, when the *Comites Civicos*, the armed forces, the COB, and enough 'politicians' came together to achieve Senate approval for its latest project. Nevertheless, the project was stalled in the Chamber of Deputies, in a political dispute which placed on one side the now resonating demands of civil society for 'democracy' (deepening of political reform) and, on the other, the 'political class' and its party apparatus, seeking to preserve its traditional prerogatives of power and influence. It would take several years of debate before this impasse was broken with the passing of two complementary pieces of legislation: (i) the Popular Participation Law, which legislated the existence of Organizaciones Territoriales de Base (OTBs) that were allocated the authority – and corresponding revenues – to make decisions that relate to conditions that directly affect the local community or municipality;[46] and (ii) the Administrative Decentralization law, which constituted the institutional framework for 'popular participation' and municipal autonomy, in particular a nexus between the national and local municipal governments – for the sharing of public service and accountability. According to some, these two laws as combined and in their political conditions has created a contradictory and problematic situation for the proponents of local democracy and participatory development. On the one hand, the measures instituted with these two laws have transferred to the local government responsibilities related to the meeting of social demands and the resolution of social conflicts while retaining for the central government effective control. The problem, according to some COB intellectuals, is that in theory decentralization involved 'a process of transfer of responsibility and resources...to the...provinces, cantones, ayllus and communities...so that the rural population, on the basis of its own efforts can overcome its present situation of stagnation, and incorporate itself as an active force of national construction'.[47] However, in practice, by allocating the authority to make decisions and the financial resources that go with it to the municipality, a political-administrative unit of local government, the federal government has tended to undermine and weaken the authority and functioning of 'the community', the social unit with which most Bolivians, and particularly the country's numerically important indigenous peoples, identify and to which they are fundamentally tied.[48] On the other hand, the Popular Participation Law has opened up a political space for which the organizations of civil society have waged a long and hard struggle. In this context, the state is more permeable to social demands and closer in its decisions to local realities, which not only provides the national government a measure of legitimacy but it provides the basis for better government as well as a degree and form of local participatory development. At the same time, the political reforms instituted by these two laws have had a demonstrated tendency to weaken traditional community-based or solidarity organizations and the functioning of unions that articulate interests beyond the merely local.[49]

In this context, a twofold political dynamic can be discerned. On the one hand, social movements of community-based civil organizations have managed to achieve a greater measure of 'democracy', that is, political space to operate freely with more avenues for popular participation. On the other hand, in this process social movements of class-based organizations that are generally oriented towards and seek social transformation rather than the extension of democracy and more freedom often as in Bolivia have been disarticulated and weakened in their capacity to challenge the power-structure and to effect change. In effect, the capacity of people to participate in policy-making decisions and to act politically becomes involuted and restricted to local issues, reversing the apparent gains made in democracy. As a result, the political Left is placed in a quandary, unable to oppose a political development that opens up avenues of popular participation but that restricts the form and level of this participation, inhibiting the participatory democracy to which many (the 'social Left') are committed.

THE LIMITS OF COMMUNITY-BASED PARTICIPATORY DEVELOPMENT AND LOCAL DEMOCRACY

UNRISD, the UNDP and other operating agencies of the UN system (in their conception of Human Development); the World Bank (in its new social policy); ECLAC (in its model of Productive Transformation with Equity); and the global network of NGOs and other proponents of Another Development all converge on the need for and centrality of popular participation in the process of development. In this intellectual context, despite enormous differences in conception as to the path to be taken towards such a participatory form of development, as well as questions as to its appropriate agency, these diverse approaches to national and community-based development have generally looked favourably upon the global trend towards decentralization of government and the associated change in the given relationship of the state to civil society. But our review of numerous studies of this experience shows that the rationale for such decentralization in most cases, and the dominant impulse behind it, is the search by national or central governments for either economic efficiencies in the provision of public services which they can no longer afford or increased legitimacy in the context of a redemocratization process and associated pressures from well-organized groups in a reconstituted civil society. However, notwithstanding this reality and the conservative (anti-change) political forces ranged behind it, the consensus view (among the various proponents of participatory development that generally share the view of the need for change) is that decentralization has created – and creates – necessary conditions for a more human and participatory form of development as well as the political space for corresponding democratic politics. The institutional basis for such participatory development, in the context of decentralization, is the municipality, a political-administrative unit of local government that most closely corresponds to, or is close to, the 'community', the social unit to which most people belong, with which they generally identify, and where they live their everyday lives and the socio-economic conditions which, for most, need to be improved or changed.

In the context of the decentralization process, the municipality is generally regarded as a privileged space for democratic politics and participatory development. This is the case for the World Bank, concerned as it is with the design and targeting of enlightened government policy, a cost-effective implementation of its New Social Policy. It is the case for CEPAL, concerned as it is to find an organization that is constituted at a level and on a scale compatible with popular participation, allowing for an equitable form of development which is not likely or simply not possible at the level of the nation-state. And it applies to all those intellectuals and development practitioners involved in the ubiquitous search for Another Development who have turned to, and generally rely on, the protagonism of grassroots community-based organizations.

In different ways these diverse organizations have ended up drawing a similar or the same picture of the decentralization process and its possibilities. However, our review of existing studies on this process indicates that there is something wrong with this picture. For one thing, it does not correspond with the facts, which appear to be as follows.

First, the municipality, the political-administrative unit targeted for strengthening and empowering, does not constitute a 'community' – the social unit which most people belong to or identify with. In this connection, the advocates of democratic decentralization see the municipality as 'the natural space where the community and government are brought together'.[50] And, indeed it is. However, they are brought together under conditions that serves the purpose of government (delegate and share responsibilities related to the provision of public services, cost-effective administration, down-the-line accountability and control, legitimacy, regulation of social demands) but tends to undermine and weaken – even destroy – the organizational and political capacity of traditional community- or class-based organizations, and, in the process, weakening the ties of people to their increasingly fragmented communities.[51]

Second, the community as conceived of in development discourse (as an organic unity bound together by social bonds, relations of mutual obligation, common interests, and shared social identity) does not seem to exist, except perhaps, to some extent, with respect to the small-scale societies constituted by the indigenous peoples in the Andean highlands of Peru, Bolivia, and Ecuador; the Amazonian rain forests, or Guatemala and the Southeast of Mexico. The sociological and anthropological literature on this point by now is enormous but it seems to have entirely escaped the attention of scholars and practitioners in the field of development. What many of these studies tend to show is that most so-called communities are anything but; or when examined closely that they tend to dissolve into diverse relations of power and conflict, with (i) a minority in control of the means of production and political authority – and power; (ii) various middle strata dependent on petty production or public service within the locality or oriented towards and dependent on connections to the outside world (in terms of communications, culture, and often even with respect to economic activity or employment); and (iii) large numbers of segmented and poorly organized low-income small producers, low-wage hunters and gatherers, and an underclass of landless or otherwise marginal workers, many of them forced to migrate in search of subsistence.[52] As Smith (1989) has detailed and shown so convincingly in the case of one Peruvian community, the existence of class divisions and relations of conflict within a community (or territorial social unit, to use a more general and descriptive category), does not mean that at certain conjunctures, and for certain purposes and common interests, cannot come together and form fairly representative social and political organizations. They can and do. However, the construction of any community-based strategy or development program, or political organization, needs to take into account the conditions and social relations under which the 'community' is constituted both in itself and in its connections with the outside world – the broader society. Thus, for example, in a World Bank institution-strengthening project designed to benefit a 'community' in the outskirts or environs of Potosi, La Paz or Cochabamba in Bolivia, it might be discovered that the effective if not intended beneficiary might be certain elements of the local oligarchy who do not favour the access of indigenous peoples and peasants to *el Consejo Municipal del Pueblo* and have no intention to share resources or political power with them.[53]

Third, a decentralized form of political development focused on the municipality, in the context of conditions given in Latin America, more often than not seems to have the effect – if not the aim – of restricting the scope of political action to local issues, effectively incapacitating people from organizing for more fundamental change. In this context, for example, the political conditions needed to implement CEPAL's model of Productive Transformation-with-Equity do not exist and are not available. As it happens, in the course of structural reforms implemented at the nation-state level over the past decade and a half, the productive apparatus of Latin America's economies indeed has been transformed.

However, this transformation has been without equity, or, not to make too fine point of it, with considerable inequity – converting the CEPAL model into 'a new fairy tale for the 1990s'.[54] Under the conditions created by the process of government decentralization, the capacity for people in the region to organize, be mobilized, and act in their collective interests beyond any purely local issue (such as building a school or clinic) has been undermined. And the development that has occurred in the process has been neither equitable, participatory, people-led, or human.

CONCLUSIONS

Decentralization of government (policy-making and administration) is viewed by CEPAL, the institution which more than any other has led the search for an alternative to neoliberal capitalism in Latin America, as a necessary condition of participatory development and as such the 'missing link' in its proposed development model ('productive transformation and equity').[55] However, our review and brief analysis of existing studies allows us to conclude that CEPAL's solution ('development from within', as Osvaldo Sunkel[56] defines it) is not supportive of the agenda set by the proponents of Another Development. Rather, it is supportive of the agenda pursued by the World Bank and other such institutions (of the 'international financial community'), and implemented by virtually every regime in Latin America. This is to say, it is a case of development 'from above and the outside' rather than 'from below'. In this context we have found, and argue, that the participatory model in Latin America, as designed and implemented on the basis of government decentralization, has failed to shift power and control from the state to the people. As we see it, there are two dimensions to this failure. On the one hand, the model is constructed on the basis of, and with reference to, an administrative unit (the municipality) rather than the sense or existence of real communities. The connection between the two often is problematic if not non-existent. On the other hand, the democratic impulse embedded in the decentralization project – and process – is very convoluted. As a project that is designed as much on 'the outside' (by economists from the World Bank) as 'the inside' (CEPAL economists), and implemented 'from above' (as a government initiative), decentralization has resulted in a highly limited and ineffective form of democracy. The secret of 'local power' (based on mechanisms of popular participation) is precisely in that decision-making and administrative capacity is localized – restricted to local issues. In this context, the process of (re)democratization and participatory development is hijacked, subordinated to the economic agenda and political goals of the existing neoliberal regimes. The capacity of people to participate in decisions relating to larger-than-local issues, and to effect change in larger nation-wide structures, has become increasingly limited. In short, in the Latin American context decentralization has tended to limit rather than extend the institution of democracy. It is, we suggest, a question of myth and appearance over reality.

5 The Dynamics of Neoliberal Electoral Politics

Throughout Latin America there is a deepening popular disenchantment with neoliberal governments that have entrenched themselves across the continent over the past decade or more. Yet one of the paradoxes confounding analysts of the region's politics has been voter reluctance to repudiate these regimes at the ballot box: devastating socioeconomic failures have been no obstacle to the election of successor regimes committed to the same kinds of policies.[1] Another paradox is just as striking: while political oppositions, exploiting voter hostility, have waged successful election campaigns to oust incumbent neoliberal governments, once in power the new regime has invariably and systematically repudiated its critical electoral posture in favour of deepening the neoliberal agenda of its predecessor.

This chapter explores the pattern of reproducing neoliberal regimes in Latin America and poses the question of whether there can be a 'resolution' to this debilitating political cycle. The latter is linked to, and interrelated with, upward and downward socioeconomic spirals which, in turn, are closely associated with a key part of the neoliberal repertoire – the so-called structural adjustment programme (SAP). Based on an examination of their real socioeconomic impact, we argue that too much attention has been paid to the SAPs as part of a purported economic strategy rather than comprehending them as primarily motivated by a class directed political strategy.

THE NEOLIBERAL POLITICAL CYCLE: FIRST-WAVE REGIMES

Neoliberal electoral regimes have followed a cycle of ascendancy, decay and reproduction. Three broad waves of such regimes can be identified. For most countries the first-wave began during the 1980s, roughly coinciding with the negotiated transitions from military dictatorships to civilian governments that were taking place across the continent. The second-wave followed toward the end of the decade through the first half of the 1990s. A third neoliberal wave has begun to take shape in the current period.

Fernando Belaunde and Alan Garcia in Peru, Raul Alfonsin in Argentina, Miguel de la Madrid in Mexico, Julio Sanguinetti in Uruguay, and Jose Sarney in Brazil were prominent among those who headed the first-wave of neoliberal electoral regimes that rode to power on the surge of euphoria accompanying the 'redemocratization' process and the electorate's expectation that political change and economic opening would promote freedom and prosperity. Sooner or later, however, each of these 'reformist' governments did an about-turn, jettisoning their populist campaign rhetoric in favour of extending the free market agenda originally proposed by the military dictatorships which they replaced. Exhibiting a new found willingness to implement the 'stabilization' and structural adjustment programmes (SAPs) prescribed by the International Monetary Fund (IMF) and the World Bank, they began to dismantle social welfare programmes, weaken labour legislation, take the first steps toward dismantling the state sector and permit large-scale foreign buyouts of public enterprises, and give priority to repaying the foreign debt at the expense of social and economic development at home.

But what was striking about this first-wave of neoliberal regimes was their common failure to generate sustained, dynamic growth based on a more equitable distribution of wealth and income. As their terms reached conclusion, each confronted serious economic crises, in some cases compounded by major corruption scandals, producing widespread voter malaise and a burgeoning electoral and extra-parliamentary opposition. The cases of Peru and Brazil are illustrative of these developments. In Peru, Belaunde's election to the presidency in 1980 was in large measure due to his ability to attract the votes of workers, peasants and the urban poor with promises of jobs, improved living standards and greater freedom to unionize. Once in office, though, he quickly signalled a new priority agenda: freeing the market, privatizing state enterprises, encouraging foreign investment, meeting international debt obligations, and imposing austerity-stability measures in return for new loans from the international financial institutions. By 1984, Belaunde's neoliberal policies had produced neither growth nor development. Instead, the economy was mired in a severe recession: while approximately 50 per cent of export earnings were being siphoned off to maintain the foreign debt payments schedule, agricultural and industrial production had plummeted downward. The social costs were equally devastating: growing unemployment, rising food prices, declining real wage levels and a dramatic increase in reported cases of malnutrition and tuberculosis. The electoral support for the candidate of Belaunde's party in the 1985 presidential election collapsed to less than 10 per cent.

The APRA Party's Alan Garcia won the 1985 contest on a platform that promised to reverse the process of economic decline and improve living standards by employing a strategy that combined austerity measures with increased government spending. During 1986–7, Garcia presided over a limited but fragile economic recovery (lower inflation, rising employment, increased purchasing power of the masses) but it soon began to falter against a background of stagnant investment, capital flight, and balance of payments difficulties. Between 1988 and 1990, the regime dumped its populist pretensions and enacted three IMF-style structural adjustment programmes in a failed effort to bring resurgent hyper-inflation under control. The third and harshest of these economic packages included massive overnight price increases in basic food items and consumer goods with the predictable devastating consequences for living standards. The austerity shock treatments impoverished a large segment of the population. This time, the neoliberal experiment triggered a major resurgence of political and class struggle: hundreds of thousands of workers in the mining, textile, education and state sectors participated in waves of strikes throughout the country.[2]

In Brazil, the sequence of events was much the same: from short-term, limited reforms to full-blown neoliberal policies and the collapse of the regime's political base. Through a combination of price freezes, currency reform and other measures, the Sarney government (1985–90) temporarily succeeded in bringing inflation under control and increasing real wage levels. By early 1987, however, most constraints on prices were lifted, signalling a major policy shift. By late 1988, the return of hyper-inflation had devastated workers' purchasing power, the economy was in a state of crisis, and charges of government corruption were rife. Meanwhile, Sarney seemed more concerned with renegotiating payments on the country's massive $121 billion foreign debt, which involved new austerity measures in return for new loans from its international creditors. As inflation once again spiralled out of control hundreds of thousands of organized workers took to the streets, engaging in strikes and other protests against the consequences of neoliberal policies. To re-impose 'law and order', the regime increasingly resorted to use of the army and police. In public opinion surveys conducted prior to the November 1988 municipal elections, in which the ruling Brazilian Democratic Movement Party suffered heavy losses, Sarney's approval rating hit a new low of 5 per cent.[3]

The crises of first-wave neoliberal regimes did not induce the pre-eminent international lending agencies – the IMF and the World Bank – to critically reassess the consequences of the initial 'economic reforms' or 'free market policies'. On the contrary, they clung to their original diagnosis and found fault not with the prescriptions offered, but with the failure of the first-wave regimes to implement the neoliberal policies in a sufficiently forceful, consistent and sustained fashion. This diagnosis, however, posed a major problem for the foreign financial aid donors, so influential in shaping the Latin American development agenda, and their local collaborators, insofar as the majority of the electorate felt that the 'bitter medicine' prescribed for future prosperity was bitter enough, especially given that prosperity still seemed a distant prospect. The political issue facing the international actors and the emerging domestic electoral opposition who would form the second-wave of neoliberal regimes revolved around pacifying the electorate sufficiently to get elected in order to implement a new and more radical neoliberal agenda.

THE NEOLIBERAL POLITICAL CYCLE: SECOND-WAVE REGIMES

The second-wave of neoliberal electoral politicians – Carlos Andres Perez in Venezuela, Carlos Menem in Argentina, Fernando Collor in Brazil, Alberto Fujimori in Peru, Jaime Paz Zamora in Bolivia, Luis LaCalle in Uruguay, Carlos Salinas in Mexico – solved the dilemma of submitting to the electorate in order to serve their economic rulers by dividing the political process into distinct sets of activities. The *electoral campaign* was characterized by sharp populist attacks on the *consequences* of *neoliberalism* (poverty, stagnation, capital flight) in order to diffuse popular discontent over the first-wave of neoliberal regimes and mobilize sufficient votes to gain office. The *post-electoral* period quickly witnessed a reaffirmation of support for the neoliberal agenda combined with a powerful indication that these second-wave presidents were not simply part of a reshuffling process but were committed to a *radicalization* of the policies of their predecessors – whether it involved support for accelerated privatization formulas, harsher constraints on trade union activities or more wage and job cuts to create a greater reserve army of cheap labour – that had savaged living standards across the region and made possible their political rulership.

After successfully campaigning for the Venezuelan presidency in late 1988 on a quasi-populist programme, including support for a debtor's cartel to limit the social and economic costs of the country's repayments to its international creditors, Carlos Andres Perez began implementing a savage neoliberal programme almost from the moment he took over the reigns of political power. In February 1989, he negotiated a $4.6 billion economic package with the IMF which reflected, in part, a decision to make foreign debt payments a high priority. Overnight, the government imposed massive increases in the cost of gasoline, transport and basic foodstuffs, triggering explosive riots which left 200 dead and more than 1 000 injured, while the elimination of price controls and food subsidies, and the freeing of interest charges halved the inflation rate during Perez' first 18 months in office, these and other austerity measures (cutting tariff barriers, eliminating thousands of jobs in the state sector, etc.) significantly eroded the living standards of both the lower and middle classes. Despite a 9 per cent increase in GDP between mid-1991 and mid-1992, Perez' public approval rate had plummeted to 6 per cent, which was not surprising given that real wage levels had fallen to half of what they were in 1988 and around 60 per cent of the population remained below the poverty line.[4] These consequences of the neoliberal reforms, together with an increasingly pervasive graft and corruption within the regime, triggered nation-wide protests and work stoppages on an almost constant basis. In May 1993, the Supreme Court ruled that sufficient evidence existed to prosecute Perez on charges of embezzlement and misappropriation of public funds. Later that year he was impeached and subsequently incarcerated on charges of corrupt behaviour in office.

In Brazil, the Collor government (1990–3) quickly dispatched its populist electoral rhetoric and outlined an ambitious free market economic plan based on deregulation, large-scale privatization, and letting the market set wages and prices. Although efforts to sell off state-owned companies barely got off the ground because of consistent popular opposition to privatizing most basic public services, the regime pushed ahead with its fiscal and monetary policies to the tune of depressed demand, falling industrial activity, rising unemployment, hyper-inflation, an unprecedented number of bankruptcies, and negative overall growth. By the end of 1991, Collor's popular support base had collapsed. As the neoliberal-induced recession entered its third year, the President was confronted by another problem: in June 1992, a congressional investigation found that he had knowingly used his public office for personal gain. In September, the Chamber of Deputies voted for impeachment; and three months later he resigned from office only to be subsequently convicted by the Senate of engaging in corrupt activities.

The Zamora government in Bolivia (1989–3) launched an aggressive neoliberal programme to 'stabilize' and 'adjust' the economy. In close consultation with the IMF and the World Bank, Zamora, seeking to attract new loans and foreign investment, eliminated controls on goods and services, cut tariffs supporting local industry, and instituted labour system changes which gave employers more authority to reduce wages and increased power over hiring and firing of workers. However, the effort to launch an ambitious privatization programme in 1992 was also derailed for some, but not all, of the same reasons that had frustrated Collor in Brazil: trade union opposition; allegations of government corruption; and military discontent over losing some of its most lucrative sources of income.

In the case of the Menem government in Argentina (1989–93), the division between the election campaign and post-election policies could not have been sharper. To win the presidency, Menem promised an economic revival and a return to traditional labour policies. He promised to increase workers' wages which had declined substantially, in real terms, under his predecessor, Raul Alfonsin; and castigated Alfonsin for allowing debt payments to consume approximately 45 per cent of the country's export earnings. He told voters his government would push for a five year 'grace period', in effect a debt moratorium. At the same time, he also favoured the sale of state-owned companies and new policies to increase foreign investment levels.

During his first hundred days in office, the order of priorities were comprehensively reversed. With the promise of new IMF assistance he turned his back on the trade union movement that had played a major role in his electoral victory and proceeded to implement a set of neoliberal austerity measures including support for massive rate increases by public utility, transport, communications and energy enterprises. Simultaneously, he retreated from his advocacy of a debt moratorium, indicating a preparedness to negotiate a new schedule of repayment terms with the country's international creditors.

In 1991, Economics Minister Domingo Cavallo launched a major programme of neoliberal market reforms intended, among other objectives, to entice greater inflows of foreign capital. By mid-1993, the regime had privatized a large number of state enterprises and, more importantly in terms of maintaining popular support, had lowered the unemployment rate and pushed inflation down from a monthly growth rate of 200 per cent in 1989 to an annual increase of only 12 per cent.[5] But cracks in the neoliberal façade began to appear during late 1993 and early 1994 in the form of rising civil unrest, including popular uprisings in the northern province of Santiago del Estero over the failure of market reforms to improve the socioeconomic lot of traditionally marginalized sectors.

Moreover, unemployment began an upward trend, reaching 18 per cent in 1996, at a time when the government announced cuts in the national unemployment fund and in welfare and health benefits for workers. In December 1994, the state pension system suffered a similar fate; two months later up to 500000 civil servants were informed that salary cuts were imminent.[6] Nonetheless, Menem was re-elected in May 1995, with nearly 50 per cent of the vote. Having stabilized the economy, presided over a GDP growth rate which averaged close to 8 per cent annually during his first administration and, above all, effectively solved the inflation problem, the electorate appeared willing to return him to power notwithstanding the austerity 'adjustments' and growing poverty that accompanied the neoliberal experiment.

The victorious candidate in Peru's 1990 presidential election, Alberto Fujimori campaigned against both his opponent, the rightist free marketer Mario Vargas Llosa, and his neoliberal predecessors. He attacked the latter for failing to address the country's social problems and, in contrast to Vargas Llosa's call for harsh 'shock treatment' measures, announced that he intended to reduce the country's hyperinflation on a gradual basis. The urban poor and rural peasantry swept him into office in a June run-off election. Within weeks, Fujimori reversed course and announced a set of stringent austerity measures mandated by the IMF and World Bank in return for new loans. Dubbed 'Fujishock', they were almost a mirror image of the Vargas Llosa campaign promises which the electorate had repudiated. The removal of subsidies on basic foodstuffs tripled prices overnight; soon after, hundreds of thousands of public sector workers were the victims of 'downsizing'. The immediate response to rising bread and milk costs, and falling wages, were mass demonstrations, riots and confrontations between Lima's urban slum dwellers and the regime's security-military forces; and strikes by public sector unions whose members had suffered big job losses.

Fujimori's neoliberal commitment also extended to repayment of a $2 billion foreign debt arrears owed to the IMF, the World Bank, and the Inter-American Development Bank. This headlong drive to regain favour within the international financial community translated into added burdens on the poor and the lower-middle class. During the regime's first 12 months, debt servicing absorbed hundreds of millions of dollars compared with an estimated $40 million spent on social welfare programmes. Meanwhile, almost 90 per cent of the work force lacked stable, full time employment and the proportion of the population living below the poverty line more than doubled. However, if the social costs of the neoliberal policies were catastrophic for many Peruvians, they did halt runaway inflation and bring it under control for the duration of Fujimori's first term in office.

By late 1994, Fujimori had successfully privatized a large part of the state sector, established an enviable inflation-fighting record, and produced growth and a stable economy, all of which contributed to his landslide re-election victory in April 1995. This, despite a worsening of social conditions, more people reduced to poverty status, and the passage of new laws 'that virtually eliminated all forms of legal protection for salaried workers'.[7]

The 'adjustment' and 'stabilization' measures promulgated by the second-wave of neoliberal regimes effectively took on the character of annual rituals, each new round further shredding the remaining vestiges of the social net. Emblematic of deteriorating socioeconomic conditions in major capital cities such as Buenos Aires, São Paulo, Caracas and Mexico City were the extraordinarily high levels of open and disguised unemployment. While deflationary economic policies, international bank loans and the influx of speculative capital stabilized these economies in the short term, all too often such recoveries were soon after followed by new rounds of structurally induced crises.

As the 'economic reforms' polarized these societies, the second-wave neoliberal Presidents also began to increasingly centralize legislative and executive power. The prototype was the Fujimori 'autogolpe' (self-induced coup) which was executed while maintaining the framework or facade of a bargaining electoral system. In April 1992, with the full backing of the military high command, the Peruvian president dismissed the Congress, closed down the judiciary, suspended all constitutional guarantees, and rewrote the constitution to permit his re-election to a second term.

This willingness to impose policies by executive fiat, over-riding legislatures, and violating constitutional norms and individual's civil rights was a defining feature of these second-wave neoliberal regimes. In the single-minded pursuit of an ideological doctrine, their leaders were often impervious to large-scale public protests or abysmally low public opinion ratings. Argentina's Carlos Menem, for instance, stated on more than one occasion that nothing – whether general strikes or collapsing popular support – would deter him from pursuing his free market agenda. Such rigidity and scorn toward any notion of a consultative regime was accompanied by the beginnings of a move to strengthen coercive institutions and remilitarize civil society. This shift, and its parallel creation of an increasing 'bunker mentality' among neoliberal regimes, becomes more entrenched with the advent of the third-wave neoliberal presidents.

Two kinds of opposition emerged as the second 'wave' regimes declined: well-financed political parties who condemned the 'harshness' of the austerity programmes, but once again were preparing a wave of neoliberal experiments; and growing social movements desperately struggling to salvage the remnants of the social wage and avoid falling into deeper poverty. In the face of regime rigidity and the elimination of serious public interlocutors, even pro-regime conciliators among trade unions, civic associations and neighbourhood groups associated with clientilistic politics begin to organize protest activities. While a majority of the public increasingly favoured a break with neoliberalism, the majority of the political opposition remained deeply embedded in that framework, unable to elaborate new initiatives outside of the 'globalized' economies that they would ultimately administer. The option facing the third-wave of new or reelected neoliberal presidents was, and is, the further deepening of the free market exploitation and an increasing risk of organized social upheavals.

THE NEOLIBERAL POLITICAL CYCLE: THIRD-WAVE REGIMES

The third-wave neoliberal regimes that came to power between 1993 and 1995 range from those of Alberto Fujimori in Peru and Carlos Menem in Argentina, both reelected to second terms, to the administrations of Ernesto Zedillo in Mexico, Rafael Caldera in Venezuela, Gonzalo Sanchez de Losada in Bolivia and Fernando Henrique Cardoso in Brazil. Like the second-wave neoliberals, what they continue to demonstrate is that the SAP is not a passing phenomena, that social sacrifice is *not* a *temporary* condition on the way to long term, large scale prosperity; that what the lower-middle and working classes are now experiencing is a c*ontinuous spiral of declining living standard*, as temporary 'stabilizations' are followed by new sets of 'adjustment' measures that further erode living standards. Increasingly, intellectuals and professionals experiencing downward mobility realize that SAPs do not serve the development project. Rather, they facilitate an upward spiral of the very wealthy, creating polarized societies and destroying any remaining illusions about the classless rhetoric of neoliberal 'modernization'.

In Peru, while the international financial institutions continue to lavish praise on Fujimori for his relentless commitment to neoliberal reforms, more than half the population subsists below the poverty line and less than one in ten Peruvians has stable, full-time employment despite a sustained period of economic growth.[8] Urgently needed social projects have been abandoned as the informal economy grows apace. By April, 1996, Prime Minister Dante Cordova and more than half of the Cabinet had stepped down from their posts over Fujimori's failure to proceed with his commitments to create more jobs and tackle the poverty issue.[9]

Determined as ever to brook no opposition to his neoliberal policy agenda, Fujimori has kept up the pace of 'reforms'. Having already privatized approximately 173 of the 183 state-run companies that were operating in 1990,[10] the government announced in May 1996, that an irreversible decision had been taken to sell-off the state oil company and all remaining public enterprises by 1998. This, despite a public opinion poll taken that same month which showed almost 70 per cent of the population opposed, and an even greater majority demanding a referendum on the issue. To eliminate the referendum option, the government rammed an amendment through the Congress to block any such bid.[11]

In Argentina, in August 1996, with the labour movement now in more or less open revolt against the Menem regime over its austerity policies and the accompanying large-scale unemployment, the newly appointed Economics Minister, Roque Fernandez, a University of Chicago-trained monetarist, announced a further package of measures which included an increase in fuel and gas prices, cuts in industrial and export promotion incentives, and the elimination of export subsidies and tax concessions for manufacturers and importers of capital goods. He also declared that no general strike, such as the one organized by the General Confederation of Workers (CGT) earlier that month, would weaken the government's resolve to push through stronger spending cuts and higher taxes to deal with the main priority: the growing fiscal deficit. In late September, the CGT staged another highly effective general strike, supported by the country's two other umbrella organizations, to protest the regime's economic policies. Menem denounced the strike, reiterating his determination to proceed with the neoliberal economic programme.[12]

According to the National Statistic Institution (INDEC), the pattern of income distribution has become more skewed than ever during Menem's hold on political power.[13] The Argentine Center for Macroeconomic Studies estimates that 45 per cent of the working age population are currently without jobs or underemployed or do not earn enough to meet basic subsistence needs.[14] Meanwhile, graft and corruption charges are threatening to engulf the regime. Some cabinet ministers have been publicly accused of engaging in illicit activities for private financial gain, including corrupt involvement in the privatization of government services.

The successful passage of at least five major legislative proposals to facilitate the hiring and firing of workers, and generally give capital greater power over labour, has been a hallmark of Menem's two administrations. Employers have also been the major beneficiary of every collective agreement since 1991: more than 90 per cent of the clauses involved cost-cutting initiatives, changing job requirements, lowering wages, extending working hours and binding employees to increase productivity. In late 1996, Menem signalled his intention to submit a new package of labour 'reforms' to Congress, ostensibly to solve the unemployment problem. Described as 'flexibilización', the legislation seeks to further strip workers of hard-won gains and increase their vulnerability to capital's profit-making requirements. The two key features that have provoked powerful trade union resistance are the proposals that would eliminate the current rules on severance pay; and abolish the principle that new collective agreements cannot be negotiated 'downwards', that benefits gained in previous agreements cannot be removed.[15]

The transition from Perez to Caldera in Venezuela witnessed a re-run of the gap between campaign promises and the new regime's policies. Confronted with an economy in recession, a ballooning deficit, and surging inflation, Caldera quickly sidelined his election commitments to anti-poverty, social reform measures in favour of 'going to the IMF'. With over 70 per cent of families living below the poverty line and close to 50 per cent of the economically active population eking out a living in the informal economy,[16] the prescribed remedy was another round of neoliberal 'adjustment' measures to 'stabilize' the economy. Price controls were eliminated, gasoline costs increased, and in July, 1996, an approving IMF released a $1.5 billion standby credit in return for another round of austerity measures. As the year drew to an end, the socioeconomic circumstances of close to three-quarters of Venezuela's populace could only be described as catastrophic. Unemployment among the lower and middle classes ran into the millions. Meanwhile, the neoliberal solution had pushed the crime rate to new heights: while drug trafficking remained the most profitable business sector, car theft had pushed petroleum from second to third place.[17]

Campaigning for the presidency of Bolivia in late 1993, Gonzalo Lozada, a mining magnate and principal architect of the country's 1985 stablization programme, told voters he would continue the Zamora regime's economic restructuring programme while simultaneously addressing a raft of social concerns (including the lack of access of half the population to potable water and sewer systems) which he accused his predecessors of neglecting. Once in office, however, neoliberal economic policies assumed priority status, generating a level of popular discontent which led the government to declare a state of siege, suspend all constitutional rights and assume extraordinary powers in April, 1995. Against a background of wage stagnation, escalating unemployment, and nationwide demonstrations by workers protesting against 'downsizing' and other deflationary economic measures, Lozada received yet another loan from the IMF under the enhanced SAP in April, 1996, to support his neoliberal 'reforms'.[18] Among the latter was a highly unpopular decision to privatize selected public enterprises, including the state petroleum company (YPFB). Neither opposition political parties nor the trade union movement were able to prevent Senate approval of the YPFB partial privatization bill in May.

Populist rhetoric and a commitment to social reforms were also instrumental in Fernando Cardoso's election as Brazil's new president in 1995. And, similar to other third-wave regimes, they were quickly subordinated to a preoccupation with economic stabilization which, in turn, has triggered growing popular opposition. Workers in both the public and private sectors embarked on a series of strikes over government plans to 'downsize' the bureaucracy and inadequate minimum wage increases. But the key issue was the neoliberal regime's failure to address the unemployment problem. The trade union's statistical department, DIESSE, calculated that as of April, 1996, more than two million people were unemployed in five of the country's major cities: São Paulo (where industrial recession had pushed the rate up to almost 16 per cent), Porto Alegre, Belo Horizonte, Curitiba and Brazilia. According to the national statistical institute, IBGE, unemployment increased by more than 39 per cent between mid-1995 and mid-1996. This largely explained the results of two public opinion polls in May [1996] which revealed that Cardoso's popularity had crashed to 25 per cent from a high of 68 per cent.[19]

Like his predecessor, an important factor contributing to Cardoso's eroding political base has been the sustained popular (and parliamentary) opposition to efforts to accelerate the privatization process. The limited contraction in the overall weight of the state sector between 1990 and 1995 is partly explained by this fact: state firms accounted for 60.4 per cent of the assets of the top 500 companies in 1995, a decline of only 7.4 per cent; and 30.5 per cent of the turnover of the top 500 companies in 1995, a fall of just 7.1 per cent. The focus of current nationalist opposition is the government's recent announcement that it plans to sell-off the mining conglomerate CVRD, one of the top ten publicly traded companies in Latin America and with an enviable operating reputation.[20]

In Mexico, the third-wave neoliberal regime of Ernesto Zedillo has been no more successful than Salinas or de la Madrid in improving the socioeconomic conditions of the mass of the population – whether in the areas of jobs, wages, prices or public services. To meet the strict economic and fiscal conditions imposed by Washington and the IMF in return for a multi-billion financial 'bailout' following the post-December, 1994 economic crisis, Zedillo introduced a new austerity plan which included budget cuts, increases in food and electricity prices, and a rise in the value-added tax. These measures, together with a devaluation of the peso, further impoverished the working and middle classes. Between the onset of the crises and mid-1996, a combination of price jumps for basic goods and a decline in real wage levels of more than 50 per cent had thrown an additional five million Mexicans below the poverty line.[21] In common with a number of other neoliberal regimes, however, Zedillo has been forced to backtrack, at least temporarily, on the pace and scope of his privatization ambitions. In October 1996, he was forced to bow to widespread pressures from trade unions, opposition political parties, and even sectors of the governing PRI, and revise his plans to sell-off all of the state-owned petrochemical industry (PEMEX).[22]

The shift toward a more militarized version of the neoliberal approach during the second-wave regimes has become more marked with the advent of the third-wave presidents. In February 1996, for example, Caldera used the Venezuelan military to savagely put down street protests in Caracas and kept it on alert to crush any anti-government opposition getting out of hand. In April, Brazilian police opened fire on landless peasants occupying uncultivated property in the state of Para, resulting in at least 19 deaths. Weeks later, President Cardoso warned that future land occupations would be treated as a national security issue, and the armed forces would be used to evict squatters.[23] Nor has Argentina's Menem been reluctant to fill the streets of Buenos Aires with soldiers and tanks to block peaceful demonstrators taking part in general strikes. Last, but not least, Zedillo's method for dealing with the socioeconomic conditions that created the basis for the emergence of the Zapatista guerrillas in Chiapas has been to militarize a broad swath of southern Mexico.

Popular support for virtually every third 'wave' neoliberal president has collapsed or declined significantly since they entered office. Barometro Iberoamericano, a survey conducted jointly by 14 political firms in late 1996, revealed the extent of regional hostility toward these proponents of the free market agenda. Menem (79 per cent), Lozada (63 per cent) and Caldera (60 per cent) received the highest disapproval ratings, but even the most 'popular' of the group, Alberto Fujimori, experienced a 15 per cent fall in his approval rating (to 58 per cent) over the preceding 12 months.[24]

Unlike the first- and second-wave social protest movements who participated in anti-regime actions that were typically sporadic, sectoral and defensive, the third-wave of liberal politicians confront organized popular power with a social revolutionary perspective. In Mexico, the Zapatista guerrillas revealed the depth of the socioeconomic crisis and posed a fundamental challenge to the national political system; in Brazil, the landless rural workers' movement (MST) currently occupy rural properties in 22 of the country's 26 states, in an aggressive response to government inaction over agrarian reform;[25] in Bolivia, the Chapare coca-growers played a leading role in opposing the 1996 agrarian reform bill which included a 50 per cent reduction in land tax and other concessions to property-holders.[26]

These and other movements across the continent not only illustrate a new type of revolutionary democratic opposition to neoliberal electoral politics, but have been successful in attracting important sectors of the downwardly mobile lower-middle class previously hesitant, if not hostile, to radical politics and direct action, and a prime base of electoral support for the neoliberal regimes. In Mexico, the debtors organization of small and medium farmers (Barzon), and business people and professionals, have developed links with the Zapatistas; in Brazil, sectors of national industry and commerce have expressed support for the landless rural workers' demands for agrarian reform; in Bolivia, small and medium size business groups have expressed support for the coca farmers; in Paraguay, professionals, journalists and teachers articulate the interests of peasant movements.

The degree of middle class alienation in the big cities varies. Deep seated prejudices toward radical movements of the poor and a continued belief in old discredited liberal-democratic models of social consensus momentarily block any rapid shift to the left. Nevertheless, as one set of so-called 'center-left' pragmatists fails to prevent the fall of the middle class into poverty, there is a perceptible questioning of electoral politics and the viability of the neoliberal model – hastening the move, especially among affected public sector employees, toward extra-parliamentary politics. As the neoliberal cycle plays itself out, the electorate is becoming increasingly distrustful toward the political class and its capacity to define a new politico-economic project.

The duality of neoliberal politics – populist electoral campaigns and austerity free market regimes – has bred general cynicism toward all politicians. At the same time, the class perspective toward politics has gained ascendancy in the social movements, challenging a basic tenet of neoliberal doctrine that there are 'no alternatives'. The social movements are increasingly moving toward defining an alternative political project – moving from protest against neoliberal policies toward the politics of social revolution. In Brazil, the MST is debating a programme which goes beyond agrarian reform to self-managed socialism. In Bolivia, the coca farmers have organized a new political movement, the Alliance for the Sovereignty of the People, which incorporated the autonomy of the Indian nation, social ownership and free market production of coca. In Paraguay, the National Peasant Federation has openly defined a socialist programme in which rural co-operative and public ownership are counterposed to Stroessner-style 'statism' and the Wasmosy government's liberalism. The division between 'social movement' and 'politics' is coming to an end The political definitions of the social movements are taking place without looking to external oracles and encompass searching debates and the exploration of new terrains of discussion.

FROM CRITICS TO CELEBRANTS: ENTRENCHING THE NEOLIBERAL AGENDA

In analyzing the contemporary Latin American political cycle it is important to address the question of why the apparent voter opposition to neoliberalism translates into the election of successor regimes espousing the same policies.

First, as we have observed in virtually every case, neoliberals do not campaign for political office on their programme; they do *not* promise to lower salaries, dismantle the welfare state, reduce pensions, increase prices of essential food items and basic social services. On the contrary, neoliberals disguise themselves as populists, flay the incumbent neoliberals and promise to change course. In the quest for the presidency, populist and nationalist slogans predominate; candidates promise to address the problems of poverty and unemployment; proponents of the free market doctrine are vigorously denounced. But once in office, the reformist commitments are subordinated to IMF-style 'adjustment' and 'stabilization' programmes as severe as any of the outgoing neoliberal regimes which were denounced for all to the accompaniment of dismantled social welfare systems, the elimination of laws protecting labour, downward wage spirals, rising unemployment and the growth of the informal economy, and greater impoverishment of populations.

Electoral campaign programmes are inversely related to post-election politics. Neoliberalism has *debased* the *electoral* process as much as it has *marginalized the legislature* in the *post-electoral* period. Under neoliberalism, electoral politics has become meaningless as a method of providing meaningful choices to the electorate, in which voter expectations are correlated to electoral outcomes. The result calls into question the whole issue of representative government. Electoral non-representativeness is a result of the fundamentally elitist character of neoliberalism: its socioeconomic policy is incompatible with free elections. Under military rule, neoliberal measures could be announced openly and imposed. Under civilian rule, they must be disguised and then imposed via the fiction of the electoral mandate. The pseudo-legitimacy of neoliberal regimes rests on the false assumption that the government was 'freely elected'. But politicians are legitimately elected only as representatives of a publicly defended position. Stripped of political context, the electoral process loses its legitimacy as would any other instance of political fraud. To the extent that neoliberal electoral campaigns are manipulated to secure voting outcomes diametrically opposed to those supported by the majority of the electorate, it is not only a violation of trust but of the very notion of representative government.

The neoliberal cycle – the reproduction of neoliberal regimes – is thus based on its practitioners' capacity to distort the electoral process through conscious deception; it deepens the gap between voter preferences and the practices of the political class, between electoral processes and policy outcomes.

The second reason public opposition to neoliberalism translates into the election of neoliberals is the political power of economic groups organized 'outside' of the electoral process. The main determinants of political decisions are not voter preferences, but are embedded in the socioeconomic structures in which elected politicians operate. The latter, committed to working within existing capitalist property relations, international circuits and financial networks, automatically seek to accommodate their policies to the basic economic interests of this configuration. The key capitalist actors – international and national, productive and financial – base their investment decisions on the perpetuation of the neoliberal model. The result is that capitalist politicians who attempt to 'regulate' or change the rules of investing to accommodate the social interests of the majority of voters inevitably provokes capital flight, declining investment and reductions of external financial flows. The elected politicians, anticipating a possible crisis of 'investor confidence', move swiftly to repudiate their campaign promises and implement the 'other', hidden agenda.

In today's executive-centred political system linked to the neoliberal, free market 'model' there is little or no institutional space for countervailing social forces proposing alternatives to a capitalist strategy. The ease with which 'reformist' or 'populist' politicians repudiate their campaign rhetoric suggests that organized social forces or institutions capable of holding them to political accountability, at least via the electoral process, are very weak.

The third reason why neoliberalism reproduces itself despite widespread electoral opposition can be found in the accommodationist behaviour of center-left politicians. Despite electoral mandates to change, an ideology that purports to oppose neoliberalism and a prior political trajectory of opposition, the center-left quickly adapts to the neoliberal power configuration.

Past history (social background and struggles) are not as influential on center-left political behaviour as immediate contextual factors; ideological commitments are less important than narrow political interests; electoral mandates are not as relevant as self-enrichment. Contextual factors, political interests and self enrichment have taken on such prominence in today's world because they resonate with the dominant ethos of the time. Center-left politicians denounce neoliberalism in the abstract: in practice, they are strongly attracted to the ethic of quick and easy fortunes made through public-private transactions. This process is facilitated and legitimated by the privatization discourse. For the petty bourgeois (and not a few ex-workers), upward social mobility through politics has been a staple practice. In the past, this opportunism has been controlled to some degree or checked by strong class institutions (which held leaders accountable) and sanctioned by stern moral prescriptions. Today majoritarian popular discontent is not institutionalized; class ethics have been eroded. As a result, center-left politicians are free to drift across the political and social map redefining the terms for 'opposing neoliberalism'. Such terms are sufficiently vague as to allow various forms of pro-capitalist 'modernization' stratagems to surface that are hardly popular 'alternatives'.

The reproduction of neoliberalism can also be analyzed in terms of institutional continuities between the military regimes and the new electoral system. The debate on 'transitions' from dictatorship to democracy have typically ignored or falsified a key element: the continuity of socio-economic power, state institutions and the development 'model'. The electoral regimes were neither able or willing to confront the rigid policy parameters established by international and domestic capital. To do so would call into question the very origins of the 'political pact' that allowed electoral politicians to emerge from obscurity. This historical legacy and recognition of the policy boundaries has become part of the revived electoral political culture. Transgressors of the 'political pact' face the prospects of a crisis of investor confidence and, beyond that, the threat of a return of military rule. Under neoliberal hegemony, the new rules of the electoral game allow opposition parties free rein to attack neoliberalism in *pursuit* of government office, but insist on 'responsibility' for accelerating the model *after gaining* office. Freedom, in the market democracy sense, involves talking to the people in electoral campaigns and working for the rich in power.

IMPOVERISHING SOCIETIES: THE CRISIS MULTIPLIER IN NEOLIBERALISM

The fundamental problem of neoliberalism is that it is not able to create a stable predictable policy with any foreseeable take-off into sustained growth and incremental benefits that would allow for long-term consolidation. Though regimes espousing this approach have revealed an uncanny capacity to reproduce themselves, this has invariably led to a further radicalization of the 'adjustment' and 'stabilization' measures accompanied by a slow, but sure, growth of socio-political opposition movements challenging their rule and their 'model'.

The basic question that proponents of the 'model' must answer is why does neoliberalism enter into a deeper crisis with each new wave of 'adjustments' rather than to an economic 'take off' and prosperity? The key to understanding the SAP is reconceptualizing it in terms of a political and class strategy because its prime effect is to alter the terrain of social struggle and reconcentrate political power, as well as to widen the wealth gap between rich and poor. The discourse of socio-economic development is a peripheral consideration. SAPs are preceded by 'stabilization' measures which are political in character, establishing the terrain for the more profound 'adjustments' that follow.

The typical 'stabilization' measure creates barriers which make popular resistance to the SAP much more difficult. 'Stabilization' induces an economic crisis which forces the working and middle classes to concentrate on the struggle for existence. It also weakens popular movements by targeting bastions of organized labour, notably public sector, mining and petroleum unions. In such an environment, labour leaders may be quickly outflanked and intimidated into accommodation. In Argentina, Brazil and Venezuela, where trade unions administer multimillion dollar health and welfare budgets, those in charge are disinclined to mobilize political opposition to 'adjustment' as their organizational and monetary resources are put in jeopardy by 'stabilization'.

Rather than assume the economic rationale of the SAP, it is more relevant to stress the political logic undergirding 'stabilization' policies and their socio-economic consequences. The neoliberal policies have little to do with economic development. Privatization or the sell-off of public assets adds little to new productive facilities. At best, additional investments may occur, but most of the original inflow of resources is counter-balanced by outflow through larger remittances to the home office (resulting from the depressed Latin markets). Capitalizing privatized enterprises is accompanied by a greater de-capitalization of the economy, creating balance-of-payment problems, not solutions.

Trade liberalization, the unilateral elimination or drastic reduction of tariffs, has not usually created 'competitive' enterprises. It has led to a massive number of bankruptcies, the dominance of the market by a small number of large enterprises and/or heavy dependence on foreign imports. Between 1986 and 1994, exports failed to keep pace with imports, transforming the region's large positive trade balance into an $18 billion deficit (Green, 1995: 80). The 'opening of trade' assumes that the shock of competition will spur enterprises to catch up technologically, upgrade their labour force, discover overseas markets in a time frame and global context that far exceeds the capacity of any country or firm at a comparable stage of development. The application of open trade policies independently of the historical specificities and capabilities of a country reflects their origins in doctrinal belief systems rather than any historical or empirically situated context.

The liberalization of financial flows has not contributed to new investment capital in large scale, long-term productive activities. Most new financial flows have been directed at short-term high interest bonds and government notes to strengthen foreign reserves, meet debt payments or balance external accounts. In 1990, portfolio investments accounted for a mere 3.7 per cent of all foreign investment in Latin

America; during 1993 to 1995, that figure jumped to between 42 per cent and 62 per cent.[27] Financial deregulation is frequently associated with the growth of speculator capital: easy entry and quick exit. These speculative practices are imitated by local investors who take advantage of de-regulation to move their capital to and from overseas accounts on the basis of shifts in interest rates that are integral to the 'opening', increasing the costs of borrowing for local producers and stifling entrepreneurial behaviour by shifting earnings from profits to interest payments. As a result of increased indebtedness to banks, productive capital usually exerts pressure to lower salaries and social payments to labour. Many employers subcontract to the so-called informal sector or divert capital from slow-maturing productive investments into high turnover commercial activity or lucrative interest-bearing government bonds. In other words, the neoliberal strategy has more to do with concentrating private wealth and increasing foreign and monopoly ownership than in stimulating entrepreneurial skills, productive investment or well paid employment.

Even less convincing is the neoliberal argument that 'downsizing' social sector budgets helps employers and investors by eliminating excessive costs that hinder accumulation and growth. Cuts in social programmes undermine labour productivity and lead to an increased turnover of workers and the loss of expertise associated with stable employment. The strategy encourages labour-intensive investments which, in turn, weakens the incentive for research and development that creates new technological innovations. The growth of neoliberalism has spawned a vast army of 'informal' employees (stripped of social benefits) who have no future and frequently engage in drug and contraband activities. In Brazil, for example, the 'informal' economy accounted for almost 30 per cent of the monies circulating in the country's financial system in 1992, equivalent to approximately 60 per cent of the annual GDP, most related to drug trafficking, illegal financial activities, corruption and smuggling.[28] Higher profits that do accrue are not likely to be invested in depressed domestic markets with large numbers of low income workers/consumers. Hence, the interest in overseas markets (Mercosur, NAFTA) and speculative global investments.

Neoliberalism is premised on the notion of prioritizing external debt payments over and above any domestic development. The argument is that overseas investor/creditor confidence is central to securing strategic inflows of capital to rebuild the economy. In practice, the obligation to make full, prompt debt payments has led to the massive deterioration of the physical infrastructure: roads, transport systems, educational and health facilities have deteriorated, leaving only private facilities for the elite. The transport market 'grids' that linked productive sectors have been replaced by a central 'spoke' system linking productive enclaves to export-central cities directed toward overseas markets. Enclave development may result in high export growth statistics and adequate debt payment performance, but it leaves the bulk of the provincial economies in shambles. The deterioration of the infrastructural shell, related to cutbacks in state capital investment in communication and transportation, discourages productive investment particularly outside of the capital cities. The decline of public education and the expansion of elite private education is also linked to a specialized economy catering to overseas markets and speculative services. Social cuts enlarge the role of enclave based capital. Speculator capital and foreign debt holders preside over a stagnant economy populated by an impoverished labour force.

The opening to foreign capital (particularly the elimination of protected strategic sectors) through deregulation, tax incentives and free trade zones, induces investment in export production with little value added (assembly plants, mining, forestry, fishing, agriculture). The elimination or lowering of multinational corporate taxation results in declining state revenues and increased taxation on local business and wage earners. The attempt to compensate for declining corporate revenues through social cuts fuels social unrest which in turn dampens the climate for long-term, large-scale productive investment. Neoliberalism creates an investment culture in which perpetual low labour/social costs is a specified condition for new or sustained investment. The lowering of labour costs is not merely an enticement for entry capital but a built-in and assumed condition for 'normal' capitalist investment.

Thus, working class sacrifice is not a short term precondition for general prosperity but a long-term structural condition for concentrating income. With declining internal markets, high rates of business and agricultural bankruptcy, greater import dependency and high fixed money costs (due to debt payments, external imbalances, flight capital) neoliberal regimes confront domestic budget deficits and a need to seek external borrowing. To secure external financial support, however, they must apply a new SAP, which in turn recreates the conditions for a new crisis. The process continues in a spiral that constantly keeps wages declining and social conditions deteriorating, while those classes in the state and private sector linked to the new circuits grow richer. Foreign ownership of basic resources multiplies, while high profits and interests continue on an upward spiral creating a new class of super-rich billionaires.

CONCLUSION

Neoliberalism is, in essence, about the 'adjustment' cycle: a downward spiral for the working and middle class and an upward spiral for the multinational corporations, bankers and domestic ruling classes linked to the state and external circuits. The dialectics of 'adjustment' are expressed in a highly polarized class structure. As salaries decline and domestic resources are taken over by foreign capital, public officials and the political class cannot accumulate wealth through 'normal paths'. Neo-liberalism, then, becomes an attractive doctrine for facilitating corrupt practices, including commissions and partnerships for the public officials presiding over the privatization process, financial 'rewards' from local capitalists for trade and resource concessions, and support for pro-business labour agreements.

The 'new ethics' of private enrichment underlines public virtue and converts most conventional electoral politicians into neoliberals. Exiting from the public sector means appropriating the greatest amount of wealth in the shortest time – before the private sector takes it all. In turn, state corruption facilitates the accumulation of private wealth which becomes the basis for partnerships with those in the private sector who benefit from the sell-off of public enterprises. Given such behaviour a political reading of SAP provides a more appropriate frame work for understanding neoliberalism than its purported treatment as an economic strategy.

The neoliberal electoral cycle and the socioeconomic spiral continually intersect, each time around more 'radical' conditions for social and political action. A rupture in these cycles as we have shown is not structurally pre-determined, but depends on the conscious political intervention of the growing pool of downwardly mobile classes. The politics of 'opposition' have been deflected at each point of neoliberal crises because a systemic (socialist) alternative has been absent. The process of movement beyond neoliberalism not only in the 'social sense' but in the political has begun. As our analysis suggests, the new socio-political movements have their greatest chance of success outside of the electoral framework because of the tight constraints and limitations within which the latter operates. The break with neoliberalism is likely to take place in the extraparliamentary arena by political forces that move beyond the pragmatism of the centre left.

6 New Social Movements in Latin America: The Dynamics of Class and Identity

INTRODUCTION

The insurrection of indigenous peasants in Chiapas on the first of January in 1994 has had a profound impact. Not only did it put an end to the ruling class's – and party's – illusion of social peace and stability, and brought on centre-stage the long and hard struggles of indigenous peoples in Mexico and elsewhere, but it had a significant impact on what we could term the sociology of social movements – the way in which movements of resistance and social change are conceived. In the immediate context, the uprising seriously undermined and tarnished the glow that surrounded the government's neoliberal policies of structural adjustment which just a month earlier had been lauded by president Clinton at a summit of Latin American heads of state as a model for other governments in the region to follow. In the same context, it raised serious questions about the feasibility of armed struggle, a tactic that had all but been abandoned by the Left as a result of the repeated failures and the destruction of the many organizations that had taken up arms in the 1960s and 1970s.

The flood of studies and interpretations that have been produced in the wake of the initial resurrection and the subsequent process of political transition and transformation, each seeking to draw out some of its vital 'lessons', can be placed into two categories. First, there are all those many studies (and published reflections) that have focused on and debated the politics of armed struggle. The obvious and clear 'success' of the uprising in placing the demands of indigenous people on the political agenda, and in forcing the government to seriously negotiate these demands as well as its relations with and treatment of these people, tended to revalidate the tactic as a form of resistance and struggle. And, in fact, similar organizations to the EZLN subsequently have formed and appeared in several places, especially Guerrero and Oaxaca, where similar conditions to Chiapas exist.[1] However, the left wing of what in Mexico is termed 'the political class' (referring to the intelligentsia and the PRD, the major centre-left political party in the country), was manifestly shaken and generally gave the EZLN an ambiguous response, sympathizing with its aims but objecting to its methods. Critically important support within the country for the EZLN came from other quarters including some intellectuals associated with a plethora of civil associations, community-based or national organizations of Mexico's vibrant civil society that in the end forced the government to reject its policy of armed confrontation and enter into a process of negotiations with the EZLN.

A second category of more widely ranging and internationally scattered studies have tended to focus on what is 'new' and distinctive about the EZLN's organization and its internal dynamics, with respect to the social movement of indigenous peoples – a movement that has ramifications and resonance well beyond Chiapas and Mexico.[2] The theoretical perspective of these diverse studies is diffuse and has numerous permutations, but in its critical dimensions is based on or is affected by variations of what has come to be known as 'postmodernism', a perspective that in the 1980s displaced Marxism as the dominant approach to the sociological study of peasant communities and their social and political dynamics. The essence of this perspective is that the Chiapas uprising, like the 'new social movements' that emerged throughout Latin America in the 1980s, represents a radically new form of organization and politics that highlights the postmodern condition: a radical subjectivity of experience and the self-constitution of a new social subject, a social actor seeking to define and express itself on a largely self-constructed stage.

With reference to these two bodies of literature, the aim of this chapter is to (i) identify and cut through what is at issue in the emerging (or by now well-established) debates; and argue that (ii) the Chiapas uprising constitutes or represents not so much a 'new social movement', as conceived by proponents of postmodernism, but a resurgence of class-based social movements in Latin America; (iii) that this latest wave of social movements, the third in the post World War II Latin American context, is led by peasants and revolves around their struggle for access to land and other productive resources, freedom or democracy, and social justice – eminently 'modernist' and class demands predicated on the need to establish a new relationship to existing society and its state or to restructure that state itself; and (iv) that in the context of these peasant-based and -led movements that the tools of class analysis need to be reconstituted and are validated. In effect, it will be argued that despite its constitution of a number of salutary principles, postmodernism does not provide a useful theoretical perspective or analytical framework for understanding, and explaining, the dynamics of social and political struggles in Latin America. In fact, what it contributes, and its major effect, is intellectual immobilization and political demobilization. The dynamics of the on-going and new social struggles in Latin America require and dictate a reconstituted form of class analysis.

This argument is constructed as follows. Part I reconstructs the critical elements of the postmodern perspective as relates to an analysis of new social movements in Latin America. Part II provides several counterpoints to this perspective, with specific reference to class formations and social movements in the rural sector of Mexican society. Fragments of class analysis are here introduced. Part III places these formations and movements in a broader Latin American context and identifies critical features and the class dynamics of an emergent social movement of peasants and indigenous peoples. This social movement is shown to be 'new' in a number of respects and representing the most dynamic forces in Latin American society of resistance and opposition to the neoliberal agenda. The chapter concludes with a statement of several lessons that can and should be drawn from our exploratory analysis.

THE POSTMODERN AGENDA: A NEW PIVOT OF SOCIAL ANALYSIS

The sociology of development, like its counterparts in economics and politics, is the product of intellectual (and political) developments in the post World War period but can be traced back to an intellectual project of the 18th-century Enlightenment: modernism. The process associated with this project (modernization), and reflected in the 18th-century idea of 'progress', has three critical dimensions: (i) *economic* – the expansion of society's productive forces, the growth of output, and on this basis an improvement in the standards of living of the population;[3] (ii) *political* – liberation from oppressive and restrictive structures and institutions, increased freedom for the individual (the institution of democracy) and thus greater capacity for self-realization;[4] and (iii) *social* – the creation of a society which, in Rousseau's words, 'creates conditions equal for all', or that provides equity and social justice (in the distribution of society'(s resources).[5] The process involved in the realization of this project and its conditions[6] is alternatively conceptualized as (i) industrialization (the shift from agriculture to industry and the associated transformation of the structure of production) and capitalist development (the institution and spread of wage labour and the market, the 'motor' of the development process – the most efficient mechanism for the allocation of resources – and private enterprise, the conductor of this motor); (ii) modernization (the transformation of a system whose functioning is based on 'traditional' values into one based on 'modern' values);[7] and (iii) democratization (the institution of a democratic system of governance). No matter how conceived, or what aspect and dimension is emphasized in analysis, modernization – the road to modernity (in which people are free, equal, and able to satisfy their basic needs and realize their human potential) – is the essence of the project involved, the object or goal of the associated process of change and development.[8]

In the late 1950s, faith in the idea of 'progress', in the notion of a development process, either was lost or gave way to the notion that the process of modernization was at an end, that it had exhausted its limits and was giving way to a new 'postmodern period', in which, as C. Wright Mills, among other sociologists, argues, all the historic expectations that have characterized 'Western culture' are no longer relevant and the Enlightenment faith in the united progress of reason and freedom, together with the ideologies grounded in that faith (liberalism, socialism) 'have virtually collapsed as adequate explanations of the World and ourselves'.[9]

Not all sociologists at the time shared or went along with this notion and perspective of an emerging post-modern, post-industrial, or post-capitalist society. Indeed, the sociology of development and its theory of modernization, was but in its infancy. Over the next two decades sociological analysis was divided among those who, like C.W.Mills and Daniel Bell, sought to analyse the post-modern condition, and those who continued to believe in the fundamental process of modernization, on the one hand, or capitalist development, on the other.[10] However, by the 1980s, sociological theory – and development theory more generally – reached an impasse and by a number of accounts went into crisis.[11]

Within the specific though interdisciplinary field of development studies this impasse or crisis took the form of an incapacity of the theorists and practitioners in the mainstream to withstand the attacks made on their postulates and propositions by proponents, on the Left, of Marxist-oriented theories of dependency and imperialism, and, on the right, by proponents of neoclassical economics and neoliberal policies of structural adjustment. One resolution of this crisis was what has amounted to a 'counter-revolution' in theory and policy,[12] resulting in the formation of a new 'Washington consensus' on correct thinking and policy.[13] There were several other attempted resolutions, most notably by exponents of a search for an alternative form of development that is predicated on neither the agency of the state nor the functioning of the market but on community-based, human scale, people-led participatory action.[14] As for sociological analysis more generally, there were a number of critical theoretical issues, but the most salient revolved around the question of historical determination – whether human agency, the actions and projects of individuals or particular social groups and classes, were determining factors of historical development, or, on the other hand, whether these developments were determined by objectively given conditions, by the working (the 'laws' of) of the economic system on individuals.

The debate on this issue has taken numerous forms with many permutations that cut across the theoretical – and political – divide between liberal and Marxist sociologists and between advocates of materialism (structuralism) and idealism (subjectivism) in social analysis, or between a society's 'political economy' or its 'culture'. One of the more critical and intellectually consequential (although, we will argue, wrongheaded) forms of this debate revolved around French post-structuralist discourse-analysis and an associated critique of structuralism, particularly in its Marxist form of class analysis.[15] The main object of this critique was the structuralist belief in the capacity to represent in thought (and reflected in the textual discourse) conditions that are real in their effects, conditions generated by underlying deep structures that are invisible in themselves, manifest only in their effects.[16] The radical idea introduced by these post-structuralists was that the human mind has no way of determining the correspondence between the real and its representations – of 'knowing' or accessing the 'real'; and that the observed patterns and regularities captured in thought and reflected in theoretical discourse (the 'text') were determined internally, imposed by the mind (that is, had no empirical referents), and did not necessarily – or at all – represent conditions that are 'real'; in themselves; and that the 'real' is largely subjective, determined by and reflective of the particular standpoint of the particular 'historical subject'. This form of analysis,[17] which to some extent can be traced back to the nihilist philosophy of Nietsche and a long sociological tradition of idealist critiques of science (including the Frankfurt school of critical theory that emerged in the 1920s and 1930 but was transplanted and reworked at the New York School for Social Research)[18] had a significant impact on the form that analysis – and theorizing – could and would take. In its most radical form, it implied a disbelief, scepticism or agnosticism with respect to the possibility of scientific knowledge – of structural determination, and of the relevance of meta-theories predicated on structural determination or the working of a system – of objectively given, and determining, conditions.[19] It presupposes a radical heterogeneity and subjectivity – the standpoint of the historically situated individual, able to socially construct – and thus determine one's own reality.

How is this post-structuralist analysis/critique and post-modernist perspective applied in practice; that is, in social analysis? It is clear enough that it has had a significant impact in the analysis of certain issues in specific fields, such as international development and peasant studies, and in an explanation of the internal dynamics of what have been defined as 'new social movements'. For the most part these movements have been analysed in the context of societies in what are customarily regarded as industrialized, capitalist democracies in Europe and North America. However, new social movements have also been identified in Latin America, the conditions of which in the 1980s generated a spate of studies into social movements as well as the internal dynamics of peasant communities and behaviour.[20] Despite some obfuscation on the issue, this analysis was – and is – explicitly designed as a rejection and replacement of the Marxist structural discourse and class analysis that had hitherto dominated these fields.

The postmodernist perspective underlying and derived from the post-structuralist critique of structuralism and Marxism is reflected in and has taken the form of several concepts and principles enunciated as a new framework of analysis. The central concept is that of a self-constituted subject or social actor, able to draw up a script, construct an identity, improvise a corresponding role or line of action, and act it out on a stage set up in the particular setting in which participants in the action find themselves.[21] Its major principles, variously and broadly applied (as we will see) to the dynamics of social movements and peasant communities in Latin America, can be formulated as follows: (i) subjectivity – the idea that conscious experience is predominantly subjective in nature and as such both the source of social identity and the constituent (or determinant) component of social action;[22] (ii) heterogeneity – the idea that the form of consciousness and action cannot be viewed as simply the effect of some underlying cause, of a deeply embedded structure that is invisible in itself manifest only in its effects on behaviour (consciousness and action), but that it reflects and expresses the diversity of its self-constituted elements;[23] and (iii) contextuality – the related idea that forms of social action should be related to (explained in terms of) their meaning, arising in historically specific contexts, rather than their cause, which is to say, the universal effects of structurally determined objective conditions.

POSTMODERNISM AND NEW SOCIAL MOVEMENTS IN LATIN AMERICA

On the basis of these ideas – with reference to the associated principles (which were sometimes enunciated, sometimes not) – the study of peasants in the rural sector of Latin American societies and the emergence of new social movements in the urban sector of these and other societies have been placed in a postmodernist perspective, all but displacing Marxism, which in the 1960s and 1970s had dominated these fields. At the centre of Marxism was the concept of class, defined in terms of the individual's objectively defined relationship to the means of production, and applied with reference to the idea that (i) the basic structure of this relationship was based on the division between the owners of the means of production and the direct producers or workers; (ii) under capitalism, the inner secret of this structured social relation was the exploitation of labour by capital, the extraction of surplus value; (iii) that this structure produced both the objective and subjective conditions of social change, the revolutionary transformation of the capitalist system; (iv) that the working class is the active agent of this transformation, the historical subject of the revolutionary project (or, in Hegelian language, the historic dialectic); and that (v) the politics of this process required the unity of the diverse social forces accumulated by the organization of the subordinate classes – all the oppressed and the exploited – in various sectors of society.

In the context of Latin America and elsewhere in the 1980s, these propositions were generally and specifically rejected by a new (and a converted old) generation of scholars, who counterposed a series of alternative propositions that placed political developments in the region in a very different perspective. In this perspective, the notion of a structurally specific mode of production that generates objective conditions for different classes of individuals was jettisoned. The notion of coercive and exploitative social relationships such as debt peonage and wage labour was replaced with the notion of diverse social actors more or less in control of their lives, depending only on the success of their performance – on their ability to construct and project in their action a specific social identity. In this context, for example, the subjugated are widely portrayed as holding power over their exploiters (Brass, 1991). Social relations like peonage, once thought to rely heavily on coercion are viewed as symbiotic, even in the best interests of the peons themselves (Knight, 1988). Seen through the prism of postmodernist concepts and ideas (discourse, experience, agency, and contextuality), powerful peons are seen in fact to dominate the hapless *hacendados*; and exploitative class relations are replaced by notions of a moral economy, where patron and client, *hacendado* and peon, patron or employer and employee, are bound together by relations of mutual benefit, community spirit, and notions of fairness. The World Bank, for example, in its report on world labour (1995) in this constructed context of a moral economy views the jobber, who has long figured on the historical stage of rural labour markets and migrant workers as a brutally exploitative self-serving middleman or class agent, now reappears as an efficient (and honest?) broker who smoothes the useful mechanism of social exchange in rural communities.[24] In this and other contexts, the objectively given conditions of class exploitation and oppression are seen as figments of mechanistic structuralism and are reconstructed as a play of diverse actors searching for and actively constructing their social identity. In this process, mundane manifestations of social discontent and resistance are seen to alter class relations cumulatively and fundamentally.

NEW SOCIAL MOVEMENTS IN LATIN AMERICA: THE CONSTRUCTION OF SOCIAL IDENTITY VERSUS THE POLITICS OF CLASS

If one were to describe in terms of 'objective' social conditions what the 1980s meant for Latin America it would be possible to do so in terms of four assertions: (i) debt crisis, economic stagnation, and the decline of economic conditions for the majority of the population (in some cases deterioration to a level achieved in 1970);[25] (ii) the retrenchment of military and authoritarian regimes and their replacement with constitutional democratically-elected civilian regimes;[26] (iii) the widespread implementation of the SAP, an amalgam of stabilization and austerity measures (currency devaluation, anti-inflation) and 'structural' economic reforms (outward orientation, liberalization, deregulation, privatization, downsizing) designed by the International Monetary Fund and the World Bank; [27] and (iv) the refoundation of the capital accumulation process based on a radical change in the capital–labour relationship and the associated class structure.[28] These four sets of objective conditions, associated with and generated by a far-reaching economic and social restructuring process, undergone and experienced to different degrees by every country in the region in the 1980s,[29] provide the context in which 'new social movements' have been identified and analyzed. Take, for example, the retreat of the generals to their barracks and the reinstitution of liberal democracy throughout the region. In virtually every case, this process was preceded and accompanied by an explosive combination of newly formed popular social organizations and political demands for the restoration of democracy as well as specific (economic and political) demands of particular social groups. The revealing feature of these struggles is the protagonism of 'civil society' – popular organizations drawn from and formed in diverse social sectors and that had displaced the traditional organizations (political parties and unions) which had hitherto dominated the contested terrain of politics. In effect, these newly formed popular sector organizations were constituted – constituted themselves – as the 'subjects' of an unfolding political process.[30]

Although to date there does not exist any systematic comparative study of the social movement or movements constituted by these popular sector organizations,[31] it is possible to identify their salient features in terms of four criteria: their social base, their demands, the arena and specific form of struggle, the specific methods for realizing the goals of the movement; and, in postmodernist terms, the identity assumed or constructed by participants in the course of their struggle. And we could add another criterion: the political or ideological issue of the targeted adversary, what in Marxist discourse used to be defined as 'the enemy', and of the scope and orientation of action – political reform (democracy) or social transformation (revolution), or, more immediately, state power.

In terms of the first two criteria, we can identify at the base of these new social movements (NSM) various marginalized groups of the urban poor, protesting the oppression of government economic policies and the lack of democracy, and demanding legalization and title to occupied plots of land, as well as support in constructing houses and access to utilities and services;[32] women protesting the negative impact of government policy on their households and lives, sexual discrimination, exploitative and oppressive relationships and conditions, the abuse of their human and reproductive rights, and joining the demand for democracy – for democratizing social relations at all levels (Barrig,

1987; Jelin, 1990);[33] indigenous populations and communities, struggling to recover and define their ethnic and cultfural identity; and demanding autonomy, respect for their culture and institutions, social justice, and an end to exploitative practices and their oppression;[34] youth, who joined and led diverse protests of government austerity measures and the lack of democracy, as well the economic conditions of their exclusion from school or the workplace, and their cultural alienation;[35] family members of persons imprisoned or disappeared by the retreating military regimes or assassinated for political reasons;[36] supportive middle class organizations, protesting the violation of human rights and demanding respect of these rights (Calderon and Santos, 1987; Sondereguer, 1985); and new working class organizations formed in the streets of the burgeoning informal sector, as well as a few established 'workers' centres', to demand of government authorities the right to occupy the physical space needed to conduct their 'work' (in the streets) and access to the licences which governments distributed to regulate economic activity (Calderon and Santos, 1987).[37]

As indicated, the proliferation of 'new social movements' in Latin America in the 1980s requires a more detailed and synthetic study of the identity assumed by each, their internal dynamics, and the conditions that gave rise to them, as well as the form and direction of the struggles involved. However, the displacement of political parties, unions, and other traditional instruments of class struggle (and of what in Latin America is referred to as the 'political class') from the contested terrain of politics has been enough to convince an entire generation of sociologists and anthropologists of the constitution and existence of a new complex of social actors, the 'subjects' of the current struggle of resistance and for social change.[38]

From this perspective, the emergence of 'new social movements' had a double effect on progressive social thought in Latin America. On the one hand, it tended to invalidate a strict class analysis or, in postmodernist discourse, class essentialism. On the other hand, it raised serious questions about the viability or relevance of the vanguard party and other Marxist or Leninist forms of political organization which had achieved a virtual hegemony in the social movements of the 1960s and 1970s. In this context it was given that the axis of struggle, and of the construction of social movements for change, had shifted towards and was based on a new 'subject' that was at the same time more 'universal' and more politically diverse and heterogeneous than that identified and defined in terms of the Marxist concept of class (Hunter, 1995). If the industrial proletariat, which had figured so centrally in Marxist class analysis of social movements, with the reduction of wage-labour in the workforce and associated changes in the structure and organization of the working class, had more or less disappeared from the political scene (as argued by Laclau, 1995), the intellectual search for a new historical subject confronted (and ended with) the resurgence of popular sector organizations that expressed both the political potential of the oppressed (as well as the exploited and the marginalized) – being a repository of their interests and social forces for change – and the highly diverse contextually specific demands, concerns, and actions of different groups and categories of citizens.

The most critical and defining feature of these new social movements, from this point of view, was the social identity constructed in each particular case. The actions, forms of resistance, and social movements of diverse popular community-based organizations were seen to reflect the diversity of their subject positions, the localized experiences and forms of consciousness. Thus, a series of movements led and organized by women in different urban contexts expressed their self-awareness as women and their efforts to construct for themselves a social identity as women which would (and did) allow them to act and project a collective form of action... their collectively-shared experience of discrimination (and oppression) experienced in different spheres of their lives – the family, the workplace, and in the public sphere of social production and politics;[39] Likewise, in different localized contexts, indigenous peoples all across the region struggled to recover and express their cultural and national identity and demand respect for their culture, indigenous forms of organization, and their human rights.[40] Generally, in these diverse localized contexts it was discovered that the social movements did not respond to the objectively-given conditions generated by the institutionalized structures of the economic and political system or to a presumably shared position within this system.

The new social movements shared the feature of resistance, but this resistance expressed the subjective and heterogeneous conditions of self-awareness and took the form of a search for survival on a day to day basis as well as the demand for enough political space and participation in decisions that affected people's everyday lives.[41] In this context, the demand for social transformation, characteristic of class-based movements, was transmuted into demands for democracy, for more political space within which to project their social action, a space shared by the most diverse social organizations and groups of individuals; and this demand in turn was transmuted into more specific demands to meet the immediate needs of and address the concerns of people in their communities. In this process of transmutation and involution, resistance no longer took the form of explosive encounters with the guardians of the existing order or large-scale mobilizations for social transformation. It took the form of a day-to-day struggle for survival – to control the conditions of their particular situations.[42]

POSTMODERNISM IN PERSPECTIVE

With hindsight of several years it is easier and possible to place in perspective, and to evaluate, this postmodernist form of theorizing and analysis of the dynamics of new social movements. First, it is clear enough that it does indeed 'capture' a characteristic feature of the diverse movements: their limited scope, the involution of their demands for change, and the conditions that provoked or called for politically limited economically defensive actions as well as search for cultural identity, another element of this self-defence. However, at a different level, this theory of NSM profoundly misunderstood the nature and dynamics of these movements and miscast their participants or members.

As observed and argued by de la Cruz, Calderon, Laserna and others[43] it is clear enough that very few of these movements exhibited or operated with class-consciousness, awareness of their objectively-shared position *vis-à-vis* the economic system or government neoliberal policies that created objectively similar conditions for the most diverse social groups. But in terms of these 'objective' conditions it would be possible to analyze the social basis of the diverse new social movements in class terms: the major elements of its heterogeneous social base constitute fragments, strata or diverse forms of what could be loosely defined as the 'new working class', a class that has evolved in a radically different form than that analyzed and theoretically constructed in traditional Marxist analysis. However, in as much as these diverse groups and categories of individuals saw and defined themselves in different terms, and did not form a class 'identity' they did not – and, Marx would have argued, do not fully constitute a class. As Marx observed with respect to the independent rural producers in 19th-century France, to fully constitute a class requires not only a position within a system that creates objective shared conditions... but requires 'class consciousness' – the formation of a class identity, which does not spring automatically from these objective conditions but is the result of an ideological and political struggle – a contested terrain in itself.

The problem with the postmodernist interpretation and analysis of NSMs in Latin America is that in subjectifying the experience and consciousness of different social groups – and in assuming that people act almost exclusively in terms of this conscious experience and subjective interpretation – it contributed to the involution of conscious action and forms of resistance exhibited by these new social movements, to the shift from a struggle to change the broader system towards seeking democracy to seeking only redress of specific contextualized demands. There are 'objective conditions' of lived experience that help explain this process of political involution,[44] but in converting a political problem into an intellectual virtue, postmodern intellectuals effectively discarded the intellectual and political weapons needed to build an effective movement for change, contributing to the demobilization and reduced protagonism of these popular movement in recent years.

COUNTERPOINTS OF CLASS: FRAGMENTS OF AN ALTERNATIVE FORM OF ANALYSIS

Not all sociological studies of peasant communities and the dynamics of social movements in Latin America have been trapped in the rather sterile debate arising out of an economistic form of class analysis that ignores the subjective aspects of class formation, on the one hand, and an overly subjectivist and idealist postmodernist interpretation, on the other. Several such studies will be briefly touched on or summarized so as to illustrate some of the complexities and nuances of what amounts to a reconstituted form of class analysis that takes into account gender, ethnic, and development issues

Benjamin (1989), a historian, examines in the context of Chiapas, Mexico, the dynamics of a historical process in which a landowning class managed to consolidate and preserve ownership and control over the state's considerable economic resources and political destiny, and, in the process transform itself over time into government agents, bankers, and other forms of capitalists, and to acquire both wealth and power. The conditions of this process, according to Benjamin, meant and included the appropriation of the best tracts of arable land (for the production and capitalist development of cacao, coffee, cotton, sugar, mahogany....); monopoly control over capital and other productive resources; effective political control of the state and local governments and the state apparatus (the legislature, judiciary, police); the subjugation of the largely indigenous (Mayan) peasant population and their conversion into *jornaleros* (day wage labourers); and the marginalization of their communities, a function not of their geographic isolation, as so often argued, but of an actively directed process.[45] As Benjamin reconstructs it, the historical process of these developments was based on the structured relationship of different social groups to the means of production and on the symbiotic relationship between the holders of political and economic power, who he defines in terms of two interconnected elites but clearly constitute a dominant, and ruling, class.

In this context, the political upheavals of 1910–20 had little impact on the structure of economic and political power, although they did lead to the mobilization of social forces of opposition and resistance, the emergence of a socialist movement, and, in the 1930s, the formation of the Confederación Nacional de Campesinos (CNC) and the Confederación de Trabajadores Mexicana (CTM), both of which ultimately were accommodated within the corporatist structure set up by the governing party. In the 1960s and 1970s, another round of social upheavals and mobilizations led to the formation of left-wing class-based political organizations that launched and waged a long series of disconnected and ultimately unsuccessful political and armed struggles to settle demands for land and higher wages, and beyond these for control of the state and social transformation. These struggles in Chiapas were part of region-wide wave of social and political movements that formed the organizational roots of the armed insurrection of the EZLN on the first of January in 1994. They also constituted the political context of a process of capitalist penetration of marginalized peasant and indigenous communities, a process which converted large tracts of *ejido* or communal property into de facto private plots that were bought and sold within the indigenous community, generating – according to an account given by Greenberg (1989) – class divisions and an upsurge of intracommunal conflict, and converting large numbers of indigenous peasants into landless workers or de facto wage labourers, a process that was consciously accelerated by the federal government in 1992 on the basis of a constitutional reform.[46]

Another study that highlights some of the subtleties of an emerging reconstituted class analysis is conducted by Gavin Smith (1991) in a rural community in Peru. Smith develops a complex and provocative argument that the determination of class relations should not begin with an analysis of property relations and their objective conditions, with forms of consciousness, the experience of struggle and political relations added on; rather, the interplay of experience and consciousness, which so often in postmodernist discourse constitutes a vaguely defined subjective agency, is shown to be integral to the formation and transformation of productive or property relations; that is, it is a constituent, and thus determinant, element of class formation, as critical as are the objective conditions of this formation. At one level, Smith here only makes more precise what Marx had argued as a methodological principle in the 19th Brumaire. But his contribution is a welcome relief from the intellectual posturing of so many postmodernists who rarely, as it happens, leave the ethereal world of their conceptualizations to experience 'reality' in its objectively given conditions. After all, concepts have no empirical reference points in the 'world out there'.

What is most useful in Smith's analysis is his examination of the relationship between community and class, the scylla and charubdis of social analysis and of the debate (or divide) between Marxism and postmodernism. In his analysis, Smith establishes the complimentarity of the two concepts, viewing the object of his analysis (the community) as a complex of diverse class relations and not as in so much sociological analysis a vaguely defined organic whole held together and constituted by a sense of belonging and shared social identity. Smith shows in exquisite detail that members of a community can unite in a common struggle even though the interests, aims and objectives of the different classes that comprise it – and that connect it to the wider society – diverge. In the case of the struggle of the Huasicanchinos for land, a form of commonality was produced on the basis of a shared discourse but this did not mean that class differences were subsumed or replaced by community ties. Again and again he shows that divergent class interests both within and outside the community threaten to destroy the community and to undermine the commonality of its struggles (1989: 233).

In this context, Smith provides an illuminating theoretical commentary on the process of social transformation within a peasant community. At this level, his analysis has much to recommend it, a corrective to the excessive objectivism and economism of traditional class analysis and the excessive subjectivism of postmodernist discourse analysis. However, Smith's focus on the internal dynamics of class and community also contains a problem, one that is shared by many anthropologists and sociologists in their study of 'peasant communities'. The problem is that the connection of the community to the wider society – and to its economic and political systems – is not brought into a clear focus. This problem could be posed (and in the literature it often is) as a question of the penetration of economically and politically marginal and geographically remote (often indigenous) communities by outside forces. The dynamics of this penetration also have a class dimension which needs to be both conceptualized and analyzed, as they are to some degree by the studies on Mexico discussed or referenced above (Benjamin, Greenberg, Schryer). However, these studies are not immune from the ambiguity and intellectual schizophrenia that characterizes so many academic studies in this field when it comes to the marginal status of so many traditional indigenous communities.[47] On the one hand, many of these communities are geographically isolated as well as marginal in economic, social and political terms, leading many studies to view the conditions of their marginality (deprivation, poverty) as the result of geographic isolation or as self-imposed rather than as the result of social and political exclusion, discrimination, and the nature of the relationship that these communities have with the broader society, its culture, and its economic and political institutions. In these terms, these studies evoke the need of these communities to overcome their isolation and to integrate into the wider society – to be incorporated into its institutionalized practices and structure. On the other hand, the conditions encompassed by the term 'marginality' are correctly viewed as the product not of the marginal status of indigenous communities but of the specific form of their relationship with the broader society.

Take the case of Chiapas, one of Mexico's richest states in terms of natural resources, and one of the poorest in terms of the incidence of marginality, the objective conditions of which correspond to the large number of indigenous communities of peasant producers and the large size and distribution of the indigenous population. It has been estimated that at least 60 per cent of these peasants are, in fact, *jornaleros,* or wage labourers for the large *hacendado,* ranchers and *caciques* that own most of the arable land, commercial operations and productive resources in the region and control the political system[48]. And a large number of peasants, dispossessed of their access to land, have migrated to the Lacandon forest in search of wage labour associated with the country's largest petrochemical plant, hydroelectric complex, oil fields, and logging operations.[49] As Benjamin and others (Botz, 1994) have documented, the conditions of this process of what would have termed 'primitive accumulation' (dispossession of the producers from their means of production), which have converted many indigenous peasant producers into landless workers, a super-exploited semi-proletariat, or what Marx had conceptualized in a different context as 'an industrial reserve army' (an enormous reservoir of surplus labour) have been a long time in the making, at least several decades and to some extent centuries. The conditions and dynamics of this historic process make it difficult to conceive of the 'marginal' peasant community as isolated from the wider society, disconnected from its economic structure. Moreover, the largely self-subsistent base of the peasant economy, constructed within the institutional and legal framework of the *ejido* system of community landholding, also is part of Mexico's national economy. Not only does it serve to reproduce the incredibly cheap labour that so many *campesinos* are compelled to offer to the *hacendados* and capitalists across the country, but, as one consequence of Mexico's entry into the North America Free Trade Agreement (NAFTA,) it is subject to unfair competition from US producers that has crippled the local economy.[50]

It is clear enough that the complex of peasant communities constituting the economic and cultural basis of Mexico's indigenous peoples and society is very much a part of a national – indeed global – economy and deeply affected by its workings.[51] Thus it is that *subcomandante* Marcos, in the immediate wake of the *Zapatista* uprising, could speak of NAFTA as 'a death sentence' for the indigenous people of Chiapas and the country. However, the uprising and the subsequent process of negotiations – and transition of the EZLN from an army of national liberation into a new political force – make it just as clear that there is a significant 'political' dimension to the relationship that the country's indigenous peoples have with Mexican society. One of the central issues in the prolonged negotiation process is precisely the need to fundamentally change the constitutionally defined (and politically effective) political relationship of the country's indigenous peoples to the government and to the state – to meet thereby the Zapatista movement's critical demands for 'liberty, independence, and democracy – and social justice'. At issue in these clearly modernist demands[52] is the struggle of Mexico's indigenous peoples to escape the objectively given (and experienced) conditions of their exploitation and oppression; and to do so not in the subjectivity of experience (the construction of a social identity), nor even by changing their position within the operating economic system (neoliberal capitalism) and its political adjunct, but to change the system itself.[53] This is the challenge faced by the EZLN. The issue, as we will argue, is fundamentally that of class in its interconnected objective and subjective conditions.

THE LATIN AMERICAN PEASANTRY: THE EMERGENCE OF A NEW FORCE FOR SOCIAL CHANGE

The double discourse, political turns and opportunism of many political leaders on the left in Latin America have led in many parts to confusion and an absolute distrust in the 'political class' and their favourite political instrument – the party. In this context, many citizens have left the class struggle to devote themselves to the problems of every-day life, seeking at this level to survive the conditions created by austerity measures and to make a living. Some intellectuals, as we have noted, armed with a postmodernist perspective, misinterpreted this trend, seeing in it the constitution of new social subjects and the emergence of new social movements based on the politics of everyday life and the generation of non-class identities.[54]

Despite the double trend of an escape into the politics of everyday life and the election of neoliberal parties to national power, in many countries were formed movements of resistance and opposition to the neoliberal policies, more often than not in the immediate context of having just constituted a neoliberal regime. This resistance and opposition to neoliberal policies took different forms, but it had an undoubted class basis, postmodernism notwithstanding. This can be seen in Bolivia, for example, in the widespread and mounting protests of the miners and the *cocaleros* (miners turned coco-leaf farmers), teachers and public sector workers, and a new form of union tied to the social movements, and coordinating their actions with an amalgam of social organizations instead of the parties on the Left. But, above all it is evident in the emergence of new actions and struggles forming in the countryside – the centre and axis of the new insurgence.[55]

A good example of these new class-based movements is the Movement of Landless Workers (MST) in Brazil, formed on the basis of hundreds of organizations and hundreds of thousands of activists and supporters in the countryside. The MST has created a nation-wide political discussion on the issue of land, and according to most observers is the most dynamic social movement in the country, the best organized, and the most effective, with a record of concrete achievements and the accumulation of considerable social forces.[56] In Bolivia, the closing of the mines, the import of inexpensive products and widespread contraband has weakened the hitherto powerful unions of the mining and industrial sectors. In their place have been formed organizations of peasants, in particular among the *cocaleros* (many of whom are ex-miners) who are currently leading the struggle against neoliberalism, with large confrontations, marches, and general strikes that have paralyzed the country.[57] In Paraguay, the National Federation of Peasants is the principal force behind the massive mobilizations that are currently shaking the country, imposing the land issue on the political agenda...and the axis of the struggle against the neoliberal regime.[58]

Also in Mexico (in Chiapas, Guerrero, Oaxaca...) confrontations among the peasants and the State are almost a daily occurrence.[59] And in Ecuador, Colombia, El Salvador, and other countries in the region, the peasants have likewise constituted themselves as the principal subject of the class struggle. In many contexts the peasants are of indigenous origin, giving their struggle a national and ethnic character, but the base of the struggle can be found in their relationships to the means of production and to the state.

In short, the epitaph given to the peasantry by analysts and historians such as Eric Hobsbawm (1984) is premature and misinformed. The demographic argument in terms of their diminishing number in the labour force does not translate into good political analysis, at least with respect to Latin America. First, millions of families continue to live in the countryside – over six million families just in Mexico. Second, the urban crisis and their conditions of unemployment and misery is not a promising avenue or escape for peasant youth. Third, in the current context of land takeovers in Brazil, Paraguay, El Salvador and other countries there is evidence of a movement that runs counter to the traditional pattern of migration from the countryside to the city. Fourth, neoliberal policies have battered small producers all across the region with low prices, unequal competition and an unpayable debt, creating in the process social and family ties with the sons and daughters of the landless workers. And fifth, aside from structural considerations, there has emerged a new generation of peasant leaders with a notable capacity for organization, a sharp understanding of international and national politics, and a deep political commitment to changing their life situation.

Clearly we are not speaking of traditional peasant movements. First, in many cases the peasants are not divorced from urban life. In some cases they are ex-miners or displaced workers.[60] In other cases, the militants had a religious formation but abandoned the church to enter the struggle for agrarian reform as leaders of the movement of landless workers and peasants.[61] In many cases they are daughters of small peasant producers with a primary or secondary level education who decide to join (and sometimes end up leading) the movement instead of migrating to the cities to work in domestic service.[62] The new peasants, in particular the militants in leadership positions, often travel to the city to attend seminars and training schools and to participate in political discussions. In short, although they have their roots in the rural struggle, live in the camps or on the land settlements, and they are agricultural producers, they tend to have a cosmopolitan view. The number and quality of these intellectual peasants vary from country to country.

In Brazil, the MST has invested considerable resources and energy in the training of leadership cadres, with hundreds of peasants participating annually in a national training programme.[63] In other cases, as in Paraguay, Bolivia and El Salvador, the movement depends in a reduced number of leaders with savvy. In any case, what distinguishes these new peasant movements is the quality, militancy and democratic character of their leadership, which is reflected in the stated position of subcomandante Marcos that he 'mando obedeciendo' (leads by obeying).[64]

The second point critical point of these new peasant movements (NPMs) is that they are autonomous from political parties. The MST, for example, has cordial relations with the Workers Party (PT), as does the ADC in El Salvador with the FMLN. But the strength of both movements is in the direct struggle – land takeovers, the blocking of highways, marches and demonstrations, the occupation of public buildings. Their strategy, tactics, and the ideological discussions are decided within the movement, and not subject to any party line. To the contrary, it is these movements that provide the dynamism of the political struggles of the parties of the left – of their commitments to the rural struggle. At present, the NPMs in many cases constitute the catalyst of resistance to and the protests of neoliberal policies. In Bolivia, for example, the peasant organizations have broken their ties with the parties, and are actively engaged in debating the idea and the need to form their own 'political instrument'. In Paraguay, many leaders of the Peasant Federation have launched their own political revolutionary socialist movement. In Ecuador, the National Confederation of Indigenous Peoples (CONAIE) has called for a new 'national indigenous uprising' and have formed their own political instrument, even launching their own Presidential candidate in the last elections.

Third, the NPMs as a rule are involved in direct struggle and not in the electoral process. As in Chiapas, they have tended to discard it as a form of political action. They prefer to confer and to negotiate with the representatives of the state, or to coordinate with the unions, NGOs, and parties specific actions such as the organization and coordination of a general strike or proposing a certain piece of legislation. They are careful to retain control of the pace and the direction of the principal form of struggle – massive mobilizations and direct action.

Fourth, the NPMs are influenced by a mixture of classic Marxism and in various contexts by ideas related to ecology, and, in particular, the issues of ethnicity and nationality. In Paraguay, and in particular Bolivia, the class struggle of peasants and rural workers is closely tied to issues of ethnic identity, indigenous culture, the rights of the indigenous peoples, and the demand for national autonomy. In this context, internal debates as a rule are characterized by ideas of a close connection between issues of class and the nation. And in a number of contexts these issues are combined with a number of gender issues. At least in Brazil and Bolivia groups have organized within the NPM to the purpose of obtaining better representation and equality of women in the power structure and gender issues on the political agenda. In this context, these groups of women tend to think and work politically within the framework of gender-class, discarding both a bourgeois-feminist class-less perspective and an economistic form of class analysis.

Fifth, the NPMs are generally coordinated and, to a certain point united, on the basis of regional organizations such as CLOL and increasingly international forums such as Via Campesina which debate and exchange relevant experiences related to rural struggles – struggles that are increasingly shared and viewed as the same. Through these experiences and links is emerging an internationalist orientation – and practice. Thus, the militants of PT in Brazil not infrequently join with their counterparts in Paraguay and to a lesser degree in Argentina and Uruguay. And the same is occurring in the Andes, among the indigenous peoples and peasants of Bolivia, Peru and Ecuador, and in Central America.

To summarize, the resurgence of NPMs in the 1990s is not simply a return to 1960s and 1970s. In many cases the successes and the failures of those experiences have been studied and debated by the intellectuals of the NPM in the search of the lessons that can be drawn from them. Also there are elements of continuity with those struggles at the level of the surviving militants and their sons and daughters. But there are also critical differences in terms of strategy, tactics, and organization that separate the earlier movements from the new wave of peasant movements. These movements are much more aware and oriented by an understanding of the existence of a new world order and of the associated workings of neoliberal economic policies. Also they are generally more united by an awareness of the need to fight this system and to do so on the basis of a united front among indigenous peoples and peasants, and the need to join forces with other forces organized in opposition to the neoliberal economic and social order.

CONCLUSIONS

The conditions that gave rise to the Chiapas rebellion and uprising were clearly structural in source and objective enough in their effects on a population that responded not blindly and passively but actively and with a clear theoretical awareness of themselves – of who they are and represented, that is, their social identity as an exploited class and an oppressed people.[65] In the organized and active response to these conditions, the Zapatistas (the EZLN) were (and are) part of a new wave of social movements sweeping the region.[66] Although the Chiapas rebellion generated a serious (and on-going) debate as to political methods and appropriate (and viable) forms of struggle, the outbreak and the subsequent process of struggle[67] is part of a history constructed by peasants and indigenous people across Latin America. Resistance and opposition to the neoliberal agenda and the underlying capitalist system is forming and mounting in other popular sectors of civil society, including a restructured working class, but we conclude that the peasantry in its various forms and sectors is the most dynamic force for change. Its actions, as Marx had argued in 1844 with respect to a striking group of Silesian weavers,[68] bear the 'superior quality' of consciousness – theoretical awareness of what it is and represents – and the willingness and ability to act on it.

The actions and new social movements of the peasantry also relates to and allows us to address (if not settle) an on-going extended academic debate as to the objective and the subjective dimensions of social movements and the question of their class character and basis. In this respect, we conclude that the indigenous people and peasants in Chiapas and elsewhere in the region are constituted as a class under the objectively given conditions of their relationship to the means of production and to the State, protector and guarantor of this relationship. At the same time, these peasants and indigenous people have constituted themselves as a class in subjective terms, with reference to actions based on a clear awareness of themselves as a class and a people – seeking to liberate themselves (and others in the process) from the exploitative and oppressive structures of neoliberal capitalism in its Latin American form. On this basis, and in this context, as theorized by over a decade ago by Alain Touraine himself, a major influence on the postmodern generation of sociologists, the Latin American peasantry has constituted itself not only as a class, but as a social actor, the conditions of which, as he argued, are both ahead of and behind its constitution as a class (Touraine, 1984).

Under these conditions of class constitution and formation, there is no question of a radical heterogeneity or the specificity of a localized context for the Zapatista uprising. The rebellion resonated throughout the region, particularly among the peasantry and indigenous peoples who have experienced similar or comparable conditions and who are essentially engaged in the same political process of resistance and opposition to neoliberal capitalism in its Latin American forms.[69] In this context, the conditions of which, we have found, require and are very much subject to a structural (and political) class analysis, the Zapatistas (and other peasant-led social movements) have posed a major challenge for other forces of resistance and opposition to the existing economic and social order. Whether or not these forces – including those that progressive intellectuals on the Left can muster – which are generally located in the popular organized sectors of civil society, are up to this challenge remains to be seen. The political Left in Latin America and elsewhere have yet to resolve their own crisis: a lack of organic connection to the continuing struggle for social change (Petras, 1990). They are at a crossroads of history – a history constructed by (among others) the peasantry and indigenous people of Latin America. It is to be hoped that they will choose the right road leading, as Marcos has stated in expectation, to a new world in which there is life, not death – and where the modernist conditions of economic progress, liberty, democracy and social justice abound for all.

7 Neoliberalism and the Latin American Left: The Search for a Socialist Project

INTRODUCTION

The internal contradictions of the neoliberal project have generated not only diverse forces of opposition and resistance but enabling conditions for a number of alternative projects. One such project (social liberalism) is the response of social forces supportive of or with a vested interest in the existing socio-economic system. The concern here is to ensure the political viability of the neoliberal project in terms of its legitimacy and the stability of the regimes disposed towards it. The institutions ranged behind this model are run by the dominant class and elements of a middle class that are tied up and accommodated to the interests of this class. A second type of response is located in the popular sector of civil society and relies on community-based form of development based on the agency of non-government forms of organization. The *raison d'être* of these NGOs is to mediate between the grassroots and government/ outside 'donor' agencies. The essence of this type of response is to expand opportunities for popular participation in decisions that affect the community without, in effect, challenging the institutionality of the existing system. Liberal democracy at the macro- and the micro-level is what defines the goal of organizations that take this approach. This type of response is associated with what could be termed the social Left. A third type of response is associated with social forces of opposition and resistance that have also formed in the popular sector of civil society. It involves a complex of struggles and takes the organizational form of social movements. The liberal approach, by way of contrast, involves either a project-based form of development or a centre-left search for insertion into the structures and processes of the existing system. This bottom-up type of response is anti-systemic and is oriented towards changing the system itself, not just the position of different groups and classes of individuals within it. As argued in the last chapter it is associated with an emerging form of peasant-based social movement that is exhibiting considerable dynamism at the level of opposition and resistance. However, there is some question about the possibility of these movements in providing a serious challenge to the social forces entrenched in the existing system and its capacity to formulate a viable alternative socialist project, and to mobilize sufficient forces for its effective implementation. Herein, we would argue, lies the major challenge to the socialist Left committed towards substantive change and the socialist project. At issue here is not the 'political left' that continues to engage in the fantasies of electoral politics or the 'social left' that has turned to the trap of community-based development – to expand participatory spaces at the local level without understanding let alone be able to act against the larger social forces operating in the system. We conclude our review of the dynamics of social change in Latin America by turning to this question and the labyrinth of developments associated with it.

THE ITINERARY OF THE POLITICAL CLASS: FROM THE BARRICADES TO THE BALLOT BOX

A decade of protests, spontaneous and organized protests against neoliberal policies have had mixed results. Waves of spontaneous protests in some countries against a neoliberal policy of austerity measures has had little to no effect. Only in Ecuador did they not only result in a shelving of announced measures but they actually brought down the President of the country (Abdam Bucaram). In Bolivia, Brazil, Nicaragua, Venezuela and Uruguay more organized forms of protests against various privatization or other neoliberal measures did have some impact in blocking the proposed measures. But in countries like Mexico and Argentina the power of the state is so centralized in the office of the president, that the protests – and, Mexico, in particular, has experienced a lot (an average five a day in 1995) – have had little possibility of diverting the country from its neoliberal road.

However, a more serious problem for the opposition to neoliberalism is that opposition parties and organizations have not been able to present a coherent alternative program. Thus, in spite of establishing a tradition of resistance, the protests on balance have produced little more than a political vacuum and a lack of confidence in the possibility of change.

An expression of the political limits of protest is the inability to transform them into electoral victories. During the last years of protest, national elections have demonstrated what has been characterized as an 'apparent schizophrenia', with reference to a trend of choosing at the central government level rightist regimes given to neoliberal policies, and at the level of municipal government leftist regimes oriented toward opposition. In Brazil, for example, the PT (Workers Party) in the 1988 elections experienced a notable success in the municipalities of São Paulo and Porto Alegre among others. In 1992 the PT extended its control to 55 communities, converting it into the second political force at this level (although it lost São Paulo to a right-wing populist). In the 1996 elections the PT maintained its position as the second force at municipal level, while losing ground at the level of the central government (having previously lost the presidency to H.F. Cardoso, a social democrat turned neoliberal). And in other parts – from 1988 Montevideo has been in the hands of the Frente Amplio, a broad front of leftist parties, and the same has occurred in Asuncion, Caracas, and Buenos Aires, a city of 10 million that as of 1994 has been in the hands of a coalition of leftist parties.

In conclusion, the Left has acquired a modicum of local power without any capacity to control resources or of derailing the national policy of neoliberalism. However, within these limits the Left has been able to sow the seeds of a new participatory form of politics that has contributed to an explosion of more promising social movements. And in the process the left has gained a reputation for efficiency and honesty that contradicts widespread distrust of the political class. If the left can capitalize on this political resource it might have a future.

In spite of the alternative vision and proposals given at the municipal level, the reformist liberals and Social Christians allied with the social democratic opposition has not been able to translate widespread protests against neoliberalism into national power. Examples of this include Ernesto Samper in Colombia and Rafael Caldera in Venezuela, both of who ran for office as populist critics of neoliberalism. Caldera won the 1993 election with the support of MAS (Socialist Movement), which, like the Socialist Party of Chile, is 'socialist' in name only as their main purpose is to secure government posts so as to have access to the spoils of office. In the process they have lost any capacity or pretension to represent the popular forces.

What carried Caldera to power was a mix of nostalgia for the by-gone days of prosperity in the oil era and the very contradictory promises to control inflation and the fiscal deficit, increase government expenditures, and eliminate the value added sales tax. But once he had the instrument of national power in his hands, Caldera, like other populists in and out of power, made a sharp turn to the right – and neoliberal policy. In his government the most slavish followers of IMF policies is Teodoro Petbon, the leader of the MAS. The experiences of Samper, Caldera and the *concertacion* regime in Chile has made it clear that such regimes are not able to represent the forces of opposition and resistance to neoliberal policies. None of them has been able to construct or to put into practices an alternative programme. Just like Albert Fujimori in Peru and Carlos Menem in Argentina, once in power such regimes without exception ally with transnational capital and actively implement the policies of the international financial agencies and the multinationals. From mid-1996 to mid-1998 Caldera has been collaborating with Agenda Venezuela, a right-wing adjustment programme manufactured in Washington and thus bearing a striking resemblance to those in place in Argentina and Mexico.[1] Plan Venezuela is based on a policy of privatization, the end of state subsidies, and labour reforms intended to make the labour more 'flexible' in government efforts to make Venezuelan industry, that is capital, more competitive.[2]

The electoral leaders of the Centre-Left have not been able to realize an opposition programme to neoliberalism. In some contexts such as Brazil and Mexico parties with a social democratic or populist appeal, and with a rhetoric of opposition towards neoliberalism, has presented itself, and is seen by others, as a political instrument of opposition forces. As they increase their electoral strength these parties succumb to right-wing opportunism, turning towards neoliberalism with negative consequences. In the case of Mexico, in spite of the generalized cynicism and disillusionment with respect to government policy and all politicians, in 1994 the citizenry chose as their President a technocrat in the neoliberal mould and candidate of the long-governing Party of Government (PRI), and therefore representing continuity with neoliberal policies. In the context of the election campaign, Cuahtemoc Cardenas, who presented himself as a champion of nationalism and of the popular forces, and as an opponent of neoliberalism, wrote an article for the *Wall Street Journal* praising the neoliberal North American Treaty to which he had been so opposed in the past. Back home, however, he presented another face to the electorate, with a critique of NAFTA and support for the Zapatista demands. In June 1997 he subsequently won the mayoralty election in Mexico City, positioning himself well as a likely candidate for the next Presidential elections.

The Workers Party (PT) in Brazil has followed a similar course. In mid-1994 the PT's candidate for President, Lula, was ahead in the polls, with 40 per cent declared support versus 20 per cent for Fernando Cardoso, a former social democrat who in the end won the elections on the basis of the successful implementation of a new currency stabilization programme. It was an evident mistake of Lula and the PT to ignore or oppose a popular programme such as Cardoso's Plan Real which in the last analysis did control the galloping inflation which had been eating away at the purchasing power of the masses. But in the end the principal problem of the PT was the same as that of the PRD in Mexico: the lack of a coherent alternative programme that appeals to the common sense of electors. The PT succumbed to the same dynamic that has made it impossible for the political class of the Left to take power. People everywhere have lost confidence in this class and its politics due to its double discourse and swings from Left to Right, and opportunist deals with neoliberalism.[3]

In large part this continues to be the problem of the left in the 1990s, although Ruben Zamora, a leader of the Salvadoran Left, in his reflections on the process or the conjuncture approached in the 1980s by leftist parties in Latin America, argued that 'never before were so many parties on the left so close to taking power'. What prevented this from happening, according to Zamora, were 'external forces opposed to the interests of the majority'.[4] 'Never before', he further argues, had those forces 'been so determinant' in the outcome of Latin American power struggles.

Zamora could be right or at least in part: to explain the inability of the left to take national power in so many instances requires us to look beyond internal conditions. We turn to this point below.

SOCIAL ORGANIZATIONS AND MOVEMENTS

If we were to describe the significance of the 1980s in Latin America we could do so in terms of two affirmations: (i) a stagnation and economic setback, on the one hand; and (ii) an advance of civilian constitutional regimes over military dictatorships, on the other. In this context, what is most striking is, on the one side, the lack of protagonism and the structural weakness of the working class movement, the heart and the principal base of the struggles of the 1960 and 1970s; and, on the other, the explosion of social protest and action that forced the generals back to the barracks. As for the weakness of working class several explanations range from the structural (a dramatic involution in the internal structure of the class – the disappearance of the traditional full-time worker in heavy basic industry and the public sector – repression, and the reduction of manoeuvring space left to the unions; the drastic fall of employment in the formal sector, another of the devastating consequences of the adjustment process, which has favoured the adoption by labour of a purely defensive strategy) to the subjective (a failure of leadership; an inadequate response to the neoconservative offensive launched against the working class; an intellectual and ideological crisis of the left).

As for the dynamics of political and social struggle in the 1980s, the surprising and striking factor was the protagonism of the urban poor and an amalgam of social movements that moved into the vacuum left by the political parties and unions. At the social base and leadership of these movements were inhabitants of marginal urban areas; women denouncing government policy and the lack of democracy as well as sexual discrimination; indigenous communities demanding autonomy and respect for their organizations and culture; many youth excluded from school or of the work; and family members of those who had been incarcerated, tortured or made to 'disappear' (murdered) for political reasons by the military regimes in place.[5]

The emergence of these new social movements (NSMs) has created a torment of theoretical explanation, including the idea that the heterogeneity of these movements, in terms of their social bases and their demands, deligitimate a strict class analysis of these movements. In the projection of this idea it has come to be argued that something other than class analysis is needed: a new form of analysis that can encompass the complexity and the heterogeneity of these NSMs, and the dynamics of their struggles to establish their identity in local spaces and in very specific contexts.[6]

However, the attempt to banish class analysis from the study of social movements and to substitute a postmodernist, non-structural form of identity analysis, has manifestly failed.[7] To confront this failure, and to seek a reconstituted form of class analysis, we follow Jose Michael Candia (1996) in locating Latin America's NSMs within an analytical framework that classifies social movements in terms of (i) their social base (the sectors of population that constitute their base of support and action; and (ii) the type of demands that serve to mobilize the social base. With an eye to tradition (of class analysis) we could add the issue of the movement's ideological direction or scope, viz. reform or revolution.

There does not exist, and we will not attempt to create, a systematic analysis of these movements, but what is evident is that their principal demands can be classified as follows:

(i) class struggles (still the majority of cases);
(ii) regional problems, that sometimes, have a class dimension;
(iii) ethnic or gender claims for equality or the ending of oppression, the relations and conditions of which also appear, more often than not, to have a class dimension;
(iv) demands for the respect of fundamental human rights that tend to have either a class or an ethnic and/or gender dimension; and
(v) demands related to either protection of the environment or the inter-generational issues raised and addressed by youth organizations that also tend to have an ethnic and/or class dimension.

There is a pronounced lack of systematic and comparative analysis of these movements in the Latin American context, the dominant approach being the detailed description of one movement in a country without any attempt at comparative structural analysis. But we can say in anticipation of such studies that given the clear class character of so many social movements in the region the abandonment of class theory and analysis is at best premature, at worst an idealist escape from reality – from realities that most people in the region cannot escape in thought.

For sure, it is not possible or desirable to reduce an analysis of these movements, of their social base and their dynamics, to the issue of class, but then: who would do so? Certainly not any Marxist! What in fact is missing in the analysis of these NSMs is precisely the question of class. We will address this question in the following section, providing thereby some elements of a reconstituted class analysis.

NGOS AND PARTICIPATORY DEVELOPMENT: SOLIDARITY FROM BELOW

The basic elements of a model for Alternative Development (AD) were elaborated in the 1970s (see discussion in the first part of this chapter). One of their sources is the Dag Hammarskjöld Foundation that gave the initial impulse in the formation of a movement devoted to the search for an alternative development that now can be found all over the world. Ironically, the AD movement has its origins in the same year (1974) that gave place to

(i) the discovery of the World Bank of poverty as a global problem and the elaboration of a Basic Needs strategy designed so as to alleviate the conditions of extreme poverty;

(ii) the counter-offensive launched by capital against the working class (in different contexts and forms but as evident in the South than the North);[8] and
(iii) the height of the liberal reform movement and its model of growth-with-equity, its politics of state-led structural reform (land reform, the redistribution of income progressive taxation, etc.), and proposals for development and social welfare, designed to the purpose of preventing more radical solutions such as social revolution.

These liberal reform policies and programmes reached their limits at the end of the decade. In this context, the liberal-social reformers, who dominated the theory and practice of development, succumbed to the blows administered to them by the neoliberals on their right and the Marxists and Dependency theorists on their left. Unable to explain the failures of so many developing countries or the successes of the Newly Industrialized Countries (NICs) in East Asia, the reformers lost their nerve and confidence in their postulates and political and theoretical recipes, and they abandoned the scene, opening up a huge space that was in little time occupied by the neoclassical economists and advocates of neoliberalism. The counter-revolution in theory and practice had begun.[9] And so had the era of structural adjustment with its devastating attempts to restructure economies around the world in the search for conditions needed to reestablish the process of capital accumulation.

At the end of the 1980s neoliberalism entered into a species of crisis, with the emergence of resistance and opposition to its policies and their high social costs, and clearly having reached its political limits. The context for this decline, as have seen, included a social and economic crisis with a significant political dimension; a process of democratic conversion of existing military regimes; and the reconstruction of civil society, with reference to the emergence in the popular sector of organizations and social movements that are predicated on resistance and oriented towards construction of an alternative to neoliberalism – the social base of diverse proposals for alternative development.

In this new context, various forms of alternative development were advanced. As we have seen, one set of such proposals (constituting a 'new paradigm') were actually authored by the World Bank itself in conjunction with the UNDP and other operating UN agencies such as UNICEF in an effort to give structural adjustment a human face. But, although these institutions had appropriated the concepts and principles of AD (popular participation, empowerment, and so on) they could not propose an alternative model, Rather, what emerged was a rehabilitated and dressed-up form of the same neoliberal model of SAP, somewhat akin to the 'renovation' of the post-Second World War economic order in recent years that took place to produce 'the new world order'.

However, the crisis generated by the application of the neoliberal recipe was such that it generated a series of proposals not for its renovation but for a more radical overhaul, even, from some quarters, its abandonment. The social and political base of this more radical response was found in a great unfurling of community-based or directed social organizations associated with the reconstruction of 'civil society'. The critical factor in this reorganization was the growth of a complex network of NGOs, many of which had, in fact, offered themselves to institutional authorities as mediators with the grass-roots organizations of the community. For example, a forum of NGOs on the Promotion of Rural Development held at the end of October 1996, in Tepic, Nay, Mexico, resolved to create a network of civil support organizations on the basis of experience in states such as Chiapas and Oaxaca, where over 2000 NGOs had been identified. In this connection, it is estimated that in the entire country there exists over 10 000 NGOs that had proliferated in the 1980s because, as conference representatives noted, 'the people no longer want to obey and just be quiet'.[10] That is, these NGOs were formed to mobilize popular discontent – and, as we will see, to channel it.

In this situation of an oppressed people that awakens and seeks their voice, NGOs were formed not just in Mexico but all over the region to purpose of 'supporting the people' in their constitution as 'new social subjects in the bosom of the society' and in 'stimulating the processes of gestation and consolidation of their collective asocial identities'.[11]

In this reconstruction of civil society, governments in the region, together with the financial and other institutions tied to neoliberal policies, turned towards the NGOs because of their capacity to mediate relations with the base organizations and open up channels for popular participation in public policy.[12]

In turn, many of these NGOs approached and worked with the agencies of the central government, foundations and donor institutions to purpose of seeking funding, and, in the process, to provide marginalized and poor communities compensatory services to alleviate the impacts of the adjustment process. This relationship of solidarity and association ('partnership') constitute the axis of the World Bank's new approach – the new paradigm as it is widely referred to in UN agencies such as the International Fund for Agricultural Development.

Subsequent proposals from this sector – and the search for new proposals in different contexts continues – take a number of varied forms, but their essence is that the development has to be community-directed and-based; that is, it is both local and, creating thus the necessary conditions for empowering communities, constituting them as collective social subjects.

One expression of this approach – and there are numerous – can be found in the efforts and the search for what has been labelled 'community economic development' (CED). Elaboration of this approach are abundant, and in many places – especially in the US and Canada where there is no planning tradition as relates to the process of development – CED has been institutionalized as the dominant and principal policy. The institutional form of CED is established by means of political and economic decentralization, a strategy and policy that is understood as Ronald Reagan did: as the devolution of government to the local authorities and 'the people'. Within this institutionality, established in many places in the 1980s, CED has been promoted, with numerous permutations, by reference to a small business enterprise strategy and the private sector viewed as the motor or creative force of the development process, viz. entrepreneurship and job/income generating capacity.

However, in spite of the vast array of CED projects and proposals implemented all over the world there does not exist to date any systematic comparative evaluations of the strategy and associated models. The range of precise conditions needed to implement the strategy, its effectiveness and viability as a national strategy, remain unclear.

Aside from CED, which essentially is a strategy implemented 'from above', that is, from within the apparatus of government, and 'from the outside', that is, with the support of the community of international financial and donor institutions, the NGO sector has generated a great variety of ideas but no specific models for an alternative community-based and directed form of development. Insofar as they constitute a movement, NGOs have been and are generally aligned in opposition to neoliberalism and are active participants in the search for AD. An exemplar of these proposals, one of many, is the Alternative Strategy for Economic Development elaborated in September 1995 by the Civic Alliance, an amalgam of 53 social organizations in Mexico, together with some other seven NGOs. The strategy was elaborated with reference to some 425 000 signatures collected in the context of a Referendum for Freedom convoked in June of the same year and the first National Congress to Condemn the Economic Policy of the Mexican

Government. A series of Encounters against the Neoliberalism and for Humanity (Democracy), summoned by the EZLN in 1996 had the same purpose: to encourage and give form to the widespread disillusionment and dissent, and a diffuse politics of resistance and opposition to neoliberalism; and to transform this intellectual and political energy into concrete alternative proposals. The outcome is uncertain (can community-based development projects be translated into a viable national development strategy?) but will be closely monitored and awaited with interest.

NEW CLASS MOVEMENTS IN THE COUNTRYSIDE

The double discourse and the opportunism of many leaders of left political organizations have resulted in confusion and a distrust of the political class and its political instrument of choice – the political party. In this context, many citizens have abandoned the class struggle to devote themselves to the problems of their daily lives, seeking at this level the means of surviving the conditions created by neoliberalism – and to simply make a living (in many cases, in the informal sector), which is to say, the streets and, in some contexts, criminal behaviour. Some intellectuals, armed with a postmodernist perspective, have seriously misinterpreted this trend, seeing in it the constitution of new social subjects and the emergence of new social movements based on the politics of everyday life and social identity – of gender, of the ecology, of ethnicity – and, by the same token, the end of class politics.[13]

Notwithstanding the twofold tendency for so many people to both escape from politics into the problems of managing their 'everyday life' under neoliberalism and electing to power regimes that generate these problems, in many countries there can be found a growing movement of resistance and opposition to neoliberal capitalism.

This politics of resistance and opposition has also taken different forms in diverse contexts, but it undoubtedly had a class basis. This can be seen in Bolivia, for example, in the protest actions of the miners and the cocaleros, teachers, and a new type of union bound to the social movements, co-ordinating their actions with an amalgam of social organizations rather than the parties of the left. But, more than anything it can be seen in the actions and struggles that are taking place in the countryside – the apparent centre of a new wave of insurgency.[14]

An exemplar of these new class movements is the Landless Workers Movement in Brazil (the MST), formed on the base of hundreds of organizations and hundreds of thousands of activists and supporters. The MST has created – and led – a national political debate on the land and land reform issue, and according to most observers is the most dynamic and best organized social movement in the country. It is also the most effective, with a consistent record of concrete achievements and successful land occupations, allowing it to accumulate a huge reservoir of social forces deployed in direct action.[15] In Bolivia, the closure of the mines and imports of inexpensive products and contraband have weakened the hitherto powerful unions in the mining and industrial sectors organized in the form of the Confederation of Bolivian Unionized Workers (COB). In their place have been formed organizations of peasants, in particular the cocaleros (many of whom are ex-miners) that are leading the struggle against neoliberalism, with massive confrontations, marches, and general strikes that have paralyzed the country.[16] In Paraguay, the National Federation of Peasants is the principal force behind the massive mobilizations that have shaken the country, placing the land issue at the centre of the political agenda and the main axis of struggle against neoliberalism.[17] Also in Mexico there abound (in Guerrero, Chiapas, and Oaxaca...) serious confrontations between peasants organizations and the State.[18] And in Ecuador, Colombia and El Salvador, and other countries in the region, the peasants have also constituted themselves as the principal subject of the class struggle against neoliberalism. In many contexts the peasants are of indigenous origin, giving a national and ethnic character to their struggle, but the base and principal line of struggle can be found in their relationship to the means of social production – and the state.

In short, as observed in the last chapter, the epitaph given to the peasantry by analysts and historians such as Eric Hobsbawm[19] is premature to say the least and misinformed to say more. These peasant-led movements are 'new' in a number of critical respects. First, although they have their roots in the land struggle, many of the new peasant leaders have a cosmopolitan, even an internationalist, vision. Second, they are generally intent on maintaining their autonomy even from the political parties on the left with which they may have ties and a tactical alliance. The tactics, strategy, and ideological discussions of these movements in every case are decided within and are not subordinated to any party line. To the contrary, it is these movements that are providing the dynamism of the political struggles of the parties on the left and constitute the catalyst of protests against neoliberalism. Third, the NPMs engage in direct action rather than the electoral process. In fact, as in Chiapas, they have generally discarded elections as a specific form of political action. They prefer a strategy of combining direct action and negotiations with representatives of the state, or to coordinate actions or political specify with the unions, NGOs, and left parties in specific contexts such as organizing and coordinating a general strike or proposing a piece of legislation. The movements tend to be clear about the principal form of struggle – massive mobilization. Fourth, the NPMs are influenced by a mixture of classic Marxism and in various contexts by ideas relating to issues of gender, the ecology, and particularly ethnicity and nationality. In many contexts, internal debates and the politics of these movements relate to the search for ways of combining these issues in their analysis and their practice. Fifth, NPMs are generally coordinated and, to a certain point, united, on the basis of regional organizations such as CLOL and in international organizations such as Via Campesina that debate, and exchange relevant experiences of struggles that are increasingly seen as the same. Through these experiences and ties is emerging an internationalist consciousness – and practice.

To summarize, the reappearance of peasant-led social movements in the 1990s is not simply a return to the 1960s and 1970s. In many cases the successes and the failures of those years have been studied and debated in the search of the lessons that they can be drawn from them. There are elements of continuity in the NPMs with the struggles of the 1970s. But there are also differences in tactics, strategy, politics, and organization. They also tend to have a much greater consciousness of the existence of a global empire, of a policy programme (neoliberalism) that is tied to the world economic order. On this point there is a clear awareness of neoliberalism (and its imperial adjunct) as the principal enemy, and that as a result, all peasants and the indigenous people are engaged in the same struggle and need to join forces.

The Zapatista Challenge : The Dynamics of an Indigenous Movement

The armed insurrection of the Zapatistas on the first of January 1994 not only ended the 'fiesta' of the dominant political class, viz. its illusion of social peace and stability. It forcibly introduced 'the ethnic factor' into the class struggle and broke with the rules and limits for this struggle established by what in Mexico is termed the 'political class', with equal reference to its Left and Right wings of Mexican party politics. However, after two years and more of continued struggle, mostly in the form of negotiations with the central government, the Zapatistas in its political instrument, the EZLN, has reached an impasse – or at least a crossroads. In order for the EZLN not to dissipate its political forces and to disappear from the political map it has to move beyond its current politics of negotiations and skilful management of communications. Its major interlocutor, representing the Mexican state, is anxious to settle the political questions raised by the Zapatistas but determined to do so on its own terms, that is, without giving way to the Zapatista-led demand for relative autonomy of the indigenous communities within the Mexican State – and to prevent the conversion of the Zapatistas into a national political force for change.

In the current political context, the conversion of the EZLN into a political force capable of projecting the demands of the indigenous people at the national level is its biggest challenge. The road in this direction is full of dangers and difficulties. Without doubt, what finally put the indigenous people of Chiapas on the map, compelling the government to listen to them and to seriously attend to the immemorial demands of Mexico's indigenous people for freedom, democracy and justice, not to speak of their more concrete economic demands, was the resort to and carefully timed and executed use of armed force – the constitution of an army prepared to liberate the indigenous people of the Chiapan highlands and Lacandon rain forest by the force of arms. In this context, the EZLN revalidated a form of politics that many on the Left had discarded. However, it is equally true that the time for armed struggle has passed – for the Zapatistas if not other insurgent organizations in the region. The current conjuncture will not permit the Zapatistas to follow the road of arms with success and they understand this very well – as does the government unfortunately. What is required – and the Zapatistas also understand this very well – is for it to convert itself into a new political force on the national level, capable of projecting its political actions within an institutional framework of doubtful legitimacy. This is the challenge faced by the Zapatistas

A danger (one of many) in travelling this road, according to Subcomandante Marcos, consists in that up to now all armed movements that have done so have either lost their way, dissipated their accumulated forces for radical change, or cost the lives of their activists in the streets by the hands of paramilitary squads. In this context, a major problem for the EZLN is how to convert themselves into a political force capable of opening a political space at the national level in which the social organizations of the civil society can operate freely and effectively, advancing in the process the agenda of the marginalized and oppressed indigenous peoples.

It is evident that this problematic involves a process in which the Zapatistas are actively engaged, seeking to advance it –and, with more difficulty, to control it. The process is under way, allowing us to identify the following phases: (i) the formation of the EZLN; (ii) insurrection; (iii) negotiations with state authorities and the search for a new politics in civil society (iv) continuous negotiations and the transmutation of the EZLN into a national political force; (v) indigenous unity in a national policy and politics; and (vi) the coalaescence of diverse popular forces of opposition and resistance into an anti-systemic movement.

The Formation of the EZLN and the Question of Ideology

The EZLN has its origins in the rural arm of the Forces of National Liberation (FLN), one of the oldest guerrilla organizations in Mexico, formed in the 1960s as a part of the Insurgent Army of Mexico (EIM) as part of what James Petras has identified as the first political wave of the left in Latin America.[20] At the beginning of the 1980s, a group of young intellectuals, for the most part students of UNAM with a Marxist orientation, moved to Chiapas as part of a move to activate the rural front of the FLN. By the end of the decade, the front had a considerable formation on the basis of a leadership composed of intellectuals like Marcos from Mexico City, militant peasants, and, it seems, a group of activists from the archdiocese of San Cristobal. In this context, sub-comandante Marcos led the Ocisingo division of the military arm of the rural front.[1]

What is important and significant about the formation of this army of national liberation, aside from its orientation towards armed struggle, is the critical link formed with the indigenous people in the area. In this connection over the course of ten years of hard struggle and preparation Marcos – and he is not alone or the only one – achieved what no other political organization of the left in all Latin America managed: the respect and the full confidence of the indigenous peoples, and, on this basis, the formation of an organic connection with them.

This organic connection is manifest in the subordination of the military arm to the political, symbolized in the category of sub-comandante, the form of organizing politics, the dominance of the Clandestine Indigenous Revolutionary Committee, and the relation of direct democracy between this committee and the assembly of peoples united in struggle – the Tzeltales, Tzotziles, Choles, Tojolabales, who for centuries had co-existed in a state of mutual animosity.

The organic connection of the EZLN can also be seen in the position and attitude of subcomandante Marcos, who – as he puts it – 'command by obeying' (the Revolutionary Committee), and in the ideological formation of the Revolutionary Army. At the beginning, the ideology of the FLN, as all such political formations – and there have been many in Latin America – was oriented towards the class struggle and the conquest of state power by a strategic alliance of the workers and peasants. The principal enemy was imperialism, in particular that of the USA, its local allies (the big bourgeoisie), and their puppets in control of the apparatus of State and its armed forces. The social base of the revolution sought by the forces of national liberation included the oppressed, the exploited, who were locked in struggle against imperialism, the exploiters, and an oppressive state. It is probable that at the beginning the ideology of the movement had little or nothing to do with the specificity of the millenarian struggle of the indigenous peoples for land and their fundamental rights to territory, autonomy, respect of their culture in all of its dimensions, social justice, and the dignity of their person. In the course of their class struggle this would radically change.

The armed offensive launched on the first of January 1994 was not spontaneous. It was organized with ten years of careful preparation, awaiting the timely moment. But, it would seem, it was the conditions of struggle after the initial outbreak that resulted in an effective change in the EZLN's ideology, which can be viewed as an amalgam of three elements:

(i) Marxism, expressed in the Declaration of Principles under which the EZLN operated (it speaks of the dictatorship of the proletariat and the construction of socialism,);
(ii) *Zapatismo*, expressed in the symbolic appeal to a hero the Mexican of the revolution – of the armed struggle for national liberation; and
(iii) *indigenismo*, expressed in the cultural values of full and direct democracy, community, and communion with nature. Statements of the EZLN as to the reason for the rebellion and its demands, made in the initial phase of the resurrection and of armed combat, reflected the complexity of this ideology.

In their first press conference, after having taken control of San Cristobal and four other cities in the region, Comandante Felipe, the spokesperson of the EZLN at the time, the Zapatistas declared that 'we have come to San Cristobal to make a revolution against capitalism', and in the days following they spoke of the need to construct socialism. But the First Declaration of the Lacandon jungle was more precise: the war was waged against the army, the basic pillar of the dictatorship from which the people suffered, monopolized by the ruling party and headed by Carlos Salinas.

In the context of this declaration of war, the EZLN made eleven basic demands – work, land, shelter, food, health, education, independence, freedom, democracy, justice, and peace – and announced their somewhat Quixotic plan for undertaking a march towards Mexico City, freeing people on the way, summoning a process of democratic elections, and ending with the overthrow of the dictatorship. The Declaration also promised to end to the plunder of natural resources by the TNCs and the confiscation of all rural properties in excess of 50 hectares in bad condition and 25 hectares in the case of land of good quality.

After a week of struggle it was possible to detect a profound change in the ideological discourse with respect to the class struggle, which was de-emphasized, and an emphasis on the indigenous character of the rebellion.[22] Marcos himself, in answer to a question with respect to the issue, explained that the change in discourse was in response to the accusation levelled by the government against the Revolutionary Committee as to its being foreign (Guatemalan guerrillas) and 'professionals of violence'. In any event, the subsequent speech of Marcos, converted into spokesperson of the EZLN, emphasized the obvious: the EZLN was a political instrument of the oppressed indigenous people of Chiapas and the country – and of all those who shared their conditions of exploitation and oppression or sympathized with their demands for social justice, freedom, and democracy. The Zapatistas had been converted into a movement that for many symbolizes, if not leads, the struggle to create a new world in the twenty-first century.

The 1 January 1994 Uprising: A People under Arms

Without doubt the critical factor in the uprising of the first week of January was the resort to armed struggle. The uprising put an end to the 'fiesta' of the bourgeoisie and their neoliberal regime – of its illusion of peace and stability. It also raised a spectre that was thought to be buried in the last decade. Although there were, in fact, few armed confrontations and this phase of the struggle was over in ten days, it was the resort to arms that was responsible for the Zapatistas having achieved more than any other social movement, armed or otherwise, in previous decades – or the century for that matter. Chiapas now is not what it was despite the efforts of the military to harass and intimidate the people and communities under Zapatista control, the restrictive political environment in the North of the State, and the persistence of institutionalized practices that are responsible for the oppressive conditions of exploitation, marginality and poverty lived by a majority of indigenous people in the state.[23]

At the beginning, the recourse to armed struggle not only frightened the government and investors but upset many intellectuals and the politicians on the left. As a rule they sympathized with the goals of the Zapatistas but objected to their method of armed struggle. In this respect the ambiguous attitude of the PRD and many intellectuals of the left was markedly different from that found in the popular sector of the civil society, which responded to the uprising with the formation of hundreds of support organizations, occupying the huge political space vacated by the guerrillas and the parties. These organizations forced the government to order a cease-fire and to enter into a process of negotiations with the Zapatistas.

In any event, without the recourse to arms the EZLN would never have achieved what it had sought: the attention of the government, and the world, to their demands, forcing the government to take them seriously and to enter into negotiations – the next phase in the process.

Negotiations and the Appeal to Civil Society: The Transmutation of the EZLN into a Force for Democracy

The problem for the EZLN in the immediate context of ceasefire and the end of armed confrontations was not how to achieve state-power but how to transform itself into a national political force. In this respect, the EZLN has taken two roads:

(i) negotiation with government representatives, attempting thereby to create a change in the rules and the institutionality of the political game played out with respect of Chiapas' and Mexico's indigenous peoples; and
(ii) reaching out to civil society for it to assume a protagonistic role in the creation of a democratic culture and in political action.

This second road was built on the basis of the Second Declaration of the Lacandon jungle, to the purpose of forming a National Democratic Convention (CDN) that can operate as a mechanism of organizing civil society, and the third Declaration, to the purpose of forming a Movement for National Liberation, as a bridge among all opposition forces to the regime and the system that sustains it. In the context of this double road the EZLN adjusted its goal from the promotion of social transformation social and state control of the state to the search for a more substantive and more authentic form of democracy.

Transmutation of the EZLN and the Unity of Opposition Forces

In taking the road towards freedom, democracy and social justice – and responses to its demands – the EZLN needed to convert itself into a national political force. An important moment in this process can be identified in the Fourth Declaration of the Lacandon jungle of 31 December 1995, which constitutes the EZLN's response to the national consultation (for Peace and Democracy undertaken in August of the same year). The object of this consultation was to help the EZLN decide the political form that it should assume in the democratization process. The Fourth Declaration did not give' a definitive response to this question, and, in November of 1996, after a long process of stalled negotiations and several consultations the options of EZLN remained open. The Fourth Declaration opened up another debate on how to 'do politics' as profound and extensive as the one engendered by the Zapatista resort to arms.

The position taken by the EZLN on this issue caused another stir inside the political class, as much on the left as on the right. The question as to how to do politics, according to the EZLN, does not reside in the actions of a particular class or vanguard organized on the basis of some political party in search of national power. Rather, it involves the creation of a new political force oriented towards a different conception of politics, one that incorporates an indigenous vision of politics as a means of service to the community. Such a politics for the EZLN, Marcos adds, does not imply either the conquest of state power or the assumption of political positions. It implies, he notes, a profoundly democratic political culture and the creation of a new political organization able to articulate demands and advance the interest of the people – and, in the process, of creating a new world one in which reigns justice, and democracy (Marcos, La Realidad, 2 August 1996).

As for this problem, that of creating a new political culture and a new instrument of national politics – and, for the EZLN, its transformation into a new political force at the national level – the critical factor is the forging of unity among the various civil society organizations. In this regard, the formation of the National Indigenous Forum in San Cristobal in January 1996, was a major achievement and advance, as was the creation in October 1996 of the National Indigenous Congress, an organization that permitted the various indigenous peoples for the first time to speak with one voice and to co-ordinate their political activities. It could well be that the formation of the CNI has been the EZLN's most significant to the indigenous movement – a catalyst of its projection as a national political force and of a serious effort to unite diverse pluricultural and heterogeneous forces. It could also be that no matter what specific form taken by this political force, the role of the EZLN is to constitute itself as a political instrument of the social forces united by the CNI and other such organizations.

What is needed in this respect is the formation of similar organizations in other sectors of civil society such as the peasantry and the independent sections of the working class. As it happens, Mexico is the only country in the region that does not have a national organization in these sectors. The working class and the peasantry are served by a number of independent and officially sanctioned and supported organizations, at both sectoral and regional levels. It is here that we find the biggest challenge not only for the EZLN but for the Left as a whole.

While an important component of any transformation, anti-systemic socio-political movements like the EZLN, the MST and require political alliances with other social forces in the cities and urban centre. They need to develop ties to the mayoritarian urban poor, the working and salaried classes organized in trade unions. The radical changes tied to the sectoral agrarian questions need to be reformulated into a national political programme. The MST and the EZLN have recognized the limits of agrarian change and have begun the process of building a national movement. The MST in this context has convened national meetings to discuss a new programme called Project Brazil, which combines a programme of social transformation in the industrial and financial sectors with agrarian change. In Paraguay and Bolivia the peasant's movement has also convened various 'political forums' designed to build urban bridges to political allies among the urban exploited and oppressed classes.

WHAT IS TO BE DONE IN THE CURRENT CONTEXT? THE BASES OF A SOCIALIST ALTERNATIVE

In Latin America and elsewhere people are at a historic cross-roads. On the one hand, the dominant classes are engaged in a project to renovate and consolidate a system (neoliberalism) that in its global and imperialist expansion has transformed the economic and social conditions lived by the greater part of the population in its national fortresses. This system has spread across the globe but so have its internal contradictions which are generating the conditions of a possibly devastating economic crisis – and a protracted class struggle. The policies and politics that it sustains are under severe pressure, and in decline despite efforts to rescue it by means of various forms of restructuring.

On the other hand, It is possible to identify mounting forces of opposition and resistance as well as a range of responses and alternative strategies. These responses range from social liberalism based on a neostructuralist model elaborated by ECLAC and implemented by a number of political regimes in the region. The model has been designed to give the adjust process of human face and a social dimension. It aims to expand the social basis of economic development which, in the neoliberal model is restricted to those enterprises deemed to have the capacity to adjust to the new economic order, estimated to be at most 50 per cent of all enterprises and excluding both peasant units of production and urban informal activities. The beneficiaries of this neoliberal model are the owners and managers of these enterprises, the big bourgeoisie. The ECLAC model, on the other hand, is designed to incorporate a broader spectrum of social and economic groups – to convert even elements of the peasantry into productive forces. This solution/model has been implemented through the mechanisms of the electoral process – to bring to power parties oriented towards or committed to social liberalism.

A third response to the evident decay and obsolescence of the neoliberal model is based on the agency of non-government organizations. The thinking here relates to an alternative model rooted in what has been conceived as 'another paradigm', one that accepts the institutionality of the existing system but that seeks to mobilize the social forces for change within it on the basis of community-based actions – to capacitate individuals and organizations to participate in the development process.

A fourth type of response is associated with a particular variety of new social movements that relies on the agency of social and political struggle rather than the implementation of short-term development projects or participation in on-going processes of elections and globalization. As we see it, this response provides considerable dynamism as relates to forces of opposition and resistance. However, it also evinces clear limits. For one thing, there is a question about whether these forces as currently constituted are able to successfully challenge the power-structure and assume the instruments of state power. Other questions relates to the operating ideology which is needed to mobilize the social forces of change and to the general theory which can serve to direct a concrete analysis of the situation in which the workers and producers find themselves and to inform their political practice to the purpose of constructing a socialist alternative to capitalism in its neoliberal or social liberal forms. This is the challenge for the political Left committed to the institution of a democratic socialist project – to help forge a coalition of forces for substantive change, transforming the forces of resistance and opposition into a viable model of socialist development.

What are the Options Available to the Left?

We have identified a range of responses to neoliberalism in the current conjuncture. Among intellectuals there is a deep division with ideological and political dimensions. On the one hand, there are the efforts and proposals to soften its effects, to give it a human face, and to reconstitute neoliberal capitalism in a different form (ECLAC). These solutions are sponsored and supported by the multilateral financial institutions (the IMF, BM, IDB) and by the operating agencies of the United Nations (UNDP, PREALC, UNICEF). Basically, these institutions offer a limited variation on models of the roles assigned to the state and to the market. On the other side, we have identified a diverse proposals that as a whole form a movement dedicated to the search for an alternative form of development. This movement is supported by a multiplicity and great diversity of nongovernmental and community-based organizations.

We conclude that by virtue of its broad albeit heterogeneous social base this search for alternative development offers greater possibilities for effective social change than do neoliberal and neostructural strategies. As we have shown, the socio-political movements are demonstrating a growing capacity for generating the political conditions required for their implementation at the national level. At issue here are the social forces projected by the Left in its new formation, not as a political class and its organization of choice – the political party – but as a socio-political movement with a broad base in the popular sectors of civil society. In this regard, we have drawn particular attention to social movements constructed and led by peasants in their pursuit of urban allies and coalitions. These movements have a greater dynamism than any other, and in this dynamism the potential to unite the forces of opposition to neoliberalism.

These new emerging movements of the Left are engaged in the process of elaborating an alternative economic model based on social ownership of the strategic sectors of the economy and a central role for public investment and collectively-managed enterprises combined with private and cooperative forms of property ownership. The objective conditions for such a development have been created by the very expansion and incorporation of vast sectors of the population into a new social division of labour. The enormous and growing pools of wealth in the region, combined with the extension and deepening of the conditions and forms of poverty, as well as the social and political relations of this social division, are also creating the subjective or political basis for the conversion of privileged private production into democratic forms of collective ownership and control. In the same context, the 'globalization of capital' is creating the objective (structural economic) and subjective (political) basis for a collective response to the forces of imperialism mounted by workers and peasant producers the world over. This struggle, however, promises to be long and hard, posing a major challenge for the Left – to ally and work with these forces for change or to submit and adjust to the forces of reaction against these forces.

Notes

1 Development in the New Imperial Context of Globalization

1. UNRISD (1995); Watkins (1995); World Commision on Culture and Development (1995).
2. UNDP (1992).
3. Griffin and Khan (1992).
4. A number of studies such as Barnett and Cavanagh (1994) shift between and use both terms.
5. On development as a political project see McMichael (1996). Formed in the post-1945 context, the development project has three major components and dimensions: economic progress (expansion of the forces of production, growth of output on the basis of capitalism, industrialization and modernization of the institutional structure); social justice or equity (a more equitable distribution of productive and social resources) on the basis of state-led social reforms in the institutional structure of the capitalist system; and political liberty or democracy, freeing the individual from oppressive political structures and democratizing their political institutions. Within the framework of this project, the development project is closely identified with the industrialization project and modernization.
6. In this connection, Lipietz (1987: 24-35) notes that 'a system ... must not be seen as an intentional structure or inevitable destiny because of its coherence ... Its coherence is simply the effect of the interaction between several relatively autonomous processes, of the provisionally stabilized complementarity and antagonism that exists between various national regimes of accumulation'. In the same connection Aglietta (1979), another proponent of 'regulationism', theorizes the world economy not as Wallerstein and other proponents of world systems theory do, that is, as a world system, but as a system of intersecting national formations.
7. These developments were theorized within the Marxist tradition of political economy (Lenin, Bukharin, Luxemburg, etc.) in terms of the concept of imperialism.
8. Marglin and Schor, (1990).
9. Davis, 1984; Marglin and Schor, (1990).
10. Cf. the proliferation of various post-war crisis theories.
11. Aglietta (1982).
12. UNCTAD (1994).
13. *Ibid.*, 93.
14. UNCTAD (1994) 124; McMichael (1996).
15. Instituto del Tercer Mundo (1995: 48).
16. 1994: 83.
17. Strange (1994: 112).
18. UNIDO (1996).

19. The profitability of FDI is reflected in the following statistics collected by UNCTAD (1994: 29).
20. *Ibid.*, pp. xix, 3.
21. *Ibid.*, p. 123.
22. On this offensive of capital against labour see, inter alia, Davis (1984) and Crouch and Pizzorno (1978).
23. From 1973 to 1994 the GNP in the USA grew in real terms, but for three-quarters of the working population the average gross wage fell by 19 per cent and for the bottom one third the fall was 29 per cent (Simon Heard, Das Ende der Mittelklass', *Die Zeit*, April 26, 1996; cited by Martin and Schumann (1997: 118)).
24. Instituto del Tercer Mundo (1995: 28).
25. ILO (1996); McMichael (1996).
26. Montalbano (1991).
27. The Heritage Foundation's platform to establish this order had five major planks, including the abolition of the UN Centre for Transnational Corporations, a child of UNCTAD that operated on the assumption and had the audacity to suggest the need for the operation of global capital in the form of TNCs to be regulated by governments to ensure that some benefits accrue to its national hosts in the developing world. Just as UNCTAD, the one UN institution that was geared to and answerable to the Group of 77, has been subsequently restructured with a reduced mandate *vis-à-vis* the WTO, the UNCTC, to all intents and purposes, has been dealt a death blow, reduced to a minor division of UNCTAD.
28. Unfortunately, the effort to negotiate such an agreement has attracted more 'negative publicity' than its proponents would like, forcing the OECD secretariat to open up the process somewhat and to respond to the criticism that are being leveled at the MAI all over the world from a myriad of organizations in the popular sector of what appears to a new civil society being formed at the global level.
29. South Centre (1997: 2).
30. South Centre (1996 :82).
31. UNDP (1992: 82).
32. *Ibid.*, p. 87.
33. 1987: 24–25.
34. Lipietz (1987: 14).
35. Bienefeld (1995).
36. Griffin (1995).
37. World Bank (1995: 8).
38. In the late 1980s the World Bank and the IMF redesigned the Structural Adjustment Programme (SAP). On the 'New Understanding' that led to this reworking of the SAP see Salop (1992).
39. Kapstein (1996).
40. Griffin (1995).
41. South Centre (1997: 7).
42. Kapstein (1996).
43. ILO (1996).

2 Neoliberalism and the Search for Another Development

1. With respect to this process in its various dimensions see, inter alia, Bello, with Shea annd Rau (1994); Davis (1984); Fröbel, Heinrichs and Kreye (1980); Korten (1995); Lipietz (1987); Pior and Sabel (1984); and Ross and Trachte (1990).
2. As for these two paradigms and lines of analysis see Wilber and Jameson (1989).
3. Principal theorists of this school include Arthur Lewis, Raul Prebisch, Nurske, Rodenstein, and Myrdal.
4. This theory, formulated by the renowned Caribbean economist, Sir Arthur Lewis, has its basis in a model of a closed economy. In this context, production is oriented toward the domestic market, and to maintain effective demand requires a policy of wage increases to assure purchasing power and thus demand. The limits of this process are found in a democratic system that creates conditions for a more equitable distribution of resources and income. This contrasts with the two other models constructed by neoliberal theorists. In the one the economy is opened to the outside and the benefits of growth are derived not from the domestic market but world trade, conceived as the motor of the process, with the private sector its conductor, and the price mechanism as the most efficient means of achieving an optimum distribution of resources and income. The third model also presumes an open economy, but expansion depends on the capacity to attract foreign capital and investing it in the reconversion of the production apparatus. The limits to distribution are established on the basis and by means of lowering the costs of labour and the state and the market provide the essential mechanisms and conditions of the process. This mechanism was established in practice rather than theory. In theory the growth process depends on increasing the saving rate to a critical take-off point (15 to 25 per cent) and in transferring it to the hands (or the banks) of those with a higher propensity to invest their savings. The working class is assumed to consume rather than invest theirs. In practice, in the context of neoliberal reforms many countries have exhibited a pronounced tendency to transfer income from labour (wages and salaries) to capital, with a drastic reduction in the share of the former in total national income. As Amsden and von Hoeven (1994) have clearly demonstrated this income transfer process is closely connected to a process of wage compression, which is associated with a trend not towards an increase in the growth rate (the neoliberal hypothesis), but a decrease (the structuralist hypothesis).
5. This mechanism was identified in the theory of unequal exchange (Emmanuel, 1972) formulated within the framework of the political economy paradigm, and used by the dependentistas as a complement to their theory of the fact that international trade and capital flows tend to operate as a siphon, transferring surplus value from the periphery toward the centre of the global system. This theory is currently out of fashion although it has never been refuted.
6. In the 1960s and 1970s neoclassical theorists like as von Hayek and Friedmann were out of favour and in the shadow of the dominant structuralist

perspective and planning approach to development. Bauer, in this context, provided a solitary neoliberal voice, dissenting from the orthodoxy of the moment; in the 1970s his voice was not so solitary, joined as it was by the interventions of Belassi, Kreuger, Lal, and Bhagwati among other exponents of what has been described as a 'counter-revolution' in the theory and the practice of development (Toye, 1987).

One of the first laboratories of neoliberal ideas and proposals was Chile under the Pinochet regime in the 1970s. The experiment of the 'Chicago boys', technocrats formed with the ideas and proposals of Friedmann and Harbeger, implemented a neoliberal programme under the tutelage and with the advice of Friedmann and McKinnon, who, like Kreuger, worked at the World Bank.

7. On these policies in the Latin American context see, inter alia, Green (1995), Veltmeyer, Petras and Vieux (1997), and Woodward (1992).
8. This process in Latin America can be delimited from 1979 (Ecuador) to 1989 (Chile). See, inter alia, Petras and Vieux (1994).
9. As a quite typical example, in Zacatecas, Mexico, some 19.5 per cent of cattle ranchers, who constitute the principal sector of rural production, have been classified as entrepreneurs – large (7.8 per cent) and medium to small (11.7 per cent). The rest in the sector are part of a peasant economy, mostly *ejiditarios* whose economic and social conditions do not allow them to be defined as middle class. In the other states of Mexico and countries in the region, the situation of agricultural producers – and the associated class structure – is substantially similar. In the economies of the cities and the urban centres the middle class is composed mostly of the business operators, managers, merchants and professionals, but the proportions are not that different: the middle class as 15-25 per cent of the Economically Active Population (EAP), and most entrepreneurs found elsewhere – in the informal sector. There are analytical difficulties in distinguishing the middle class in terms of their relationship to production (the petite-bourgeoisie) and by their source of income. In income terms, sociologists have identified a broad middle class that is split into accommodated and low strata, with possible political ramifications.
10. In the 1970s and 1980s where there were a number of studies along these lines such as Bartra (1974) in the case of Mexico. But in recent years such studies have been scant, with so many academics having abandoned the terrain of class analysis.
11. A study by CEPAL (1991: 32) found that 47 per cent of total world exports and over 50 per cent of imports are no more than intra-firm transfers by the TNCs with no market involvement.
12. A series of studies on this theme compiled by Lustig (1995) suggests that in some cases and contexts (e.g. Argentina) the middle class was more negatively impacted by the SAP than the working class and the poor.
13. Over the long term the process of proletarianization in relation to independent producers and operators of small businesses is a process that as in other contexts is resulting in the decline and decimation of this class – of the traditional middle class. But what is more characteristic of social formations in the countryside of the countries in the Third world is a process of sub-proletarianization, manifest in the increased reliance on one

form or other of wage labour while seeking to retain access to some means of direct production. In many cases, as, for example, in Chiapas over 50 per cent of peasant producers are in this situation. And the entrepreneurs are subject to the same process, although to a lesser degree.
14. In the case of Mexico an organization and social movement of independent producers and the entrepreneurs (El Barzon) has formed with almost a million members in less than two years under conditions of a financial crisis generated by a programme of neoliberal policies. The raison d'être of this movement is excessive indebtedness, with many properties and businesses subject to foreclosures and bankruptcy, but over time the movement has expanded its scope of concern and political demands. The Coordinadora del Consejo Empresarial calculates that from the onset of the financial crisis in Mexico (December 1994) some 15000 companies have had to close their doors as a consequence of the market contraction of the domestic market (viz. the drastic fall in purchasing power) (*La Jornada*, July 12, 1996: 55). In just one sector (construction) it is estimated that as of the financial crisis of December 1994, 21 per cent of companies have disappeared and that the number of active companies have decreased from 74 per cent to 60 per cent (SNIC, *Situación de la Industria de Construcción en 1996*; reported on by *La Jornada*, 1 November 1996: 53).
15. The conditions that provoked these mobilizations are the same that resulted in the formation of El Barzon in Mexico: high indebtedness under conditions of usurious interest rates, price rises, and neoliberal policies (as well as the classical problems of crop failure, conditions that have resulted in the accumulation of nine million dollars of debt in the rural sector (*La Jornada*, 3 November 1996: 49).
16. In another essay ('El Contexto y las dinamicas...'), we identify the roots of this process in 1973–74 in the OECD under certain conditions and under others in Latin America.
17. This army takes diverse forms. Its contingents include the unemployed, which has climbed to over 17 per cent of the EAP in Argentina and Venezuela (in official statistics), and the underemployed, which, according to official sources, incorporates at least 40 per cent of the EAP in Mexico. To these figures can be added those who do not appear in as an unemployment statistic because they know full well there are no jobs to be had (in some contexts listed as 'discouraged' workers) and in countries such as Mexico official figures seriously underestimate the numbers of unemployed because they count as employed all those who in any way, shape or form (or level of remuneration) worked for even one hour a week. In any event, the surplus population constitutes a reserve army of enormous proportions.
18. The IMF itself has studied and evaluated the economic impact of SAPs to discover that if anything it is negative. Bello, with Cunningham (1994: 67) summarizes the results of a survey conducted by the IMF to the impacts of the SAP on the economic growth of third world countries. The conclusion is that many countries under the SAP experienced a significant decline in their rate of growth relative to those countries not subject to a SAP regime. However, it seems that the IMF has effectively eluded

or hidden the results of its own study as has the World Bank in its annual reports which blithely report on the advantages of the SAP without reference to the data that suggest the contrary.
19. UNDP (1992); Korten (1995: 108-9).
20. *Ibid*., p.109.
21. A revealing example of this inequality in the distribution of wealth income is Mexico, a typical case in a region that posts the greatest rates of income disparity in the world, a disparity that has deepened and become extended in the course of ten years of neoliberal reforms and the SAP. In any event, in Mexico, (i) the poorest 40 per cent of families, composed of the lower strata of the working class (labourers, ejiditarios, domestics, peons, street sellers, and others in the informal sector) in 1994 received 7.3 per cent of the national income; (ii) a second stratum that includes qualified workers in construction and manufacturing, technicians, administrative workers, entrepreneurs and merchants; and that constitutes another 40 per cent of families, receive 20.1 per cent of the income; (iii) a third stratum – a study by the Universidad Obrero de Mexico mistakenly defines it as a group (at least it is not a social group in sociological terms) – that corresponds to the low middle class, constituted by bureaucrats, specialized technicians, administrative, staff, professionals and company executives; and that consists of 20 per cent of the population, receives 27.2 per cent of income (although this sector is considered to be one of the richest, in 1994 the income of its members barely covered the basic consumption levels); (iv) the remaining stratum, a privileged stratum representing 10 per cent of families, and composed of property owners, 'entrepreneurs', professionals, department chiefs and executives, high officials of the bureaucracy, receive (rather, appropriate) 40 per cent of the national income, that is to say, an income that is 45 times superior to the income received on a per capita basis by the poorest 30 per cent of families. And as in the world economy in the distribution of income figures a stratum of super-rich, 1 per cent of the population who in the case of Mexico receive 16.3 per cent of the national income. Within this group (and they do constitute a group in the sociological sense) are found 24 super millionaires (billionaires), the owners of the biggest banks, industries and commercial chains – the top layer of the big bourgeoisie) – who appropriated an income equivalent to that received by 11 million Mexicans. With regards to these data, see the study co-ordinated by Eduardo Manzo and reported on by the UOM (*La Jornada*, 10 October, 1996: 49).
22. The connection between neoliberal policies and the extension and deepening of the rich-poor gap, is made clear in a number of studies inter alia Hernandez Laos (1992), Khan (1993), Kliksberg (1993), Morley (1995), Schwartz (1994), Vuskovic (1993), and Woodward (1992). The experiential of this connection is transparent to everybody except dogmatic believers in the magic of the market such as Ernesto Zedillo, President of Mexico, who, contrary to all the evidence, declared that 'the market economy...provides the means combat poverty and inequality...' (speech before the fourth Ibero-American Summit at Viña del Mar, *La Jornada*, 11 November, 1996: 59).

Notes

23. According to ECLAC (*Anuario Estadistico*) the share of wages and salaries (labour) in national incomes in the region in Latin America has declined from 40 per cent more or less in 1980 to 34 per cent in 1990 and 32 per cent in 1992. See Table 3.4 for more details.
24. See the figures of UNIDO (1996) which demonstrate that the majority of 'third world' countries, particularly in Latin America and sub-Saharan Africa, have suffered a dramatic fall in the real value of wages (Table A.2), and that this is associated with a radical shift in the participation of the working class in national income (in many cases it was reduced by up to 20 percentage points) and in the increased disparity in the distribution of household income (see table 2.B). According to ECLAC, in nine Latin American countries, representing 90 per cent of the regional population, the real value of the average wage for five was lower in 1995 than in 1980 (in Peru it was less than 50 per cent), and for three countries the purchasing power of wages in 1995 was less than in 1970s (Argentina, Venezuela ...). In Mexico wages have lost 68 per cent of their real value since 1982.
25. On this theme see Sachs (1995: 168ff).
26. Walton and Seddon (1994) and Veltmeyer, Petras and Vieux (1997).
27. See, for example the recent statements and the Director-General of the World Economic Forum (WEF) in the Herald Tribune (People-Centred Development Forum # 6, 16 March 1996). It is also possible to find expressions of this fear in the academic world, particularly in the circles associated with US foreign policy (see for example, Kapstein, 1996).
28. See, for example, the annual report of the Inter-American Development Bank in 1991. Also note the declarations of the commander-in-chief of the armed forces of the USA, Latin America Division.
29. Some of the clearest expressions of this model can be found in the 1991 report of the IDB and the World Bank's 1991 World Development Report. The model and the thinking behind it, viz. the call for a new paradigm of development, is also well summarized in Chapter 2 of the 1993 Report of IFAD (International Fund for Agricultural Development) on world poverty (Jazairy *et al.*, 1992). See also the Report of the International Commission of Food and Peace (1994).
30. The incorporation of women into the development process has become an absolute programme and project principle for all development agencies and donors as well as the World Bank, the operating agencies of the UN system and government agencies. There is now an extensive bibliography on this policy, but the economic reasoning behind it is that women, by virtue of their critical position in relation to the processes of production and reproduction, constitute an essential factor in the development process. As for the question of poverty, without doubt, according to studies by UNICEF (Cornia *et al.*, 1987), the poor are the most vulnerable group affected negatively by the policy of adjustment, and need to be protected as well as have the conditions of this poverty alleviated. As for participation it is essentially a question of a policy and politics of partnership with local organizations – local governments and NGOs that mediate relations with base community organizations, facilitating their 'participation' in the government's programmes and projects that are designed above all

to placate the poor and defuse their discontent, to make SAP palatable and politically sustainable. In this context, the concept of 'participation' in this model also takes the form of a direct (more democratic) relation between the central government and the social organizations of the civil society. The concept and the corresponding practice was a central topic for discussion at the International Conference on Public Policy, People's Action, and Social Development organized by UNESCO for December 1994 in Bologna. See also the 1993 Conference on a proposed new development paradigm (Griesgraber and Gunter, 1996).

An exemplar of this policy identified and discussed at the conference was the Brazil's War Against Poverty (De Souza, 1997). And, in the same context, one of the first actions taken by H.F. Cardoso on assumption of the presidency was to establish a related programme based on the principles of partnership between the state and civil society : 'Comunidad de Solaridad'. In the same context, the incorporation of women came to be an absolute principle for accessing funding for any project by the Bank and the operational institutions of the UN system.

31. Basic formulations of this model can be found in the annual and development reports issued in 1991 by the World Bank and the IDB. Also see the Report on Rural World Poverty published by the International Fund for Agriculture and Development IFAD (Jazairy *et al.*, 1992).

32. As for Chile see Leiva and Petras, with Veltmeyer (1994); Collins (1995); and Vergara (1990) that show that the NSP has had but a marginal impact on the poor and the magnitude of the problems they face under the SAP (2/5 of the Chilean population continue to be poor), although the number of those in poverty and the conditions of extreme poverty have been reduced and ameliorated. Thus, we can speak of a modest success... with several reservations about Chile's NSP (that it is not nearly as well-targeted as it purports to be, etc.). A part of this success is the capacity of the administration to increase the social investment fund on the basis of a policy of modernizing the tax and the pension systems, a major mechanisms for the high rate of national savings (and productive as well as social investment) achieved by Chile, easily the highest in Latin America. In any event, in Mexico, the NSP has not fared so well; indeed it has been a disaster, having produced a greater electoral or political benefits to the regime than economic benefits to the poor.

33. Personal communication (October 1989) with Osvaldo Sunkel, one of the architects of CEPAL's neostructuralist model. Also see Sunkel (1991a, 1991b).

34. With regard to the policies associated with these principles see inter alia Cabrera Mendoza (1996) and various essays compiled and edited by *Nueva Sociedad*, No. 142, 1996; and UNICEF (1988).

35. This concept was elaborated by the UNDP as the basis of its annual reports, as of 1990, on Human Development on a world scale. The premises of this concept the can be found in the thought and the social change project of the thinkers of the eighteenth century enlightenment: *freedom* of the individual, conceived as a potential state to be realized by means of removing the restrictions or oppressive constraints placed by the state on the individual; *equality*, in relation to the need for creating

conditions equal for all (to eliminate the class structure, replacing it with a community of free individuals in a social and political state of equality; and *social justice*, closely bound to the idea of the equality) in that it also implied radical changes in the structure of society rather than liberal reforms.

36. As for the role assumed by many NGOs in support of the politics of the World Bank and other multilateral financial institutions, see, inter alia, Castro Arze and Lea Plaza (1996); and Petras and Arellano-Lopez (1997).
37. On this problematic in the Latin American context see, inter alia, Escobar and Solari (1996), Castro Arze and Lea Plaza (1996), Carrion (1996) and Virtuoso (1996).
38. At the summit of the Heads of State of Spain and Latin America in Viña de Mar, Chile, 10 October, 1996 (*La Jornada*, 11 November , 1996: 54).
39. See, for example, the IFAD *Report on World Poverty* (Jazairy *et al.*, 1992). The report identifies 22 roots or sources of world poverty. They included international conditions, social biases and policies (it understands that at a structural level there are cases of exploitation but IFAD is careful not to use the term), but they generally originate in conditions that are outside the control of anyone or of those for whom the poor themselves can be held responsible.
40. See the evaluation of FHIS by Fuentes (1992).
41. Laurell (1994); Gordon, (1993).
42. Although the government has put an end to Solidarity (probably because of its close identification with the Salinas de Gortieri administration), the central government has designed other programmes under the secretary of Agriculture to avoid the social convulsions that derive from the hunger and the misery that prevails in the countryside. So argued a leader of the Coordination of Urban Democratic and Peasant Organizations (CODUC) (*La Jornada*, 10 October, 1996: 50).
43. *La Jornada*, 'del campo', 1 November, 1996: 10-11.
44. An analysis of the Autonomous University of Chapingo, elaborated along with the Central of Independent Agricultural Workers and Peasants, warns that to date (November 1996) about a million, 200 thousand producers, peasants in the majority, are denied credit by the commercial banks and have no or lost any government support. And a large part of those that have had access to bank credit are indebted without any capacity of paying even the rapidly accumulating interest on these debts. Hence El Barzon.
45. See the discussion on these mechanisms described by Lira (p. 10).
46. There is no doubt that the peasants are seen by the government as a drag on agricultural development and modernization of the sector, and have no role whatsoever to play in the government's scenario of a restructured economy (the government's aim, to eliminate 50 per cent of small and inefficient – that is, peasant – produces from the sector, was admitted in San Diego by the then Under-Secretary for Agricultural Affairs and currently a key advisor to the Zedillo government).
47. Corn producers, in particular, have been heavily hit by neoliberal policies (that have resulted in an increase of 24 per cent in the import of basic

grains such as corn, under conditions of falling prices in the world market, heavy subsidies of production by the US government, as well as greater productivity), provoking mobilizations across the country, particularly in Chiapas where thousands of peasants have blocked the highways in protest against low prices, with at least three dead and a promise of the leaders of the Corn Producers Council of Chiapas, representing some 50000 producers in 15 municipalities, that the mobilizations will continue (*La Jornada*, 10 October, 1996: 6).

48. In this regard, see Leiva and Petras, with Veltmeyer (1994);Vergara (1990, 1996); and ECLAC (1990).
49. See Stahl (1996).
50. FOSIS (1994).
51. See Vergara (1990, 1996).
52. This concept of economic development (economic growth) is generally measured at the national level in terms of an annual change in total product per capita, the basic indicator of development economics reflected in Table 1 of theWorld Bank's annual Report on World Development. In the first decades of the study of development (1947–67) the theories and models elaborated by economists focused almost exclusively on the dynamics of the growth process – the critical factors, necessary conditions, the obstacles, and the most effective or efficient policies and strategies.
53. In the 1970s, the concept was expanded with a social dimension, not only in relation to conditions such as health and education (seen not only as a quality of life issue, but as human capital and thus a critical factor in the process, as well as an essential conditions of human development. As for the measurement of development it has not been easy. As recent as 1990 the UNDP incorporated a social dimension in its annual report on the level of human development reached across the world, thus originating a better index than that of the World Bank. However, it does not incorporate the critical element of equity or social justice, which figures so predominantly in the rhetoric of proponents of the new paradigm.
54. This dimension either has also not been incorporated in extant development indexes. As a rule it is associated with the question of democracy – the degree of political freedom and protection of individual human rights. At the level of the community, the social base of the programmes and models of alternative development, is associated with the capacity of people to participate in decision-making ... in their self-constitution as a social subject (popular democracy, we might say). On this concept of human development as a process by which the people become empowered, realising their capacities and potential, and releasing their cultural or social energies, see the International Commission on Peace and Food (ICPF) (1994: 201) and the UNDP's Human Development Report.
55. This cultural or ethnic development factor is totally absent in the major models in the study of development, but it is a critical and essential dimension in the movement to establish an alternative form of development.
56. As of the publication in 1987 of the Bruntland Report on Sustainable Development (*Our Common Future*), this dimension has been rescued from total ignorance to convert it into a critical dimension, the essential

Notes 155

goal of any proposed strategy, government plan, or development project. At bottom, the problem is reduced to the question of the possibility of expanding production without exceeding its ecological limits. In this regard, the Bruntland Report has faith in this possibility under two conditions: (i) a better and more efficient management of the extraction and use of natural resources and the production of waste; and (ii) the technological extension of current limits. In this regard, the 'Factor 10' club has proposed for the OECD countries multiplication by a factor of 10 the average productivity of these economies within fifty years, to establish thereby the necessary preconditions of a sustainable development process on a world scale. Clearly, many analysts do not agree with this, believing in the necessity of finding a non-growth path towards development, and a radical redistribution of the consumption of world production. Some accept that this implies the abandonment of the industrialization process that has sustained the process until now or of the capitalist system and its drive to accumulate.

57. With respect to these two paradigms, see Wilber and Jameson (1989). The orthodox paradigm is better designated as 'liberal', with two extremes: orthodoxy (neoliberalism) and heterodoxy (structuralism). The other paradigm can be designated as 'radical' in terms of its ideological orientation towards an alternative social and economic system, although it should not be confused with the movement towards alternative development that formed in the 1970s. Both paradigms share some postulates and a vision as to the nature of the development process and the role of the state and the market.

58. This search for an alternative form of development arose precisely (1973) when the World Bank discovered that up to 800 million people in the world were poor and initiated its strategy of combating it with a policy and programme of satisfying the Basic Needs of the world's population; and the capitalist class launched its counter-offensive against the working class.

59. The spread and advances of this perspective can be studied from many sources, including the People-Centred Development Forum in Malaysia under the direction of David Korten, and numerous journals such as those associated with the *Third World Insurgent*; *Development Alternatives Newsletter* (New Delhi); *Development Dialogue* (Upssala), *IFDA Dossier*, and the reports of thousand of NGOs that share the vision and perspective of alternative development.

60. In the context of Latin America (and in this case, the world) ECLAC opened this topic in 1964 in Santiago of Chile with a Regional seminar on the role of Community Development in the Acceleration of Economic and Social Development, in which was made an inventory of diverse country experiences of community development, in an effort to extract therefrom a series of recommendations. But after an initial burst this movement for community development went into decline until its resurrection, under very different condition, in the 1980s. On this point, see inter alia Castro Arze and Lea Plaza (1996); Fox and Hernandez (1992); Marcos (1996); and UNICEF (1988).

61. Blaikie (1985); Chambers (1983); Cernea (1985), a sociologist who works for the World Bank; and, with specific reference to Latin

America Calderon *et al.* (1992); Machado *et al.* (1993); Stiefel and Wolfe (1994).
62. In the Latin American context this concept is elaborated by a wide range of intellectuals such as Fals-Borda, Max-Neef y Freire.
63. Thus does Friedmann (1992) define empowerment as the essence of the alternative development process.
64. In the 1970s, the emphasis on appropriate technology and small (and micro) enterprise constituted essential conditions of populism, an alternative form of economic development, viewed not as it is in Latin America (as a form of people-oriented politics) but as an economic model propagated by Schumacher (small is beautiful) and others including the ILO. In recent years it has become obvious that the transfer of technology and the generation of small enterprise are nodal points of the process of alternative development. On this see the five volume study edited by Surendra Patel (1994, 1995).
65. The SPARK experiments in China to diffuse science and technology in the rural sector, and ASTRA, a project of the Indian Institute of Science in Bangalore, have demonstrated the viability of this approach.
66. As for the production system, the focus on the domestic market is a feature of all AD proposals. In the Latin America context see inter alia Lechner (1992).
67. Sachs (1995).
68. This problematic was the object and the agenda of an international conference on Public Policy, People's Actions, and Social Development sponsored by UNESCO in December 1994 in Bologna.
69. In this regard, Sachs (1995: 1691), in the context of a UN Conference on Social Development (the social summit) held in Copenhagen in March 1995, formulated this problematic in terms of the need to give social organizations a more 'active role' within the institutions and international forums that are characterized by a lack of democracy and elite decision-making. The thousands of NGOs formed as a counter-summit (of the Group of Seven), and that meet regularly at the encounters and annual summits of the World Bank and the IMF and international UN conferences, share this agenda. Susan George, in relation to the community of international financial institutions (IFIs) has proposed the same agenda: to form at the international level a civil society composed of organizations and producer associations, workers, citizens, and NGOs to participate in the decision-making of international institutions. The problem is that George does not explain the dynamics of this proposed democratization process; in the end it is very utopian, without any realistic possibility of implementing it.
70. Efforts of ECLAC in this area (the search for AD or a new paradigm) was crystallized in the publication of *Changing Production Patterns with Social Equity* (1990) ; and ECLAC (1992, 1994); and its annual *Panorama Social de America Latina*. Also see Meller (1991); and Sunkel (1991a, 1991b).
71. 'Growth with equity' was the theoretical basis of a model policy that was widely advocated in the 1970s: to see poverty as the essential defining condition of undevelopment and Meeting Basic Needs as the basic development policy. The World Bank was the basic institutional promoter of

this approach, but it was widely adopted as the best if not only solution short of mounting pressures for a more radical approach predicated on social revolution.
72. See, for example, Leiva and Petras, with Veltmeyer (1994). Also see Collins and Lear (1995).
73. On the Southeast Asian NICs (Taiwan and South Korea) see, inter alia, Johansen (1993). As for Latin America see inter alia Fajnzylber (1990). In the 1970s, the growth-with-equity model formulated by liberal reformers can be viewed as an exemplar of this approach applied in practice, to some extent, by South Korea and Taiwan, as well as Sri Lanka and Cuba. The growth model, on the other hand, was best exemplified by Brazil.
74. On this point see Boisier *et al.* (1992).
75. In spite of these political problems, a range of Latin American intellectuals and politicos have turned towards the ECLAC proposals as the basis of an alternative programme, adding variations. One of them is Jorgé Casteneda, a professor of economics and international relationships at UN-AM. His book *Utopia Unarmed: The Latin American Left* (1993) is very critical of neoliberal policies and its ideology of the free market, but it is equally critical of the 'utopian' solutions and proposals of the left. But as for the PRD (Partido Revolucionario Democrático), the principal political party on the left in Mexico, the ECLAC model constitutes a major point of reference for Casteneda's reflections and proposals.

3 The Restructuring of Labour

1. See, for example, PREALC (1993), OECD (1994) and the World Bank (1993, 1995), the major object in this chapter. The term 'labour market flexibility' has taken on a variety of meanings over time, prompting US Labor Secretary Robert Reich to remark at an ILO sponsored meeting on June 10, 1994 that 'rarely in international discourse has the {term} gone so directly from obscurity to meaninglessness without any intervening period of coherence' (quoted by Brodsky, 1994). What it means for the World Bank, however, as an overlooked precondition for succesful structural reform is fairly clear: 'A dynamic and flexible labor market is an important part of market-oriented policies. It helps reallocate resources and allows the economy to respond rapidly to new challenges from increased competition. Moreover, freeing the labor market of distortions improves the distribution of income because it encourages employment expansion and wage increases in the poorest segments of society' (World Bank, 1993: 92).
2. Sagasti and Árevalo (1992: 1105).
3. World Bank, *Policy Research Bulletin*, 6, (4), August-October (1995: 6).
4. As we will discuss below, although it is derived from a theory formulated by neo-classical economists at the turn of and into the 20th century, in the context of the technological conversion and productive transformation that unfolded in the 1970s and 1980s and continues to do so in the 90s, this idea is but the abstraction of the new relations of production that were being formed in the process. All of the recommended changes in labour legislation and the structure of the labour market are congruent with and

158 *Notes*

specific requirements of the new post-fordist mode of production instituted on the basis of the technological revolution in microelectronics and infomatics. The literature on this new 'echnological paradigm' and associated developments is growing, but inter alia (and with specific reference to the Latin American context of these development) see Boom and Mercado (1990), Ominami (1986), and Sotelo Valencia (1995). With specific reference to pioneering developments in Brazil see De Paula Leite (1993); Chile see Olave (1994); and for Mexico see Mercado in Boom and Mercado (1990), Dutrénit and Capdevielle (1993), and Palomares and Mertens (1993).

5. The notion that wages are too high is part of a neoclassical theory that holds that when wages decline the likely outcome is a rise in employment, and, given greater production capacity, a rise in output. As Taylor (1988) notes, this theory conflicts and can be counterposed with the structuralist theory which holds that a decline in wages is more likely to result in a contraction of output.

6. The advancement of these ideas, and the advocacy of policies based on them, has involved numerous forums and takes many forms. There is probably not a country in the region where a team of economists from the WB or one of its sister institutions (the IDB in the Latin American context) has not been found delivering the same message, usually covertly, with appropriate news releases as to the promise and successful performance of such policies when adopted by the government and of the need for the government to stay the course, but occasionally, as in Argentina, all too publicly.

7. Specifically, the Bank argues that minimum-wage legislation distorts factor allocation and punishes informal sector workers, high unemployment benefits reduce work incentives, job protection provisions and the high costs of dismissal make restructuring difficult and slow, and high non-wage costs and payroll taxes act as a disincentive for entrepreneurs to expand employment and increase the international competitiveness of local firms. The Bank expands on these points in its annual (1995) Report on 'Workers in an Integrating World'. However, its discourse is highly ideological, presented in the form of a manifesto, peppered with assertions, little argument, and highly constructed and dubious data. On this see Veltmeyer (1997b).For one thing, the Bank underestimates the scope and depth of the problems it has identified (see tables 3.3 and 3.6) for an alternative statistical presentation of the data relating to these problems, and the source of these problems in the policies it has advocated and that have been put into practice at least ten years in most countries. Despite the obvious and clear association of these conditions and the SAP (see, inter alia, Alimir, 1994; Morley, 1995; and Veltmeyer, Petras and Vieux, 1997).

8. At the base of this technological conversion is what Aglietta (1982), Boyer (1989), Lipietz (1982) and other regulationists is a crisis in the fordist mode of production and the institution of new, more flexible forms of organization and the incorporation of the technological revolution in microelectronics and informatics. On this point see, inter alia, Ferrer (1993). This process of technological transformation in Latin America was initiated by Brazil in 1975, Argentina a year later, and Mexico in 1981, thus

incorporating the three biggest industrialized economies in the region. However, the requirements of this new technological paradigm for a different labour regime and the institution of corresponding legislative and labour market reforms were first realized in Chile under the military regime of Pinochet (1977–81), who was in a better position than other heads of state to establish the political conditions for these changes, to eradicate the distortions created by Latin America's labour market regime, and to pioneer the new labour regime. On this point the World Bank waxes enthusiastic: 'The Chilean experiement gained greatly in stature once it became apparent that the new democratic government... had embraced – and furthered – the main elements of the market reforms first implemented during the military regime. In the early 1990s Chile, as well as as Mexico, had clearly become important role models for the entire region' (1993: 30-1).

Throughout the 1980s the process of technological conversion and productive transformation proceeded apace, as did the political struggle to institute the corresponding labour regime. The repression and disarticulation of working class organizations and the union movement, and a demobilazation of the working class accumulated social and political forces, were essential conditions for this process – for the implementation of the the neoliberal agenda. On this political dimension of the technological restructuring process – the legislation of a corresponding labour regime and the politics of direct repression directed against the union movement – for the pioneering case of Chile see Diaz (1989) and, in particular, Leiva (1996); for Colombia see Botero (1992); and El Salvador see Arrides Palomares (1995). A number of studies have documented, if not analyzed, the negative impact of technological restructuring on Latin American labour. In this connection see, for example, De Paula Leite (1993: 98), Mercado (1990: 64), Ominami (1986: 23-4), and, in particular, Vieira (1994).

9. On the labour regime of the maquilladora in El Salvador and Mexico see, inter alia, Arrida Palomares (1995), Mercado (1990), Brown and Domínguez (1989), and various authors in Ominami (1986).
10. On the model case of Chile see Geller (1993), Herrera (1995), Leiva (1996), and Leiva and Agacino (1994).
11. The shift over the course of the 1980s in political conditions and climate relating to the labour question in Argentina is reflected well in a recent comment by the President of the Chamber of Deputies in the context of a heavy national debate and political struggle generated by the efforts of the government to legislate or decree a new labour code that extends the managers rights instituted in Law 20.744 (Labour Contracts and the National Law of Employment) and undermines further the advances made by labour over the years and that establishes the right of employers and managers to hire, fire, extend hours of work, and relocate workers in the production process without penalty. It was necessary, he argued, to support the government's proposed reform because 'times have changed... The reality is the need to make an effort to obtain jobs; before it was to protect full employment' (*La Jornada*, 7 October 1996: 59).

12. As noted above, the Bank argues that minimum-wage legislation distorts factor allocation and punishes informal sector workers, high unemployment benefits reduce work incentives, job protection provisions and the high costs of dismissal make restructuring difficult and slow, and high non-wage costs and payroll taxes act as a disincentive for entrepreneurs to expand employment and increase the international competitiveness of local firms. The Bank expands on these points in its annual (1995) Report on 'Workers in an Integrating World'. However, its discourse is highly ideological, presented in the form of a manifesto, peppered with assertions, little argument, and highly constructed and dubious data. On this see Veltmeyer (1997c).
13. In this connection, the economists of the World Bank depart from the neoclassical vision of the worker seen not as the member of a class, acting in solidarity, and making gains on the basis of a long struggle with capital, but as an individual economic agent, capacitated as a social actor in the market, seeking and able to take advantage of the opportunities it provides. To this end, converting workers into self-seeking individual economic agents, the Bank has advocated reforms designed to strip the power of union over its members, its capacity to negotiate collective agreements on a sectoral or industry basis, mandatory dues check-off, etc.
14. There are numerous variations on this theme advanced and documented by the Bank in diverse contexts. See, for example, reports on the Bank's second annual Conference on Latin American and Caribbean Development held in Bogota (FUSADES, 1996: 1), which reported on the experience of Chile, Colombia and Peru with labour market legislative reform to the effect that within a year of appropriate legislation that included the decentralization of collective bargaining as well as greater flexibility of employers in hiring and firing workers, and shifting their position in the production process as required, as well as the resort to longer hours as required, the rate of open unemployment had been significantly reduced. Most recently in the case of Argentina, a secret Bank memorandum arguing the need to reduce the excessively high wages in the key productive sectors as the solution to the country's extraordinarily severe unemployment problem (with rates as high as 17.5 per cent), added fuel to an explosive situation, including massive mobilizations and the call for a 48 hour General Strike by the country's biggest federation of labour unions, as well as the call for a continental force to combat neoliberal economic policies, created by the government's drive to introduce a new labour code to ensure greater flexibility and thus the best solution to this problem. In its public pronouncements the government clearly had adopted the bank's reasoning that high wage, which close to two decades ago was blamed as the major source of the problem of runaway inflation, is now seen as largely responsible for the unemployment problem.
15. The literature on this redesigned model of the SAP and the associated agenda is voluminous. See, inter alia, CEPAL (1992c), IDB (1993), and Lerner (1996).
16. This implementation of this agenda has also resulted in a huge and growing literature. Inter alia see Boisier *et al.* (1992), and Cook *et al.* (1996).

17. The importance and priority given to (i) the New Social Policy, designed to make the SAP more palatable and to defuse a mounting and destabilizing level of social discontent, and (ii) the modernization of the state apparatus, is reflected in the distribution of funds by the IDB, the key financial institution charged with the responsibility of implementing the SAP within the region. In 1996 40 per cent of the Bank's portfolio was directed into social investment and programme funds, 36 per cent was directed towards the region-wide government decentralization process and the associated modernization of the state apparatus, another 16 per cent went towards infrastructure support projects, and only 8 per cent went towards agriculture and other productive sectors of the economy (IPS, Washington DC, 14 March, 1997). This characteristic low priority given to production enhancement projects, also shared by public investments in the region, reflects the widely-shared ideological orientation towards the neoliberal doctrine on the private sector as the motor of the development process.
18. ECLAC (1990). This process is based on the incorporation of new labour-displacing technologies that also reduce the requirements for material components and energy, thus automatically marginalizing those countries and regions that on a global scale continue to specialize in and rely on the latter. Despite the incorporation of Latin America's biggest economies into this process, 63 per cent of the region's exports today still take the form of energy or primary products with a high material content and little value added, products for which there is a decreasing demand on the world markets, thus explaining in part the declining weight of the region in international export markets. On this point see Levitt (1990) and Ferrer (1993: 811).
19. On these advances see, inter alia, ECLAC (1990), Boom and Mercado (1990), Morales (1992), and UNIDO (1992).
20. The low level of productive investment and capital formation in the region is in part connected to the need to service the enormous if now manageable external debt, but the problem goes well beyond this need as illustrated by the case of El Salvador, where, it is estimated by the Central Bank, the country's entrepreneurs invest less than 25 per cent of their income or earnings (ECA 1994: 551: 915).
21. Even a cursory examination of the readily available and well-published figures on the growth by country of the GNP and without reference to debated questions as to the distribution between public and private sources and forms of investment, the distribution of these investments by sector, or the connection between physical and social capital formation is sufficient to establish a correlation between the level of productive investment and the rate of annual growth in production. In the 1980s, the economic and political conditions for capital formation in Latin America were generally reduced, resulting in particularly low levels of national saving and productive investment, and this included Chile which only managed to elevate its level of productive investment – and economic growth – on the basis of a brutally severe adjustment and restructuring of labour (as in the fast-growing Asian economies) in the late 1980s. Today, Chile is the only country managing a level of productive investment comparable

to the eight Rapidly-Growing Economies of East Asia, although Leiva (1996: 5) argues that much of this investment is not productive in that as part of a strategy of relying on the existence and generation of a large stock of cheap labour, it has not been used as a means of incorporating 'hard technical change'.

22. The OECD, in its annual Economic Outlook (1996) defines 'total productivity' as the weighted average productivity gains of capital and labour. However, more generally the modern (neoclassical) theory of economic growth holds that total factor productivity can be measured in terms of the difference between the productivity increase of direct production factors (capital and labour) and total productivity increase (Ito, 1997: 189–190). In this context, total factor productivity relates to factors other than capital and labour such as the change in the organization of production (increased flexibility) associated with what has been termed 'postfordism' by the French regulationists.

23. The productivity of labour in Latin America is considerably lower than in the industrialized countries within the OECD. In 1950, for example, the productivity gap between the OECD and Latin America as a whole was 50 per cent (4.4 versus 6–7 in terms of GNP per hour worked); by 1973 this gap had doubled (9.2 versus 17.1); and by 1992 it increased by another 50 per cent (9.5 versus 25.7) (Maddison, 1995: 341).

24. This neoclassical theory (see ECA, 1995: 564: 940) basically holds that under free market competitive conditions each factor of production receives in return for its contribution to production a commensurate return. In other words, the invisible hand of the market – according to Michel Camdusses, one of three pillars of IMF economic policy, the other two being the visible hand of the state and 'solidarity between the poor and the rich' – has to be left alone to assure an optimum distribution of the social product.

25. See, for example, the Plans for Economic and Social Development adopted by the governments of Chile, Bolivia, El Salvador, Mexico, among others.

26. For example, the Plan de Desarrollo Economico y Social 1989–94 presented by the government of Cristiani in El Salvador in the context of the civil war (its text is presented in ECA 564: 942ff).

27. On this see Montesinos and Gochiz (1995: 940). The problem with the theory is that despite the centrality of this variable (the marginal productivity of labour) there does not seem to be any systematic effort to determine or measure it in a specific context. On this point see Montesino and Gochiz (1995: 940) who point out that there exists neither an effective methodology or any serious efforts to measure the marginal productivity of labour.

28. See Montesino and Gochiz (1995: 945) who point out the similarities between the observations and recommendations arising from the Bogota Conference and the argument advanced by the ARENA government. More recently, the Menem government in Argentina has advanced the same argument in the context of its campaign to introduce a programme of labour market flexibility. This argument was clearly made on the basis of the secret World Bank Report leaked to

the media in the context of this campaign and the political struggle unleashed by it.
29. The idea of adjusting wages to productivity was, of course, a key element of the post-war labour-capital accord. But it was resurrected as a specific policy recommendation in the Latin-American context by the ILO (PREALC, 1993: 15).
30. The evolution of minimum wages has tracked the same pattern as average wages, although the tendency to fall has generally been even more pronounced. See, for example, the case of El Salvador traced out by Montesino and Gochiz (1995: 951). This fall in the purchasing power of wages reflects the effects of specific policies, as well as prevailing structural conditions, designed explicitly to compress wages as a mechanism of internal adjustment. The effects and social costs of this compression have been brutally severe, leading to a drastic reduction in consumption and standards of living, which is reflected in the fact that not even in 1996 had real per capita incomes in the region recovered their level achieved in 1980 and in some cases (Argentina, Peru, Venezuela) in 1970 (United Nations, 1996: 7).
31. *La Jornada*, 5 November, 1996: 39; 15 March, 1997: 48.
32. In the not atypical case of Mexico, the number of workers in manufacturing within the formal production sector of the economy in the 1980s (from 1981 to 1989) declined dramatically, 4.5 per cent a year on average, while production levels remained stagnant, with oscillations by industry, and productivity per worker increased by 5.1 per cent, presumably to some extent related to the decrease in the number of workers (Morales, 1992: 64). According to a series of Industrial Surveys conducted over the period the same pattern held for the other branches of industry as well. In the industrial sector in 1989 the number of workers had declined 13 per cent relative to 1981, while productivity rose 14.3 per cent (Morales, 1992: 71).
33. Amsden and van der Hoeven (1994), based on data collected by UNIDO (1991, 1992), show that the growth rate of manufacturing output (taking manufacturing as a proxy for broader developments with respect to output and wage patterns) declined from an annually average rate of 6.6 per cent from 1965 to 1980 to 1.2 per cent in the 1980s, and that when value-added growth is considered – and the income associated with it, then the 1980s experienced a net decrease in output and income. Data assembled by FUSADES (1996) indicate that total productivity growth during the same period (the 1980s) was variable but generally positive. In the case of Mexico, an Industrial Survey showed that in 1988 the number of employed workers in the industrial sector was 87 per cent of the number in 1981, but that productivity had risen 14.3 per cent over the same period (Morales, 1992: 71).
34. The low level of participation of capital in the production process relates to the well established pattern of a reduced and low level of productive investment in all the Latin American economies in the 1980s (see Table 3.1). As for the participation of labour, the low levels reflect conditions of falling wages and decline in the absolute number as well as the size of the labour force in the formal sector of the production apparatus.

35. In the case of El Salvador, for example, from 1980 to 1986 productivity on average increased by 8.4 per cent while wages fell by 23.4 per cent (ECA 564, 1995: 957). Subsequently, the rate of growth in average productivity slowed down while real wages recovered somewhat, but in either case there was clearly no systematic correlation between the two (see the detailed sectoral analysis of the dynamics of productivity and wages by Montesino and Gochez, 1995: 945–962). In the case of Mexico, a study by Guerrero de Lizardi and Valle (1995), showed that until around 1982 wage and productivity increases more or less were in tandem but that at that point they began to sharply diverge, wages falling drastically while average productivity tended to remain stable with a tendency for a gradual but persistent increase as of around 1987.

36. There is clear evidence of the use by the Chicago Boys of Chile of unemployment, purposefully maintained at twice the historic rate, as a means to pressure and discipline workers, undercutting and reducing their demands for decent or fair wage increases (Sanfuentes, 1987). As for inflation, there is similar evidence of it being used as a mechanism for compressing wages and transferring income from labour to capital. On this economic policies of the current Zedillo regime is revealing. Since he came into office on December 1994, the Basic Basket (*canasta basica*) has increased by some 170 per cent, while wages have been adjusted, allowed to increase, to a maximum of 71 per cent, a difference of over 200 per cent (*La Jornada*, 27 January, 1997: 42). The disarticulation and repression of working class organizations have been well-documented, albeit not analyzed in terms of a politically determined mechanism for compressing wages. For the case of El Salvador *vis-à-vis* the maquilladoras created in the mid-1980s see Arrida Palomares (1995) and the pioneering case of Chile see Leiva and Petras, with Veltmeyer (1994) and Leiva (1996).

37. This is particularly the case for Latin America but indications are the same applies elsewhere as in the European Community where until the mid-1970s the share of capital in value added to manufacturing as well as returns to capital invested in the sector had been declining. In the 1980s these trends were turned around. On this point see Fuji Gambero (1997: 48).

38. In the case of Mexico, the rate of capital formation in 1988 was only 41 per cent of the 1981 rate (Morales, 1992: 69) and more recent studies (see, for example, Petras and Veltmeyer, 1995) show that despite a resurgence of direct foreign investment as of 1992, the general level of productive investment in the region (Chile excepted) remains low. The vast bulk of the resurgent FDI, which in '97 reached $80 billion, has been used not to finance a growth of productive capacity and output but to acquire already existing corporate assets at bargain prices. According to US Securities Data (January 16, 1989) up to $71.2 billion was invested in 1997 in the purchase of corporate stock in latin America. In 1998 the oportunities for a financial killing presented by the privatization of public or state enterprises attracted a phenomenal $56.5 billion of foreign direct investment.

39. However, Leiva (1996), for one, discounts the effectiveness of this investment, emphasizing its many hidden and not so hidden costs such as the

weakening and disarticulation of the labour movement, the disproportionate growth of precarious and poorly paid jobs, the dramatically increased rates of reliance on cheap female and child labour, the increase of job and economic insecurity, and an extension of inequality and poverty.

40. In 11 of Latin America's 20 economies the size of the external debt, measured in terms of the GDP or the rate of debt service, exceeds the World Bank's 'crisis level' (over 50 per cent of export earnings). It remains a substantial drag on the development process, explaining in part the low level of productive investment characteristic of economies in the region.

41. On the dynamics of this investment see, inter alia, Petras and Veltmeyer (1995) as well as a series of studies and data compiled by the US Department of Commerce's Bureau of Economic Analysis. As for the high level of non-productive consumption, a problem that was identified as early as the 1960s by CEPAL economists, it is reflected in the huge gap between the income disposed of by the richest households and individuals and the rate of investment. On this point, INEGI, Mexico's national statistics institute, has calculated that the 23 per cent of the richest households in the country experienced an increase of 417 per cent in their income from 1984 to 1994, while the share in national income of 10.4 million families earning the equivalent of from one to five minimum wages, and constituting 53.4 per cent of all households, fell by 31 per cent (*La Jornada*, 23 September, 1996: an. supl. V).

42. Given that most of the EAP (4) is engaged in small-scale agricultural Production, the difference in RS (4) and (5) reflects the very low rates of productivity in the small-scale peasant production sector, as does the high rate of rural poverty (6). The low productivity of peasant small-scale agriculture is well known, being, in fact, the basis of efforts throughout the region to modernize agriculture (read do away with the peasant sector). However, the informal sector has generated similar concerns and policy reactions. In the case of Mexico it has been estimated by INEGI, the National Institute for Statistics, that the informal sector, encompasing 20 per cent of commercial activity and close to 50 per cent of the EAP, contributes 8 per cent of the GNP (*La Jornada* 15 March, 1997: 60). Most economists, however, would estimate its contribution to be closer to a third of the GNP.

43. The process of these developments has been well-documented and analyzed. It relates to what has been termed 'The Golden Age of Capitalism' or what the French have dubbed 'The thirty glorious years' – close to thirty years in the post-war context of continued and unparalleled annual growth worldwide of the social product (Glynn *et al.*, 1990). One key element of the context for this growth was constituted by a labour-capital accord which provided conditions of social peace in exchange for a just share in any productivity gains and a guarantee of full employment, supported by labour-demanding spending policy of the State and the institution of a programme of social welfare. In the late 1960s cracks began to appear in the foundation of this system with the onset of a 'profitability crunch' reflected in conditions of stagnant production rates, a crisis of

overproduction, and rising unemployment. As it happened, labour launched what turned out to be its last great offensive, from 1968 to 1973, in its push for higher wages and improved benefits precisely at the point of this crisis in capitalist production, provoking a counter-offensive, launched by capital in 1974 and continuing today. Key elements of this counter-offensive included a direct attack on wages and the power of unions, the welfare state, as well as the agreement to link wages to productivity gains. The rest, as they say, is history – a long history that is by no means at an end.

44. On this point, the extraction of absolute surplus value, a study by Arrida Palomares (1993: 78–80) on the labour process of the maquilladores in El Salvador's San Bartolo Free Trade Zone found an extensive and abuse use of over-time, leading in many case of workdays of 9–10 hours or 55–60 hours a week. The extensive and abusive reliance on over-time and extended work-days does not even bring up the growing patterns of double- and triple-job holding, extensive self-exploitation in the context of households and production units in the informal sector, and the dramatic growth of child and unreported female labour. For a statistical profile of these dimensions of absolute surplus value extraction see CEPAL (1995).

45. On this concept of 'super-exploitation' see Marini (1981) and Veltmeyer (1983). It is based in part on what Meillasoux (1978) in a very different context conceptualized as 'labour rents', extracted from migrant labourers on the basis of the assumption of the labourers' households outside the capitalist system of a part of the reproductive costs of the labour purchased by agro-capitalists on a seasonal base.

46. ECA 560, 1995: 971.

47. On this point see, inter alia, Veltmeyer (1983) and, with respect to Chile, which experienced a dramatic expansion of the temporero workforce in its privileged agro-export industries in the 1980s, Petras and Leiva (1994).

48. This problem is reflected in the general failure of economies in the region to recover let alone exceed the rates of growth (5.5–6.3 per cent) that it had sustained for several decades under the now discarded state-interventionist, inward-oriented and populist strategy. The entire 1980s was 'lost to development', barely averaging 1 per cent growth per annum (−0.9 per cent on a per capita basis), but each year into the 1990s, 10 to 15 years into the SAP, and not withstanding the substantial recovery of foreign direct investment and inflow of capital in the 1990s, the expected or promised economic 'recovery' and 'activation' has failed to materialize, having barely averaged 3 per cent per annum over the decade the regional growth rate of 2.8 per cent in 1998 is expected to drop down to 1.8 in 1999 (*Informe Latinoamericano*, 1 December, 1998: 559).

49. On this point, a study by Leiva and Agacino (1994) contends that during the 1990–1994 period in Chile, employers in the manufacturing sector resorted to flexible labour practices such as temporary employment, subconracting, homework, fixed-term employment and the increased use of cheaper female labour, as means of increasing their control over the labour force-by cutting production costs and weakening the negotiating power of

workers. These variations in a labour flexibility strategy are also reflected in another characteristic feature of the production and labour process in the region: the wage discrimination against women, who make up the bulk of the labour force in the maquilladores, and who are on average paid at least 30 to 40 per cent less than men in jobs of the same value and position. In the not atypical case of El Salvador, women are paid 53 per cent less than men in industry and 47 per cent less in commerce (ECA 551: 911). On this point *vis-à-vis* Chile also see Henriquez and Reca (1994).

50. For example, in Mexico's manufacturing industry, the region's third largest, the total cost of labour in the production process has been reduced to 10 per cent, with wages representing only 2.8 per cent (*La Jornada*, April 18, 1996). On an hourly basis, minimum wages in the manufacturing sector are set at $1.23 in Mexico (versus $12.60 in the US, $20.80 in Japan, $11.93 in Canada, $8.85 in France, $6.10 in South Korea – and $2.75 in Chile). In the case of Mexico, this wage rate in real terms is lower than it was in 1965 and by no stretch of the imagination (or pocket-book) covers the cost of subsistence of the workers's family – and thus the reproduction of labour power. In this connection, it is estimated that a family of three to four, below the Mexican average in size, requires the equivalent to 5 minimum wages to pay for the *canasta basica* – the package of goods to meet its basic physical needs (*La Jornada*, 5/11/96: 40). According to the World Bank, 60 per cent of Mexican families are unable to provide adequately for their basic needs, and half of this number are deprived to a level that seriously affects their health not to speak of any social capital.

51. In this regard, the World Bank and neoclassical economists generally (Belassi, Bhagwati, Kreuger, Lal) have drawn a false and entirely misleading conclusions from the success of the rapidly-growing economies of East Asia that have geared their economies to manufacturing exports. In no case was this export-oriented industrialization strategy pursued at the expense of the domestic market. In fact, this market was – and still remains – a protectorate of the state, as are the industries and enterprises that rely on it. In contrast, in Latin America the neoliberal reform process has prematurely exposed nascent and immature industries and enterprises to the forces of the world market, leading to the technological restructuring of a few but for the most part resulting in a policy of lowering the cost of labour in production and the weakening and destruction of domestic markets.

52. Under the conditions that we have identified it is possible to conclude that the phenomenon of low wages is functionally linked to a dynamic of export-oriented production, which is determined (limited by) the absorptive capacity of external rather than domestic demand: low wages provide a disincentive for the productive investment of surplus value and favours the unproductive consumption by capital.

4 The Politics of Community-based Participatory Development

1. On this 'Golden Age of Capitalism' see Marglin and Schor (1990).
2. The 'grand theory' of the discipline revolved around the dynamics of the economic growth process, with reference to its driving force, and the

facilitating and inhibiting conditions. At the centre of this theory was the notion that economic growth was predicated on increasing the rate of savings and investment – the stock of physical and social capital – to a 'take-off' point; and the active role of the state in the mechanism of this increase and in directing investment of capital towards industry, providing its infrastructure and the modernization of its institutional framework. On variations and the evolution of this 'grand theory' see, inter alia, Meier and Seers (1984) and Hunt (1989).

3. In the mainstream of development studies, theory and practice ranged between two forms of analysis: liberalism, which in its various forms was predicated on the efficient operation of the free market (laissez-faire capitalism) and structuralism, which presupposed and advocated an active interventionist role for the state in terms of planning and directing the development process. See Colclough and Manor (1991) on the precepts and theoretical models advanced within these two frameworks. In addition to these two forms of analysis in the dominant paradigm there also existed a less central tradition represented by advocates of a Political economy approach and a radical orientation towards social change or transformation of the underlying capitalist system. On this see, inter alia, Wilbur and Jameson (1978/1989).

4. See its 1975 Report (*Another Development*) and the subsequent publication of issues of its journal, *Development Dialogue*.

5. The conditions of this structural economic crisis, and of the associated crisis of Keynesianism and the welfare state, what O'Connor (1973) termed a 'fiscal crisis', led to the formulation of diverse theories. See Marglin and Schor (1990); Aglietta (1979, 1982) and Lipietz (1982, 1987).

6. On this shift in developing thinking and practice in the heyday of liberal reform, and associated models of Growth-with-equity and the Basic Needs strategy, see, inter alia, Hunt (1989).

7. These alternative approaches make up a multi-faceted intellectual movement with diverse points of reference and formulations, with literally thousands of centres of publication and dissemination. Under the rubric of AD are found approaches that are 'people-centred' (Korten), 'articipatory' (UNRISD, Goulet, Rahman), 'human-in-scale' (Max-Neef), 'people-led', 'from below', 'human' (UNDP), and 'equitable' (ECLAC). These approaches also intersect with 'populist' ideas formulated, inter alia, by the ILO and development economists like Schumacher and Lipton.

8. There are numerous alternative formulations of this concept, most notably by the UNDP in its annual Human Development Report. The concept of human development as the expansion of choice available to the individual can be traced back to an intellectual project formulated by the *philosophes* of the eighteenth century Enlightenment, a project based on the ideals (and rallying calls to revolution) of reason, freedom, and equality. On empowerment as the central concept of Another Development see Friedmann (1992).

9. On this point, among numerous studies in the Latin American context see Castro Arze and Lea Plaza (1996); Fox and Hernandez (1992); Marcos (1996); and UNICEF (1988).

Notes 169

10. See Goulet (1989), Rahman (1993), Stiefel and Wolfe (1994).
11. See the formulations of Max-Neef, Elizalde and Hopenhayen (1965) and Korten (1995) as well as Rahman (1991).
12. In general terms, the search for AD was associated with diverse approaches that coalesced around these principles. They included an emphasis on the importance of 'appropriate technology, the importance of small-scale enterprise both because of its greater economic efficiency and employment-generating and absorptive capacity (ILO, 1976) and its human-scale (Max-Neef), 'ethno-development based on respect for indigenous techno-knowledge and culture (and support for the institution of a pluri-ethnic state), 'gender and social equity', 'environmental sustainability' (or, after the Bruntland Report 'sustainable development)', development that is 'auto-centric', 'self-reliant' and above all 'human-centred' and 'people-led' or 'participatory' in form.
13. UNRISD undertook a series of investigations and organized a series of conferences on this theme between 1979 and 1984. On this see Stiefel and Wolfe (1994). In 1982, the UN organized in Lubljana an international seminar on Popular Participation, and expanded on the idea that effective and authentic participation required action 'from below' rather than 'from above' (Wolfe, 1984). In subsequent years, this theme was expanded and reworked in the context of an International Conference on Popular Participation in the Process of African Recovery and Development (Arusha, Tanzania 1990), a Seminar on Participatory Development (UNICEF, Florence 1990), and a series of seminars, conferences and publications of ECLAC, UNDP, as well as the World Bank (Wolfe, 1984, 1991).
14. Toye (1987).
15. These policies of structural adjustment, formulated by World Bank economists, with a consensus of a host of Washington-based institutions (Williamson, 1990), as of 1982 were explicitly combined with traditional IMF stabilization policies to constitute a 'reform package' imposed on any government seeking or requiring the renegotiation of its external debt or access to new capital. The literature on these SAPs and SALs is voluminous.
16. See, inter alia, Veltmeyer, Petras and Vieux (1997) and Woodward (1992).
17. The evidence provided by the few systematic comparative studies initiated or conducted by the IMF is ambiguous. An internal study by the IMF comparing countries subject to SAP and those that are not found no systematic correlation beyond a general tendency for non-recipient countries to perform better than recipient countries. The only Latin American country that has experienced a relatively sustained recovery of economic growth is Chile, but it was not until 1992 that Chile managed to recover the capacity lost in the deep recessions of 1974–75 and 1981–82. On this see Collins and Lear (1995) and Leiva and Petras (1994).
18. The authors have argued elsewhere that a restructuring of the capital–labour relation has been the major mechanism for internal adjustment of countries in Latin America. This restructuring was expressed in the decline of wages as a share of both national income and value added to manufacturing production, the conversion of a greater share of national income into capital, and the decomposition of this capital. As for the

share of wages in national income for many countries in the 1980s it was reduced from the share of wages in value added experienced a similar decline. In many cases (Brazil, Chile, Peru...) the share of wages was reduced to under 20 per cent, a level that competes with China (15 per cent in 1993) and Ghana for the lowest relative unit costs of labour in the world. On the recomposition of financial capital in Latin America see, inter alia, Morales (1992) and Petras and Veltmeyer (1995).

19. In many countries like Argentina and Mexico wages lost over 60 per cent of their real value as the result of neoliberal reforms in the 1980s and 1990s. According to el Centro de Analisis y Proyecciones Economicas para Mexico the compression of wages in Mexico over the course of fourteen years of crisis and structural reform was so brutal as to set the country back three decades in terms of the loss of purchasing power (*La Jornada*, 11 December, 1996: 47). As a result of this compression, reflected in the decline of per capita household income, most countries in the region by 1993 had not yet recovered a standard of living achieved in 1980 and in a number of cases in 1970.

20. The statistics on this polarization are dramatic. Prior to the structural reforms of the 1980s, Latin America as a region exhibited the greatest income distribution disparities in the world – the ratio of income received by the top 20 per cent of households on average being over ten times that of the poorest 20 per cent and in a number of cases up to 26 times greater (in the case of Brazil), as compared to an average ratio of 4.5-6/1 for countries such as Taiwan or South Korea and the OECD group, or for that matter Subsaharan Africa (Veltmeyer, 1997b). But these disparities were extended and deepened, leading to an even greater polarization, in the 1980s and 1990s, and, as a result, the sprouting of a handful of super-rich billionaires on the one pole and a massive number of people living in abject poverty on the other. On this polarization see, inter alia, Lustig (1995), Morley (1995), and Vuskovic (1993).

21. ECLAC-UNDP data, cited in *Latin American Special Reports* (SR-92-5), Oct. 1992.

22. Walton and Seddon (1994) and Veltmeyer, Petras and Vieux (1997).

23. See, inter alia, the 1991 annual report of IDB. By 1996, after the showcase experience of the Zapatista rebellion in Chiapas and the emergence of new guerrilla groups in several states of Mexico and elsewhere, the Commander-in-Chief of the US armed forces in the region added his voice to the chorus of concern from international investors, international organizations and governments.

24. *Finance & Development* (1992).

25. One of the clearest and most systematic expositions of this 'new paradigm' can be found in the 1991 Annual report of the Inter-American Bank, the institution that has assumed responsibility for ensuring the implementation of the SAP in Latin America. But see also the 1991 World Bank's World Development Report and the 1992 report on world poverty by the International Fund for Agricultural Development (Chapter 2, 'The New Paradigm of Development' provides a succinct summary exposition of the thinking behind the new development model). Also see

the 1994 Report of the International Commission on Peace and Food. The political agenda behind the new development model is not normally articulated but see the IDB and WB Reports of 1991, which point towards the political dimension of the IMF's 'New Understanding' as the need to give SAPs a 'human face'. For UNICEF it was a matter of principle: to protect the most vulnerable groups in society from the brutal effects of free market policies. However, the IDB and World Bank Reports of 1991 suggest that the primary concern for revision of the SAP was political: the need to defuse widespread social discontent and avoid its political mobilization, viz. its destabilizing effects in terms of a hospitable investment climate and continued commitment by the political regimes in the region to the SAP.

26. On various permutations of the ECLAC/CEPAl model see ECLAC (1990, 1992) and CEPAL (1987, 1988, 1989, 1991). Also see the work of Sunkel (1991a, 199b), one of the chief architects of this CEPAL model based a reworking of the structuralist principles that had characterized CEPAL's thinking for over thirty years. The new approach, 'neostructuralism', had its most definitive expression in ECLAC's proposal for 'productive transformation-with-equity', a reworked update of the 'growth-with-equity' approach of the 1970s, based on the acceptance of and convergence with the neoliberal model of the World bank (according to a personal communication). In its 1990 formulation, ECLAC proposed: (i) the systematic incorporation of technical advances in the production apparatus (productive transformation), to achieve thereby international competitiveness; (ii) arresting and reversing the tendency for falling wages, to both strengthen the domestic market and achieve a measure of social equity. As ECLAC sees it, the necessary conditions for this productive transformation with equity is pluralist and participatory democracy, allowing the state to respond to the needs of the poor, and providing diverse social actors a voice and a fair share in the distribution of productive resources and income. As Wolfe (1984, 1988, 1991, 1996), has observed, ECLAC theorists questioned the capacity of the state at the national level to implement equitable policies, arguing the necessity for a more decentralized, community-based and participatory form of development. In this context, ECLAC defines 'participation' as more than traditionally understood (as 'access to collective decision-making'), but as 'control over their own situation and life project (as a social actor) by intervening in the initiatives and actions that affect the vital context in which this situation and project unfolds'. (CEPAL, 1991: 8).

27. The incorporation of women into the development process in the 1970s was formulated and came to be understood as an absolute principle and in such terms was formulated as a condition of access to any project or programme funding by the World Bank and other bilateral and multilateral development agencies. By now, the bibliography on this issue is immense but the basic reasoning behind this policy is that women because of their stategic position *vis-à-vis* food and subsistence production and the social institutions of basic health service, primary education, and family welfare, needed to be incorporated into the development process both as a social subject and beneficiary for economic and social reasons. As for the

poor, studies by UNICEF (Cornia et al., 1987), demonstrated that together with women and children who made up an estimated 75 per cent of the population, they were the most affected and the most vulnerable social category and group in society vis-à-vis the painful adjustment process that every society was experiencing. It was clear that policies had to be devised to protect them from naked market forces and to ensure a measure or minimum level of welfare, alleviating the worst effects. As for 'participation' it was viewed primarily as a matter of dialogue and partnership with local governments and intermediary non-government organization. The concept of 'participation' in this model is also formulated in the context of changing the relationship between the state and civil society, democratizing political institutions at each level. This concept was advanced and extensively discussed at the International Conference on Public Policy, Popular Participation and Social Development organized by UNESCO in Bologna, December 1992.

28. One of the most clear and systematic formulations of this model was presented in the 1991 Annual report of the IDB.

29. Modelled on Bolivia's Economic Emergency Fund set up in 1985, the NSP generally has taken the form of a social investment fund (SIF), financed primarily by the multilateral financial institutions and UN agencies, and, except in the case of Chile, placed under the control of the President's office. With its inception in Bolivia, SIFs were set up in Mexico (Pronasol) and Chile (FOSIS) in 1989–90 and soon thereafter in virtually every country in the region. These SIFs were implemented within the framework of the World Bank's new model for social policy based on three principles: (i) 'targeting' the poor (ii) privatization of social services and (iii) decentralization (partnership with local governments and NGOs).

30. As pointed out by Friedmann (1992) the concept of 'empowerment' central to Another Development, has been appropriated by the World Bank and the UN operating agencies as a critical element of their discourse. Indeed even Ronald Reagan in the office of US President used the term, quite emptying it of its intrinsic meaning as given it the search for Another Development.

31. These conditions, reflected in a trend towards increased disparities in the distribution of income and an extension of various forms and degrees of poverty, have been extensively documented and analyzed in the Latin American context. See, inter alia, Kliksberg (1993), Lustig (1995), Veltmeyer, Petras and Vieux (1997), Vuskovic (1993) and Woodward (1992).

32. On this process, which in the Latin American context can be dated from 1979 (Ecuador) to 1989 (Chile), see, Stepan (1988), Petras and Vieux (1994), and Touraine (1989).

33. The literature on the SAP in Latin America, in terms of its implementation and social impacts, is voluminous, but see Veltmeyer, Petras and Vieux (1997).

34. The objective conditions of this development are reflected in a dramatic shift in the relative shares of labour and capital and labour in national income and value added in the production process, and further reflected in a significant transformation of the working class. For some reason, the

objective conditions of this shift and transformation although well understood, have been documented only with respect to changes in forms of labour and working conditions, and have not been systematically analyzed either in macro-economic terms (changes in the structure of production and the shift in income participation shares) or in sociological terms (changes in the class and social structure).

35. On this Popular Economy see Razeto (1985).
36. The literature on the dynamics of this 'informal sector' of the urban economy in Latin America and elsewhere is voluminous. Inter alia see Infante and Tokman (1994).
37. Guerra Rodriguez (1994).
38. See Blaikie (1985) on this point.
39. On this redemocratization process in Latin America see, inter alia, Stepan (1988) and Petras and Vieux (1994).
40. Although scholars who have studied and reported on these developments do not establish the dynamics of the process it is likely that various regional, if not local, government organizations and organizations of civil society generated pressure and demand for these changes, although it is equally probable that the World Bank and the IDB, as in neighbouring Ecuador and Venezuela, and in both Bolivia and Chile, were directly involved in pushing its new strategy of partnership with local governments and intermediary institutions. The issue clearly needs further closer study.
41. Castro Arze and Lea Plaza (1996)
42. Carrion (1996: 142).
43. In this respect see the Ley Organica de la Administración Publica Federal, the Ley de Planificación, Programa de Descentralización de la Administración Pública Federal; and in 1993 the Convenios Unicos de Desarrollo CID-COTESU-MCTH (1993).
44. CID-COTESU-MCTH (1993).
45. It is estimated by INEGI, the National Statistics Institute, that there exists 1500 or so such communities with a high marginality index and characterized by a high incidence of extreme poverty. It includes over 1500 municipalities (58 per cent of the total number), encompassing 24 million people – and 78 per cent of the country's indigenous peoples (Sedesol, *Regiones Prioritarias*; *La Jornada*, Noviembre 11, 1996: 23). Together with FOSIS in Chile, the now-abandoned Pronasol has been considered a model of the NSP in Latin America. For an evaluation of its impacts see Laurell (1994).
46. On these initiatives and innovative experiments in self-sufficient local democracy see Cabrero (1995).
47. Within a year of the Law's promulgation, 10 500 OTBs had been legally recognized. The critical issue, as with the 1979 Constitution in Peru, is the legal recognition of traditionally constituted forms of organization and communities as OTBs for the purpose of municipalization of local power. In Peru, the 1979 constitution at least recognized the existence of peasant and indigenous communities – the new 1993 constitution makes no reference to them whatsoever – allowing them to participate as such in the Regional Assemblies. Unfortunately, real power was not placed or

did not reside in these assemblies but in the Regional Councils in which these communities did not participate. Thus, as in Bolivia through one means or another the power of decision-making, and the purse, is channelled into political units where the Central government is able to meet – and control – the community (see Marcos, 1993, 1994; Olivera *et al.*, 1991).
48. Veltmeyer (1997a).
49. For a similar argument with respect to Peru see Marcos (1993).
50. The Popular Participation Law applies only to locally applicable social issues, political issues being the province and sphere of action for the political parties.
51. The Mexican Association of Municipalities (AMMAC) conducted a public campaign in the form of a public letter (newspaper ad) addressed to the Chamber of Federal Deputy, and coordinated with the Association of Presidents of Democratic Municipalities, to convince the legislature if not the executive to implement the protocol agreement laid out in the document '20 Contracts for Democracy' signed by the government (*La Jornada*, December 5, 1996: 40). An article of agreement was to increase the municipalities' share of public funds from its current level of 4 per cent to 20 per cent.
52. This point is argued, with substantial evidence by Marcos (1993, 1994) and various contributors to Olivera *et al.* (1991) in the case of Peru. See also Veltmeyer (1997a).
53. On the class relations and divisions within traditional communities see Breman (1994), Rus (1995), Smith (1991) and Wolfe (1996).
54. In this context, it is easier for an Aymara like Victor Hugo Cardenas to sit next to the President, as vice-president, in a cabinet meeting than for an indigenous person to sit in a Consejo Municipal de pueblo.
55. Guimaraes (1989).
56. ECLAC (1990).
57. Sunkel (1991a, 1991b).

5 The Dynamics of Neoliberal Electoral Politics

1. A 1996 study by ECLAC concludes that poverty, unemployment and various other social problems plaguing the region had either worsened or remained unchanged during the last decade of market reforms. See Gabriel Escobar, 'Latin America's Poor Not Helped by Reforms', *Washington Post*, April 13, 1996, p. A15. Another recent United Nations study observed, somewhat ironically, that during 'a period of economic recovery' (1985–90), the incidence of poverty in Latin America rose from 23 to 28 per cent (UNDP, 1992, 1996: 60).
2. On the Belaunde and Garcia presidencies, (see Rudolph, 1992).
3. 'Brazil's democracy in the balance', *Washington Report on the Hemisphere*, December 7, 1988, p. 4.
4. 'No end to Perez's misfortunes in sight', *Washington Report on the Hemisphere*, June 17, 1992, p. 5.

5. 'Menem speeds reform for Argentine vote', *Washington Report on the Hemisphere*, June 25, 1993, p. 1.
6. 'Menem's second term off to a rocky start', *Washington Report on the Hemisphere*, August 18, 1995, p. 4.
7. Guillermo Rochabrun, 'Deciphering the enigmas of Alberto Fujimori', *NACLA Report on the Americas*, July/August 1996, p. 17.
8. Manuel Castillo Ochoa, 'Fujimori and the business class', in *Ibid.*, p. 27.
9. 'Free markets spur political upheaval', *Washington Report on the Hemisphere*, April 12, 1996, p. 6.
10. Ochoa, 'Fujimori and the business class', p. 27.
11. 'Region begins new privatization drive', *Latin American Regional Reports: Andean Group*, May 23, 1996, p. 4.
12. 'Economic problems in Argentina', *Washington Report on the Hemisphere*, September 21, 1996, pp. 1, 6; 'Menem Toughs it Out' *Latin American Monitor: Southern Cone*, October 1996, p. 4; 'Menem unmoved by general strike', *Latin American Weekly Report*, October 10, 1996, p. 458.
13. 'Official: incomes pattern is worse', *Latin American Weekly Report*, February 1, 1996, p. 47.
14. Howard LaFranchi, 'Argentines Dig Up Dirt That May Bury Reforms', *Christian Science Monitor (International Weekly Edition)*, December 13–19, 1996, p. 6.
15. Argentina's new labour squeeze', *Latin American Regional Reports: Southern Cone*, October 17, 1996, pp. 4–5.
16. 'Trying to count the unemployed', *Latin American Regional Reports: Andean Group*, June 29, 1995, p. 7.
17. 'Venezuela's weak financial structure', *Washington Report on the Hemisphere*, October 16, 1995, pp. 1, 6; 'Gas and gunpowder', *Washington Report on the Hemisphere*, November 30, 1996, p. 4.
18. 'IMF approves second annual loan', *Latin American Monitor: Andean Group*, May 1996, p. 12.
19. 'Cardoso tries to placate his critics', *Latin American Regional Reports: Brazil*, June 6, 1996, p. 6; 'Two million jobs lost in seven years', *Latin American Regional Reports: Brazil*, July 11, 1996, p. 2.
20. 'How much is still in state hands', *Latin American Regional Reports: Brazil*, September 19, 1996? pp. 4–5; Epstein, 1997:7.
21. 'The uncertain road to Mexican recovery', *Washington Report on the Hemisphere*, May 16, 1996, p. 4; 'Land lessons from Chiapas', *Washington Report on the Hemisphere*, October 9, 1996, p. 5.
22. 'Opposition forces Zedillo to curtail, but not cancel, the petrochemical sell-off', *Latin American Weekly Report*, October 24, 1996, p. 481.
23. 'Cardoso threatens to halt invasions', *Latin American Regional Reports: Brazil*, July 11, 1996, p. 2.
24. 'Joint union protest highlights discontent', *Latin American Weekly Report*, October 24, 1996, pp. 486–487.
25. 'Brazil's landless movement wins support in cities', *NACLA Report on the Americas*, November/December 1996, p. 1. Also see 'MST goes back to direct action', *Latin American Weekly Report*, September 19, 1996, pp. 428–429.
26. 'Agrarian law forced through congress', *Latin American Weekly Report*, October 24, 1996, p. 482.

27. 'FDI Flows but "lumpy"' *Latin American Weekly Report*, October 10, 1996, pp. 462–463.
28. 'Multi-billion dollar underground economy exposed', *Latin American Monitor: Brazil*, September 1996, p 5.

6 New Social Movements in Latin America: The Dynamics of Class and Identity

1. In Guerrero, there have surfaced at least three groups that have resorted to armed struggle. The most important of these is the ERP, which appeared on the first anniversary of a massacre of 17 peasants by government police forces. The ERP also builds on a long tradition of armed struggle in the State.
2. This literature is voluminous, much of it focusing on statements by subcomandante Marcos and the series of declarations made on behalf of the EZLN, all of which were made available nearly instantaneously through the medium of electronic communication and a number of computer-networks that provided a broad international audience almost day-to-day accounts and interpretations of the process that the EZLN was engaged in. With respect to this electronic communication and networking of scholars and supporters all across the world, the Chiapas rebellion is seen by some as the most novel social movement to have appeared in recent years, the bearer of the form that social struggles will take in the twenty-first century, at least with respect to the factor of international support and solidarity networks among people all over the world able to intellectually engage the Zapatista struggle through their laptops and desktops in their offices.
3. In the analysis – and 'grand theory' – provided by the pioneers of development economics (see Meier and Seers, 1984), economic progress or 'growth' is generally associated with the process of accumulation of physical (and social) capital, on the basis of increasing the rate of savings (to a critical or 'take-off' point), and investing these savings in capital-intensive industry, inducing a process of industrialization (and an associated structural transformation), modernization and capitalist development (the institution of wage labour and the market, regulated or freely operating). On the postulates and propositions – the body of grand theory – produced in the immediate post-war period (the 1950s and 1960s) and the subsequent period of reworking and a counter-revolution in theory and policy, see, inter alia, Meier and Seers (1984) and Hunt (1991).
4. Whereas the strictly economic dimension of modernization is reflected in the indicator of growth in per capita output (see the World Bank's annual World Development Report), this dimension of 'development' or 'modernization' has both an economic and a political aspect, the conditions of which are reflected in the concept of 'human development' formulated by the UNDP (see its annual Human Development Report) as 'increased capacity to make choices, to realize the individual's human potential, a concept that in turn reflects the Enlightenment ideal of 'freedom' and the need to be freed from limiting or oppressive conditions.

Notes 177

5. While economists and political theorists have tended to focus on the economic and political dimensions of the modernization process, Sociologists have tended to focus on this dimension of the process, with reference to the idea of 'equality' (in the context of the nineteenth century labour struggles against exploitation and of women and other groups of individuals for the suffrage and political participation) or 'equity' (in the context of contemporary development).
6. Although these developments are conceived of, and taken up, as an intellectual and political project, that is, as the result of specific actions taken to a pre-defined end, most scholars view them as the product of a 'process'. That is, the workings of a 'system', 'objectively given structural conditions' which operate on people in terms of their position within the system on the basis of its 'laws', which are grasped by scientific analysis. Whether these 'laws' (and the objectively given conditions which they specify) are determining factors in historical developments or whether actions of individuals on the basis of ideas and ideals are determining has always been – and remains – a central theoretical problem of sociological analysis.
7. Analysis of this aspect of the modernization process was the specific contribution of sociology, made within the theoretical perspective and analytical framework of structural-functionalism established in particular by Talcott Parsons. On this contribution, and specifically the theory of modernization, see, inter alia, Hoogvelt (1984), and, in particular, Frank (1987).
8. In the analysis of this process in different contexts it is often assumed that there is fundamentally but one road to modernity (industrialization technological transformation, capitalist development, social and cultural transformation, and democratization), with lots of variations, paths and sidetracks (see, for example, Hobsbawm 1984).
9. Cited in Meiksins Wood (1995: 1). See also Daniel Bell in *The End of Ideology* (1960), subtitled: 'On the Exhaustion of Political Ideas in the 1950s'. As Bell saw it: 'all universalistic, humanuistic ideologies of the nineteenth century, especially Marxian socialism, are exhausted'.
10. The sociology of development, by definition, was advanced by those who fundamentally believed in the existence of a process of development – of incremental change and the accumulation and unfolding of conditions of social transformation. Of course, theorists and practitioners (analysts) were divided paradigmatically between those whose point of departure was a theory of modernization and those whose analysis was predicated on variations of a theory formulated by Marx. Variations of these two schools of thought and theories dominated the sociology of development throughout the 1960s, the 1970s and the 1980s.
11. Booth (1985); Corbridge (1990); Schuurman (1993).
12. Toye (1987).
13. This consensus (see Williamson, 1990) took the form of a programme of stabilization and structural adjustment measures (liberalization, privatization, deregulation, austerity and downsizing/modernization of the State), formulated by the economists of the World Bank and the IMF as loan conditionalities imposed on borrowing countries. On these measures, the

thinking behind them and their impacts, see, inter alia, Bello (1994), Korten (1995), Veltmeyer, Petras and Vieux (1997), Woodward (1993).
14. For some unknown reason, there does not yet exist a systematic review and examination of this wide-ranging and multifaceted intellectual movement of Another Development. A more radical resolution of this crisis within development theory is expressed in Sachs (1992), contributors of which more or less share the view that development, as a concept, as an intellectual project, and in practice, is a misbegotten enterprise that, as Deepak Lal and other neoliberal critics of development economics argued from a radically opposed perspective, is 'bad' for 'developing countries'.
15. Post-structuralism, like its main object of criticism, structuralism, and the currently dominant form of political economy, regulationism, is a French school of thought, with both philosophical and sociological formulations that have become intellectually fashionable. See in particular Baudrillard (1983), Derrida (1982) and Lyotard (1987), and more ambiguously, Michel Foucault (1986). As far as far as Marxism and the identification and analysis of 'new social movements' is concerned of particular importance are the reflections of Laclau (1985, 1989, 1990, 1995), a former exponent of structural Marxism in the form of a modes of production approach, which in the late 1970s was the major Marxist alternative to Latin American dependency theory.
16. Among the clearest expositions of the logic of structural analysis in its Marxist form are the writings of Louis Althusser, the object of intense debate and criticism in the 1970s. On this debate see, inter alia, Banet (1989) and Veltmeyer (1978).
17. The tendency of this form of analysis to dissolve in thought conditions that are 'real' is clearly and dramatically reflected in a remark by Gayatri Chakravorty Spivak, a translator of Derrida, at a seminar at the pembroke Center for Teaching and Research on Women, at Brown University (March 1988, cited by Nugent, 1995: 124–125): 'class is the purest form of signifier', implying that class is but a linguistic symbol with no concrete referent in the material world. In this post-structuralist discourse, the idea of class as a structure is just that: an idea imposed on but no basis in the immediacy of lived or experienced reality.
18. The intellectual antecedents and the range of ideas encompassed by 'postmodernism' is subject to debate and interpretation, but it has basically has two centres of reference: a set of conditions associated with the culture of late-capitalist society – postmodernism as condition (Harvey, 1989; Jameson, 1991), and as a new form of knowledge and analysis (Derrida, Lyotard, Baudrillard, Foucault) based on what we would interpret as an idealist epistemology that in social analysis can be traced back to some extent to German historicism (Dilthey, etc.) and the Frankfurt School and beyond that to German historicism (Dilthey, etc.), Nietzchian nihilism and irrationalism, the Early Works of Marx and a philosophy enunciated in different ways by Kant and Hegel. On this see Veltmeyer (1979).
19. Postmodernism in this form (Lyotard, 1987; Baudrillard, 1983) not only rejects the 'grand narratives', 'totalising' ideas or 'meta-theories' – reflected

in liberal and socialist ideologies and appeals to universal standards such as progress, freedom, humanity, justice, and equality – but gives up any idea of an intelligible historic process and causality, and with it any idea of 'making history'. There are no structured process accesible to human knowledge; there are only, as Derrida (1982) emphasizes, disconnected, anarchic, and inexplicable 'differences'.

20. See, for example, Escobar and Alvarez (1992), Scott (1985), Slater (1985), Camacho and Menjivar (1989).
21. There are diverse formulations of this concept, which can be, and in analysis is, contrasted with the central concept of Marxist analysis – class. See Touraine (1984, 1988), whose formulations have been absorbed by or is central to the analysis of many Latin American sociologists (see, for example, Tironi and Lagos, 1981).
22. This principle is diametrically opposed to the first principle (objectivity) of historical materialism, formulated by Marx as the idea that 'in the process of social production, people enter into relations that are indispensable and independent of their will...that correspond to stages in the development of the material forces of society...and to which correspond certain forms of consciousness...which, in general, are determined by the form {objective conditions} of {people's} social existence'. In this context, despite the protestations or obfuscation of some, and of other attempts to actually combine materialism and postmodernism, the former, we would argue, is fundamentally idealist in its epistemology and form of analysis, denying the objectivity of the conditions of social existence and of class relations generated by the workings of a system.
23. This principle of structural determination, which is critical to Marxism as social science, is fundamentally antithetical to postmodernism, the main object of its theoretical and methodological critique of Marxism.
24. For a critique of this appropriation by the World Bank of the concept of a moral economy developed by Scott (1976, 1985) see Breman (1996).
25. These conditions, reflected in a trend towards increased disparities in the distribution of income and an extension of various forms and degrees of poverty, have been extensively documented and analyzed in the Latin American context. See Kliksberg (1993), Lustig (1995), Veltmeyer, Petras and Vieux (1997), Vuskovic (1993) and Woodward (1992).
26. On this redemocratization process, which in the Latin American context can be dated precisely from 1979 (Ecuador) to 1989 (Chile), see Stepan (1988), Diamond et al. (1989), Petras and Vieux (1994), and Touraine (1989).
27. The literature on the SAP in Latin America, in terms of its implementation and social impacts, is voluminous. Inter alia, see Veltmeyer, Petras and Vieux (1987).
28. The objective conditions of this development are reflected in a dramatic shift in the relative shares of labour and capital and labour in national income and value added in the production process, and further reflected in a significant transformation of the working class. For some reason, the objective conditions of this shift and transformation although well understood, have been documented only with respect to changes in forms of labour and working conditions, and have not been systematically analyzed

either in macro-economic terms (changes in the structure of production and the shift in income participation shares) or in sociological terms (changes in the class and social structure).
29. On this process see, inter alia, Veltmeyer, Petras and Vieux (1997).
30. See, inter alia, Escobar and Alvarez (1992), Hunter (1995), Muro and Canto Chac (1991).
31. Fairly well documented and systematic case studies of these movements can be found in Eckstein (1989) and Dominguez (1994). However, neither discuss the theoretical issues involved in the construction of new social movements. Escobar and Alvarez (1992) do, but in their focus on the new cultural dimensions of Latin American social movements they fail to conceptualize and ignore (theoretically reject) the resurgence of class-based social movements. Theoretically, the most ambitious comparative study of new Latin American movements is Assies *et al.* (1991), although like most studies of new social movements the focus is entirely on the urban question.
32. In the worst phase of the Pinochet dictatorship in Chile, the *colonos* of the '*poblaciones*', the shantytowns formed on the periphery of Santiago and other cities, confronted the military police in direct street action and led the political struggle of resistance and opposition abandoned by the political parties and unions that had been banned, broken up or placed in recess by the regime (Petras and Leiva, 1986; Tironi and Lagos, 1991). At the beginning of the 1980s, in Argentina pobladores in large marginal zones that are referred to 'gran Buenas Aires' organized themselves in the form of mutual – or neighbourhood associations to demand the legalization of the land which they had 'occupied' and help in building houses and accessing electrical, water, and sewage services. Soon thereafter, the urban poor took to the streets in the very centre of Buenas Aires and to government buildings downtown to press these demands in the form of direct action and confrontation with the police and the army which the government had called into service. In Chile and Peru, and elsewhere, similar popular economic organizations were formed to set up communal soup kitchens, and survival and defence systems for the poor, as well as organizations to press political demands of various sorts, including the restoration of democracy and to do so on the basis of direct action. On these struggles of the urban poor inter alia, see Garcia Delgado and Silva (1985), Fara (1985), Petras and Leiva (1986), Jacobi (1985), Moises and Kowarick (1981). A more global view of this process can be found in Hardoy and Portes (1984).
33. Together with the urban poor generally, women were the major protagonists of these urban local struggles. On this protagonism, and the self-constitution of women as a new social actor, see, inter alia, Barrig (1987); Del Carmen Feijoo and Gogna (1985), Saffioti and Ferrante (1985); Escobar (1985); Prieto (1985); Molina (1986); Prates and Rodriguez (1985). On these diverse struggles see also Delgado and Silva (1985) and Zambrano (1987).
34. See, for example, Rufino dos Santos (1985); Vives (1985). These ethnic struggles can be placed into two categories: oriented towards the demand for cultural and ethnic 'identity', mostly within an urban context (see Calderon,

1987) and those oriented towards social and national liberation, the vindication of their economic rights and demands. Many of these diverse struggles took place in the countryside and more often than not were combined with the peasant movement and its class organizations. See, inter alia, Chiriboga (1985) and Calderon and Jelin (1987).
35. Although rarely analyzed in these terms, youth constituted a major element of the street and neighbourhood struggles of the urban poor and for local democracy throughout the 1980s.
36. A year after the 1976 military coup in Argentina, las Madres de la Plaza de Mayo (still active 20 years later on the basis of a now generalized highly radical and militant opposition to the neoliberal economic model as well as demand for the redress of human rights violations, political immunity, and corruption) provided the first marches against the dictatorship at a time when neither parties or unions had the capacity or were able to muster the resources to combat the military regime, to resist its hardline policy of repression, assassination and 'disappearances' – up to 30 000, according to Human Rights organizations.
37. One of the more obvious and critical changes wrought by conditions and government policies in the 1980s was in the form, organization and conditions of work related to a change in the structure of the urban working class. Salient features of this change include the growth and proliferation of informalization, characterized by the predominance of work 'on one's own account' (self-employment), payment on commission, the lack of or short-term contracts, and the absence or inoperability of government regulation or social protection. Numerous studies by ECLAC, the ILO and various generations of sociologists (as well as a few economists) have determined that in the 1980s jobs in the industrial sector (manufacturing and construction) as well as government service, the backbone of the 'traditional' working class – and what have been labelled 'good jobs' (well-paying, offered on indefinite full-time contracts) – suffered an absolute decline and that the 'informal sector' accounted for the vast bulk if not 100 per cent of the job growth. At a regional level, in 1980 the informal sector constituted around a third of all jobs; by the end of the 1980s, they constituted over 40 per cent – an incredible growth, with considerable social – and political – ramifications. The critical structural – and political – feature of these changes is the shift from the factory and office to the streets. As far as political conflict and acts of protest are concerned, the demands of the 'new' working class no longer are concerned with wages and working conditions but have tended to revolve around the issues of physical space, the right of 'vendedores callejeros or ambulantes to work the streets, and the distribution of licenses to sell goods or operate taxis or buses, etc. These demands have also formed the nucleus of the struggles of plumbers, electricians, shoemakers, and the producers of such 'traded services'. Apart from such 'work-related issues, this new urban working class, who make up the bulk of the "new urban poor" (the 40 million or so that have been added to official register of the poor in Latin America since 1982), tends to mobilize around consumption-issues (the price of fuel, public transportation, food, etc., affected by government policy – austerity measures, etc'.

38. On these new social movements see, inter alia, Slater (1985); Escobar and Alvarez (1992).
39. Jelin (1990); Waylen, (1993).
40. Chiriboga (1992); Van Cott, (1994).
41. On this critical aspect of new social movements, see Scott (1985), Herzon et al. (1986), Borja et al. (1989), Tovar (1987).
42. Scott (1985).
43. In Camacho and Menjivar (1989).
44. Calderon (1995) attempts to explain the decline of class analyzes in studies of social movements in South America and the continued (and even increasing) importance of class in studies of social movements in Central America in terms of a political condition (the relative stability of the former and the upheavals in the latter). However, this is a very superficial explanation, and they avoid coming to terms with the serious theoretical issues involved in explaining the political dimensions of the economic and social restructuring process undergone in South America, the objective conditions of which could explain the forms that conflict and the politics of resistance and opposition, and social movements took. This analysis, like an analysis of the changes wrought in the social and class structures, have not been undertaken and very much needs to be.
45. In Mexico today there have been identified by the government itself as marginal zones, characterized by conditions of extreme poverty (low income, malnutrition, illiteracy, lack of adequate housing and access to electrical power and other services, etc.). 70 per cent of the country's estimated 14 million indigenous people are found in these zones, the largest number of which are found in Chiapas, Oaxaca, Guerrero, precisely the states with the highest proportions of indigenous population, and, as it happens, in the case of Chiapas, with the greatest concentration of natural resources such as hydroelectric power.
46. At least 60 per cent of indigenous 'peasants' have been converted into *jornaleros*, a semi-proletariat, dependent on both access to land and some form of wage labour. A similar penetration of indigenous communities and society by capitalism, and with it the state, occurred in other parts of Mexico and throughout the region. Another anthropologist, Frans Schryer, has studied the impact of such penetration in Hidalgo, with reference in this case not to coffee-growing but cattle-raising. As in Greenberg's account of developments in Chiapas, the penetration of capital and capitalism, the institutions of money and the market, is seen by Schryer as a source of intra-community conflict that combined with equally rampant inter-community forms of conflict. In the context of these conflicts, Schryer's study, like Greenberg's, and Benjamin's, demonstrates that although class is modified by a complex matrix of other factors within a peasant community, it remains a primary consideration in examining how and why people resist and rebel. The process of conversion of peasants into wage-labourers or landless workers was greatly accelerated by the agrarian reform initiated by Salinas in 1992 in order to modernize the agricultural sector, i.e., expel surplus peasant labour and production, and concentrate arable land

into larger-scale internationally competitive units of profitable and efficient production.
47. In Mexico, for example, at least 70 per cent of the country's estimated 14 million indigenous peoples live in what are officially characterized as 'marginal zones', areas characterized by higher than average indices of low income, malnutrition, illiteracy, and other conditions of poverty such as high rates of child mortality and lack of access to adequate housing, electricity, potable water and other services.
48. Although Chiapas is home to the country's largest hydro-electric and petrochemical plants in the country, the basis of the state and regional economy is ownership and productive use of the land, most of which is controlled by a small number of ranchers and *hacendados*. In the 1930s, during the presidency of Lazaro Cardenas millions of hectares of land was redistributed, raising the number of families on *ejidos*, or collective communal farms, in Chiapas from 710 000 in 1950 to 148 000 in 1970. Nation-wide there were more than 3 million 'beneficiaries' of the land distribution programme arising out of a commitment of the Mexican Revolution and constitutional response to the revolutionary demands of peasants for 'tierra y libertad' in the form of article 27 of the 1917 constitution which promised land reform and the protection of communal landholding. By 1992, on the eve of the constitutional repudiation of the Salinas regime of this revolutionary commitment, opening up the *ejido* to the free market, the 'social sector' of Mexican agriculture controlled more than half of the country's total stock of arable land and accounted for 55 per cent of total domestic production of maize, the subsistence staple of Mexican society. However, in many places, the land so distributed had the poorest soil, and without financial support the productivity of the *ejido* system remained very low, generating a species of agrarian production crisis which motivated the neoliberal regime of Salinas to begin a 'modernization' programme that entailed the expulsion of the inefficient small producer and the conversion of the *ejido* into large export-oriented farms and commercial operations. The indigenous peasant had no role to play in this modern world, creating intense pressures for their very survival, and these pressures were at their most intense in Chiapas, where nearly half of the total land area was controlled by just 6000 ranchers, less than 1 per cent of the population; and these ranchers, together with the big landlords, hired thugs to intimidate the Indians and make them relinquish what remained of their land and either drive them out or convert them into wage labourers. These conditions clearly were 'objective' in their effects, helping to generate the Chiapas uprising.
49. In 1960 the Lacandon forest was home to 12 000 people, but, unable to make a living on the land thousands of peasants were driven into the Lacandon forest. Today the forest, an important centre of the Chiapas rebellion, has 300 000 people (La Botz, 1994, 1995: 6–8), mostly indigenous *jornaleros*.
50. This economy is based on the production and local marketing of corn, the economy of which has been devastated as a direct result of the opening and deregulation of US imports produced under very different technological conditions, with a much higher rate of productivity, lower per

unit costs, and considerable government subsidies, allowing, in fact, Texan producers to dump their surplus product even on the local markets low-scale small producers in Chiapas, with devastating effect. Similar problems exist in other sectors of the economy, such as coffee production, much of which, in the case of Chiapas is in the hands of highly vulnerable small producers (the large producers control the export sector of the country's coffee production, the bulk of which is found in Chiapas) and cattle-raising both in Chiapas, central states like Zacatecas and the northern states.

51. Unlike Burbach (1994), who has interpreted the Zapatista uprising as history's 'the first postmodernist political movement', the Zapatistes are painfully aware of the systemic and structural basis of their struggle. For the Zapatistas there is no question of cultivating their subjectivity, or constructing their identity; the issue for them is how to do battle against a 'system' (defined by them as capitalism in its neoliberal form) and its conditions which are very much experienced as objective in their effects. On this point, see the First Declaration from the Lacandon jungle... and subsequent declarations as well various encounters and forums organized in 1996 'against neoliberalism... and for humanity'.

52. The characterization by Burbach (1994) of the Zapatista uprising as 'a postmodernist political movement' is made with reference to the 'fact' that (although postmodernists like Nietzsche would tend to argue that 'facts do not exist, only interpretations') unlike traditional guerrilla armies of national liberation the EZLN did not 'seek state power' or social transformation, but only 'an authentic or fuller democracy' (which, oddly enough given the illogic of his argument, is one of the defining characteristics of the modernization paradigm and the modernist project). In his postmodernist interpretation Burbach also makes an unspecified reference to the 'new forms of making politics', which is as unilluminating. To speak of 'facts' *vis-à-vis* the EZLN it is clear that there is nothing contextually specific about the Zapatista uprising; it is universalist in its key demands for democracy, freedom, and social justice, and both its organization and politics bespeaks of the structural forces operating not only on indigenous peoples in Chiapas but on indigenous – and other classes of – people all over Latin America and the world. The only possibly meaningful reference to postmodernism in the social movement of the EZLN is its effective use of electronic computer-based communication, which allows for instantaneous transmission all over the world, the same 'postmodern condition' that led the New York Times to characterize the December 1994 financial crisis and meltdown in Mexico as 'the first postmodern financial crisis in history'. Most unilluminating, not to say any more.

53. In the context of its transition from an armed force into a new political force able to speak and negotiate demands on behalf of all indigenous peoples in the country, the EZLN's political demands have also been transmuted from a call for social transformation into a call for full democracy. However, this shift reflects the Zapatistas' effort to open up a political space for civil society, the protagonism of which, it is hoped, will be able to create the conditions for social transformation. That is, the Zapatistas

recognized that in its limited organization and social movement it did not have the resources and the force needed to take over the state, let alone induce a process of social transformation.
54. See, for example, the essays collected by Escobar and Alvarez (1992) and Slater (1985). This line of interpretation of Latin American NSMs through its theoretical formulations seek to resolve the theoretical impasse of which Schuurman (1993) and others speak. The movement in search for Another Development has its origins in the dead-end and impasse reached by proponents of liberalism and structuralism, the two dominant lines of theory and analysis in the field. But the proponents of Another Development are also unable to explain the dynamics of international development and resolve the theoretical crisis, which as Booth (1985) has argued, also, and in particular, has affected Marxist thought.
55. The following analysis makes reference to and is based in part on an as yet unpublished essay by James Petras, who visited Bolivia and Brazil to interview the leaders and rank and file members of these peasant unions and social movements. Reference to the peasant movement in Paraguay is directly taken from Petras' essay.
56. As for the internal dynamics of the MST see Veltmeyer, Petras and Vieux (1997).
57. The history of the MST can be found in Stedile and Frei (1993) and the MST, *Documento Basico do MST* (1994).
58. *Informativo Campesino* (Asuncion), No. 91, April 1996.
59. For some documentation of these struggles see *La Jornada*, 10 August, 1996: 3; Chiapas, No. 2 (Mexico, 1996); *La Jornada*, 19 October, 1996.
60. Interview by Petras of the leader of the *cocaleros*, Evo Morales, June 10, 1996.
61. Interview of regional leaders of the MST taking the first block of the leaders training course, March 19–29, 1995 (Instituto Cajamar, São Paulo).
62. Interview by Petras of women landless workers at a conference on Peasant Struggles in the Countryside, Cajamar, São Paulo, June 22, 1996.
63. MST, National Office. *Como Organizar a la Masa São Paulo* (1991); *Documento Basico do MST*. São Paulo, 1994. The authors have taken part in a number of visits and short courses offered at the National Leaders Training School at Caceres, Santa Catarina.
64. Hernandez (1992) and Mejia and Sarmiento Silva (1987), among others have noted the profoundly democratic character of the leadership in Latin America peasant movements, which is also reflective of indigenous values and forms of organization.
65. The conditions in question (they are not at issue) are reflected in the well-known facts of the state's high incidence of marginality and poverty, that correlate with the relatively high proportion of indigenous peoples in the population and their dependence on agriculture, in both cases the highest in the country. As for these conditions – which are not at all specific to the state, merely more concentrated – 19 per cent of the economically active population receive no income at all, another 40 per cent earn less than the federally mandated minimum wage of $3.30 a day, and another 15 per cent earn only twice this amount, resulting in an average

per capita income that is a little more than 50 per cent of the national average. A third of the population is illiterate, without access to health care or electricity (in a state that accounts for more than 25 per cent of the country's source of electric power); and the conditions of poverty are endemic and widespread. Samuel Ruiz, the controversial bishop of San Cristobal estimates that in the year leading up to the rebellion over 15 000 'indios' died poverty-related of hunger, disease and violence (Roberts, 1994: 10–11).

66. The authors have argued that these peasant-led movements constitute the vanguard of a reconstituted political Left, and as such part of a third-wave of Left politics, the first, in the 1960s and 1970s, based on class organizations (unions, parties) and actions, the second, based on the protagonism of social organizations and social movements in the 1980s.

67. The phase of armed struggle was over in about a week of encounters. Subsequently, the EZLN has constructed and entered a path of negotiations with the government, appeal to civil society for active support and increased protagonism in the struggle for democracy, and conversion into a new political force able to operate on behalf of the country's indigenous peoples at a national level. In this context, the most critical contribution made by the EZLN in the process of its conversion from an armed force into a new political force able to operate at a national level is the formation in 1996 of the *Congreso Nacional Indigena* (CNI), a forum with the capacity of forming a political instrument for uniting the diverse forces of Mexico's indigenous peoples and pressing their collective demands. On the dynamics of this process see, inter alia, Botz (1994).

68. Prior to this 1844 strike of Silesian weavers Marx was at one with his colleagues in intellectual arms (self-proclaimed young or Left Hegelians) in thinking that the 'subject' or 'active force' of social revolution (the emancipation of 'man') was constituted by 'philosophy', the intellectuals like himself, armed with theoretical awareness of what the working class (the proletariat) represented (the alienation or practical negation of the human essence), and that the proletariat constituted its 'object' or material basis. However, in the strike Marx discovered a working class that combined within itself, its own action, the objective and the subjective conditions of social revolution; that was theoretically aware of itself and what it represented (class conscious), leading Marx to formulate his theory of proletarian self-determination, reformulated some fifty years later by Georg Lukacs in his conception of the working class as 'the identical subject-object of history'.

69. Without a doubt, the major significance of the Zapatista rebellion has been to (i) place on the national agenda the long established demands of indigenous people for 'freedom, democracy, and social justice; (ii) to force the government to negotiate a new relationship with the indigenous peoples not just of Chiapas but of the whole country; and (iii) creation of the conditions for the formation of the *Congreso Nacional Indigena*, a forum and a potential political instrument for giving the indigenous people of the country a united force and the basis for concerted political action; and (iv) the creation of a new way of 'doing politics' based on a radical direct internal democracy, which is reflected in among other

developments the subordinate relationship of the military arm of the movement to the civilian arm (the Clandestine Revolutionary Indigenous Committee) composed of representatives from each ethnic community involved in the struggle. However, the rebellion has resonated widely and deeply in the rural sectors of different Latin American societies. For example, In Brazil, a leader of one of the MST's largest operations (the invasion and occupation by over 300 hundred families of Hacienda Formosa in Curionpolis in West Amazonia), said that they had adopted 'Zapatista characteristics' and that 'there is a similarity between us and the Mexican guerrillas in that we are also fighting for social justice' (a highly modernist and universalist demand, we could add) (*Latinoamerica Press* 28, 10, March 21, 1996: 7).

7 Neoliberalism and the Latin American Left: The Search for a Socialist Project

1. As for Mexico, see, for example the words of Michel Camdusses, General-Director of the IMF: 'The IMF is preparing a program that will serve as a framework for assuring the growth of the Mexican economy during the years ahead, … as for the micro-economic details and the development priorities they are matter well taken care of by my friends at the World Bank and the Inter-American Development Bank' (*El Financiero*, 27 September, 1996).
2. In Venezuela, as in Argentina the probable cause of a drastic fall in the value of wages and an increase in poverty, according to the minister of finance, is a marked increase in the rate of unemployment (17 to 20 per cent) and increases in the price of basic commodities (36–50 per cent) (*La Jornada*, 21 October, 1996: 52). The Minister of Finance in Argentina, where unemployment currently has hit 17.1 per cent a little while ago declared in the same terms. In Mexico, the situation is the same, notwithstanding the view and statements by Camdusses, the US under-secretary of State, and David Rockefeller about the 'positive performance' of Mexico's key macroeconomic indicators (*La Jornada*, 30 October, 1996) and a relatively low level of official unemployment (4–5.8 per cent).
3. These cases are discussed by Petras (1996). They include the Movimiento Izquierda Revolucionario in Bolivia which in the 1980s entered in an alliance with the ex-dictator Hugo Banzer; the Socialist Party in Chile which forms part of the Christian Democratic *concertacion* regime; MAS, in Venezuela, which has backed Caldera's Plan Venezuela in exchange for government posts.
4. Zamora (1995: 11).
5. See, for example, De la Garza (1994).
6. On this poststructuralist (or postmodernist) perspectives, see inter alia, Escobar and Alvarez (1992).
7. An example of the absurdity reached in these efforts is the classification and analysis by Burbach (1994) of the Zapatista social movement in Chiapas, Mexico, as 'the first postmodern political movement' of history.
8. As for this counter-offensive in the countries of the European Community see Davis (1984).

9. On this counter-revolution see Toye (1987).
10. *La Jornada*, 24,10,96: 42.
11. Schuldt (1995: 70). There are diverse formulations of this problematic in different contexts. In the Latin American context, see, inter alia, Restrepo (1989), Tironi and Lagos (1991), Escobar and Alvarez (1992).
12. The critical role of NGOs in World Bank projects is evident in the fact that two of each five projects of the Bank with governments of developing countries in the 1990s involve NGOs (Nelson, 1995). The World Bank's policy of partnership with NGOs derives from a strategic decision made towards the end of the 1980s in a context of a 'new understanding' as to the necessity of protecting the vulnerable groups, particularly the poor, in the process of adjustment (*Finance & Development*, December 1992). In this regard the Bank elaborated a consensus document in 1987, and initiated a Working Group of NGOs, giving them a measure of autonomy, with their own permanent in Geneva, to give the Bank advice and consultations... and strategic albeit critical collaboration. In this regard, see Arruda (1993). Despite its relationship with the Bank the NGO Working Group is generally guided by a search for an alternative form of development to that espoused by the Bank.
13. See, for example, the several essays compiled by Escobar and Alvarez (1992) and Slater (1985). This perspective on the new social movements of Latin America aims to move beyond this impasse and crisis. In this regard, see Schuurman (1993). The basis of this theoretical crisis is the impasse reached in theory and practice by the proponents of both (neo)liberalism and (neo)structuralism. The AD movement has its origin precisely in an effort to escape the impasse created by these lines of thought, in the form of the constitution of a new paradigm. On this point see, inter alia, Griesgraber and Gunter (1996). But this effort, just as similar efforts taken by proponents of diverse theories and actions in the radical political economy paradigm, signally failed to move beyond the theoretical impasse and explain the dynamics of the world capitalist system and the development process. On this entire problematic see, inter alia, Sachs (1992) and Schuurman (1993), who point towards diverse attempts to resolve the impasse related to an entirely different line of thought that denies the existence of any intelligible structure or a historic process rooted in the workings of a system.
14. The following analysis derives from interviews and discussions held by the authors with leaders and members of the movements referred to.
15. A history of the MST can be found in Stedile and Sergio (1994) and MST, *Documento Basico do MST* (1991). As for its dynamics and itinerary of struggle see Veltmeyer, Petras and Vieux (1997).
16. See, for example, Contreras Baspineiro (1994).
17. Informativo Campesino (Asunción), April 1996, No. 91.
18. *La Jornada*, August 10, 1996: 3; Chiapas, No. 2 (Mexico, 1996); *La Jornada*, October 10, 1996.
19. Hobsbawm (1994).
20. As for the origins of the EZLN there is little documentation, but the government of Mexico published some internal documents of the FLN that

suggest that at the beginning of the 1980s it was organized at four levels: (i) a national directorate; (ii) a politburo; (iii) an urban front called Students and Workers in Struggle; and (iv) a rural front called the Zapatista Front of National Liberation (Oppenheimer, 1995). Oppenheimer and various documents suggest that the FLN had a Maoist orientation towards a protracted popular war in which guerrilla action in the urban and rural fronts would be combined with massive protests of the civilian population across the country so as to provoke a crisis in the central government and to demolish it. A group of students of with a Marxist orientation, many of them students of philosophy and sociology at UNAM, moved to Chiapas in 1980 to put into operation the FLN's rural front, whose commander-in-chief was Comandante German in Mexico City.

21. Together with two divisions, according to internal documents published by the government, the rural front had an army of 25 000. It is very difficult to know who can be relied on here. The CIA, it would seem, was well aware of the existence of an armed force in the area, but it discounted its importance and its capacity to act effectively even in the local area. As for the question of why Chiapas, Oppenheimer (1995: 67) recounts an interesting history about a Josefina Jimenez, administrator of a Monterey investment funds relating to Emerging Markets, that had invested in Chiapas some 70 thousand dollars. On the basis of visits to Chiapas, she estimated that those who organized the rebellion in Chiapas did not choose Chiapas at random; in the final analysis indigenous people submerged in misery could be found across the country. They chose Chiapas, she concluded, because they would be strategically located in terms of the national economy, Chiapas producing 60 per cent of the country's hydroelectric power and the state monopoly formed by PEMEX depended on the state for its abundant resources of natural gas. She visualized acts of sabotage against the economy, leading her to advise a pullout of all investments.

22. The writer and journalist Oppenheimer draws the conclusion (that is, he speculates) that a sympathizer of the rebellion, probably someone connected to the church, advised Marcos to moderate their socialist rhetoric and to plays their indigenous card as a means of attracting intellectuals and human rights organizations to the movement. However, this is pure speculation. It is probable, as explained by Marcos, that it was a decision of the Revolutionary Committee to changing the emphasisis from class to ethnicity.

23. The conditions that affect the indigenous population of Chiapas and that pushed them towards insurrection affect indigenous peoples all across the country: economic and political marginality, poverty, and the lack of respect for their human rights, and cultures. 78 per cent of the indigenous population live in zones of high marginality in which are found 24 million people and encompass 58 per cent of all municipalities (SEDESOL, *High-priority Regions*; *La Jornada*, 11 November, 1996: 23). Within these zones, indigenous peoples have an illiteracy rate of over 30 per cent; almost 50 per cent of the school age population do not know how to read; 44 per cent do not have either drainage or inside toilets; 87 per cent of the infantile population has physical deficiencies; 30 per cent of houses lack

electricity (and Chiapas produces 50 per cent of the country's hydro-electric supply); 42 per cent of the houses does not have piped water; 68 per cent without adequate housing; 50 per cent receive less than one minimum wage, which is set at well below the poverty level.

Bibliography

Afshar, Haleh and Carolyne Dennis (eds) (1992) *Women and Adjustment Policies in the Third World*, New York: St. Martin's Press.
Aglietta, M. (1979) *Theory of Capitalist Regulation*, London: New Left Books.
Aglietta, M. (1982) 'World Capitalism in the 1980s', *New Left Review*, 136 (November–December): 5–41.
Alimir, Oscar (1994) 'Distribución del Ingreso e incidencia de la pobreza a lo largo del ajuste', *Revista de CEPAL*, 52 (April): 7–32.
Alvarez, Alejandro (1987) *La crisis global del capitalismo en Mexico*, Mexico: ed. Era.
Amsden, Alica and Ralphj Van der Hoeven (1994) 'Manufacturing Output and Wages in the 1980s: Labor's Loss Towards Century's End', Working Paper 3, University of Wisconsin-Madison, Global Studies Program.
Arellano-Lopez, S. (1990) *El rol de las organizaciones no-gubernamentales en la promocion de conservacion y desarrollo: relaciones con agencias internacionales, instituciones estatales y organizaciones nativas*, Working Paper 61, Binghamton, NY: Institute for Development Anthropology.
Arrida Palomares, Joaquín (1995) 'Economía y sindicalismo. Significado económico del marco de relaciones laborales Salvadoreño', *ECA*, 551.
Arrighi, Giovanni (1990) 'Marxist Century – American Century: The Making and Remaking of the World Labour Movement', in Samir Amin *et al.*, *Transforming the Revolution*, New York: Monthly Review Press.
Arruda, Marcos (1993) 'NGOs and the World Bank: Possibilities and Limits of Collaboration', Geneva: NGO Working Group.
Assies, Willem *et al.* (1991) *Structures of Power, Movements of Resistance: An Introduction to the Theories of Urban Movements in Latin America*, Amsterdam: Center for Latin American Research and Documentation.
Banet, E. T. (1989) *Structuralism and the Logic of Dissent*, London: Methuen.
Barnet, Richard and John Cavanagh (1994) *Global Dreams: Imperial Corporations and the New World Order*, New York: Simon & Schuster.
Barrig, Maruja (1987) 'Democracia emergente y ovimiento de mujeres', in Eduardo Ballon (ed.), *Movimientos sociales y democracia: la fundación de un nuevo orden*, Lima: DESCO.
Bartra, Roger (1974) *Estructura agraria y clases sociales en Mexico*, Mexico City: Era.
Baudrillard, Jean (1983) *Simulations*, New York: Semiotext.
Bello, Walden, with Shea Cunningham and Bill Rau (1994) *Dark Victory: United States, Structural Adjustment and Global Poverty*, London: Pluto Press.
Benjamin, Thomas (1989) *A Rich Land, a poor people: Politics and Society in Modern Chiapas*, Albuquerque: University of New Mexico.
Bienefeld, Manfred (1995) 'Assessing Current Developmernt Trends: Reflections on Keith Griffin's "Global prospects for Development and Human Security"', *Canadian Journal of Development Studies*, XVI(3).

Blaikie, P. (1985) 'Why do Policies Usually Fail?', *The Political Economy of Soil Erosion in Developing Countries*, London: Longman.

Boisier, Sergio *et al.* (1992) *La descentralización: el eslabón perdido de la cadena Transformación Productiva con Equidad y Sustentabilidad*, Santiago de Chile: Cuadernos de CEPAL.

Boom, Gerard and Alfonso Mercado (eds) (1990) *Automatización flexible en la industria*, Mexico: ed. Limusa Noriega.

Booth, David (1985) 'Marxism and Development Sociology: Interpreting the Impasse', *World Development*, 13(7), (1985): 761–87.

Botero, Libardo (1992) 'Apertura económica y reforma laboral', in L. Botero *et al.*, *Neoliberalismo y subdesarrollo*, Bogota: El A'ncora.

Boyer, Robert (1989) *La teoría de la regulación: un analísis crítico*, Buenos Aires: ed. Humanitas.

Brass, T. (1991) 'Moral Economists, Subalterns, New Social Movements and the (Re)Emergence of a (Post) Modernised (Middle) Peasant', *Journal of Peasant Studies*, 18, 2.

Breman, Jan (1994) *Wage Hunters and Gatherers: Search for Work in the Urban and Rural Economy of South Gujerat*, Delhi: Oxford University Press.

Brodsky, Melvin (1994) 'Labor Market Flexibility: a Changing International Perspective', *Monthly Labor Review*, (November).

Brown, Flor and Lilia Dominguez (1989) 'Nuevas tecnologias en la industria maquiladora de exportación', *Comercio Exterior* (Mexico), 39(3) (March).

Burbach, Roger (1994) 'Roots of the Postmodern Rebellion in Chiapas', *New Left Review*, 205.

Burbach, Roger (1997) 'Socialism is Dead, Long Live Socialism', NACLA, XXX(3).

Burt, Jo-Marie (1996) 'Local NGOs in Peru Devise Alternative Anti-Poverty Program', *NACLA Report on the Americas*, 29, 6 (May–June).

Cabrero Mendozo, Enrique (1995) *La nueva gestión municipal en Mexico: analisis de experiencias innovadores en gobiernos locales*, Mexico DF: Parrua/CIDE.

Cabrero Mendoza, Enrique (1996) 'Las politicas descentralizadoras en el ambito internacional. Retos y experiencia', *Nueva Sociedad*, 142 (April–May).

Calderon, Fernando (1987) 'Movimientos etnicos y cultura', in *El desafío de la étnidad en en el siglo XX: auto-determinación, gobierno y estado*, Paris: Asociacio Internacional de Ciencia Politica.

Calderon, Fernando (1995) *Movimientos sociales y politica*, Mexico: Siglo XXI.

Calderon, Fernando and Elizabeth Jelin (1987) *Clases y movimientos sociales en America Latina. Perspectivas y realidades*, Buenos Aires: Cuadernos CEDES.

Calderon, Fernando and Mario dos Santos (eds) (1987) *Los conflictos por la constitución de un nuevo orden*, Buenos Aires: CLACSO.

Calderon, Fernando, Manuel Chiboga and Diego Pisiero (1992) *Modernización democraáica e incluyente de la agricultura en América Latina y el Caribe*. Documento de Programa No. 28, San Jose, CR: ICCA.

Camacho, D. and R. Menjivar (eds) (1989) *Los movimientos populares en America Latina*, Mexico City: Siglo XX.

Candia, Jose Miguel (1996) 'Empleo Precario y Conflicto Social. ¿Nuevas Formas de Organizacion Popular?', *Nueva Sociedad*, 142 (March–April).

Carrion, Fernando (1996) 'La descentralización: un proceso de confianza nacional', *Nueva Sociedad*, 142 (April–May).

Casteneda, Jorge (1993) *Utopia Unarmed: The Latin American Left after the Cold War*, New York: Alfed Knopf.
Castro Arze, Miguel and Mauricio Lea Plaza (1996) 'La hora de lo local en Bolivia', *Nueva Sociedad*, 142 (April–May).
CEPAL (1982) *Economia Campesina y Agricultura Empresarial*, Mexico City: Siglo Veintiuno.
CEPAL (1992a) *El perfil de la pobreza en América Latina a comienzos de los años 90*, Santiago de Chile: CEPAL.
CEPAL (1992b) *Estudio Económico de América Latina y el Caribe 1990*, I–II, Santiago de Chile: CEPAL.
CEPAL (1992c) *Focalización y Pobreza: nuevas tendencias en la política social*, Santiago de Chile.
CEPAL (1993) *Balance preliminar de la economia de América Latina y el Caribe*, Santiago de Chile, December.
CEPAL (1995) *Panorama Social de America latina*, Santiago de Chile: CEPAL.
CEPAL (various years) *Anuario Estadistico de America Latina y el Caribe*, Santiago: CEPAL.
CEPAL-INEGI (1993) *Informe sobre la magnitud y la evolucion de la pobreza en Mexico, 1984–1992*, Mexico: CEPAL-INEGI.
CEPAL (1991) 'Internacionalización y regionalización de la economia mundial: sus consequencias para Latina America', LC/L 640, 3 September.
Cernea, Michael (ed.) (1985) *Putting People First: Sociological Variables in Rural Development*, New York: Oxford University Press.
Chambers, Robert (1983) *Rural Development. Putting the Last First.*, London: Longman.
Chiriboga, Manuel (1985) *Crisis económica y movimiento campesino y indígena*, Quito: CERLAC.
Chiriboga, Manuel (1992) 'Movimiento campesino e indigena y participación politica en Ecuador: la construcción de identidades en una sociedad heterogenea', *Sintesis* (AIETI) (January–April).
Chossudovsky, Michel (1997) *The Globalisation of Poverty,* London: Zed Books.
CID-COTESU-MCTH (1993) *Politicas Sociales y ajuste estructural: Bolivia 1985–93*. La Paz: CID-COTESU-MCTH.
Colclough, Christopher and James Manor (eds) (1991) *States or markets? Neoliberalism and the Development Policy Debate*, Oxford: Clarendon Press.
Collins, J. (1995) *Communal Work and Rural Development in the State of Oaxaca*, Geneva: ILO.
Collins, Joseph and Jon Lear (1995) *Chile's Free Market Miracles: A Second Look*, Oakland, CA: Food First.
Contreras Baspineiro, Alex (1994) *La Marcha Historico*, Cochabamba: CEDIB.
Cook, Maria Lorena *et al.* (eds) (1996) *Las dimensiones políticas de la reestructuración económica*, México: UNAM., 39–106, 293–432.
Corbridge, Stuart (1990) 'Post-Marxism and Development Studies: Beyond the Impasse', *World Development*, 18(5).
Cornia, G. Andrea, Richard Jolly, and Frances Stewart (eds) (1987) *Adjustment with a Human Face*, Oxford: Oxford University Press (for UNICEF).
Cornia, Giovanni Andrea (1993) 'Is Adjustment Conducive to Long-Term Development? The Case of Africa in the 1980s' in Gianni Vaggi (ed.), *From the Debt Crisis to Sustainable Development*, New York: St. Martin's Press.

Crouch, C. and A. Pizzorno (1978) *Resurgence of Class Conflict in Western Europe Since 1968*, London: Holmes & Meier.

Davis, Mike (1984). 'The Political Economy of Late-Imperial America', *New Left Review*, 143 (Jan–Feb).

De la Garza Toledo, Enrique (ed.) (1994) *Democracia y Política Economia Alternativa*, Mexico, DF: Centro de Investigaciones Interdisciplinarias en Humanidades, UNAM.

De Paula Leite, Marcia (1993) 'Innovación tecnológica, organización del trabajo y relaciones industriales en el Brasil', *Nueva Sociedad*, 124 (March–April).

De Souza, Amoury (1997) 'The Social Agenda at Century's End', in Riordan Roett (ed.), *Brazil Under Cardoso*, Boulder, CO: Lynne Rienner.

Del Carmen, Feijoo and Monica Gona (1985) *Las mujeres en la transición a la democracia*, Buenos Aires: CEDES.

Derrida, Jacques (1982) *Margins of Philosophy*, Chicago University Press.

Diamond, Larry, Juan Linz and S.M. Lipset (eds) (1989) *Democracy in Developing Countries*, Boulder, CO: Lynne Rienner.

Diaz, Alvaro (1989) 'Chile: reestructuracion y modernizacion industrial autoritatoria. Desafios para el sindicalismo y la oposición', in *Industria, Estado y sociedad*, Caracas: Editorial Nueva Sociedad.

Dominguez, Jorge (1994) *Social Movements in Latin America: The Experiernce of Peasants, Workers, Women and the Urban Poor, and the Middle Sectors*, New York: Garland Publications.

Dutrénit, Gabriela and Mario Capdevielle (1993) 'El perfil tecnológico de la industria mexicana y su dinámica innovadora en la década de los ochenta', *El trimestre Económico* (México), LX(239) (July–September).

ECA (Estudios Centroamericanos), 551 (September 1994); 560 (June 1995); 564 (October 1995).

Eckstein, Susan (1989) *Power and Popular Protest: Latin American Social Movements*, Berkeley: University of California Press.

ECLAC (1992) *Social Equity and Changing Production Patterns: an Integrated Approach*, Santiago de Chile: CEPAL.

ECLAC (1990) *Productive Transformation with Equity*, Santiago de Chile: ECLAC.

Emmanuel, Arghiri (1972) *Unequal Exchange: A Study of the Imperialism of Trade*, New York: Monthly Review Press.

Epstein, Jack (1997) 'Brazil Asks: Is Mine Sale a Sell-Off or Sell-Out?' *Christian Science Monitor*, (January): 3–9.

Escobar, Arturo (1992) 'Reflections on "Development": Grassroots Approaches and Alternative Politics in the Third World', *Futures*, 2495.

Escobar, Arturo (1995) *Encountering Development: The Making and the Unmaking of the Third World*, Princeton, NJ: Princeton University Press.

Escobar, Arturo and Sonia Alvarez (eds) (1992) *The Making of Social Movements in Latin America: Identity, Strategy, and Democracy*, Boulder, CO: Westview Press.

Escobar, Cristina (1985) *Movimientos de mujeres*, Bogota: CINEP.

Escobar, Santiago and Ricardo Solari (1996) 'El Municipio y la democracia moderna', *Nueva Sociedad*, 142 (April–May).

Fajnzylber, Fernando (1990) *Unavoidable Industrial Restructuring in Latin America*, Durham, NC.

Bibliography

Fanelli J., R. Frenkel and G. Rozenwurcel (1990) 'Growth and Structural-Reform in Latin America. Where We Stand', *Documento CEDES*, No. 57, Buenos Aires.

Fara, Luis (1985) *Luchas reivindicativas urbanas en una contexto autoritario*, Buenos Aires: CEDES.

Ferrer, Aldo (1993) 'Nuevos paradigmas tecnológicos y dersarrollo sostenible: perspectiva Latinoamericana', *Comercio Exterior*, 43(9) (September).

Figueroa, Victor (1986) *Reinterpretando el subdesarrollo. Trabajo general, clase y fuerza productivo en América Latina*, Mexico DF: Siglo XX.

FOSIS (1994) *Memoria FOSIS 1994*, Santiago de Chile: FOSOS.

Foucault, Michel (1986) 'The Subject and Power: an Afterword', in H. L. Dreyfus and P. Rabinow (eds), *Michel Foucault: Beyond Structuralism and Hermeneutics*, Brighton: Harvester Press.

Fox, Jonathan and L. Hernandez (1992) 'Mexico's Difficulties: Grassroots Movements, NGOs and Local Government', *Alternatives*, 17(2).

Frank, André Gunder (1987) 'The Development of Underdevelopment', *Monthly Review*, 41(2).

Friedmann, J. (1992) *Empowerment: The Politics of Alternative Development*, Blackwell, Cambridge, MA /Oxford, UK.

Fröbel, Folker, Jürgen Heinrichs and Otto Kreye (1980) *The New International Division of Labour: Structural Unemployment in Industrialised Countries and Industrialisation in Developing Countries*, New York, NY: Cambridge University Press.

Fuentes, L.A. (1992) 'El Fondo Hondureño de Inversion Social: una nueva modalidad de gestión pública', in *Fondos y Programas de Compensación Social: Experiencias en América Latina y el Caribe*, Washington, DC: PAHO: 185–225.

FUSADES (1996) *Boletin Economico y Social*, No. 128 (July), San Salvador: FUSADES.

Garcia Delgado, Daniel and Juan Silva (1985) *El movimiento vecinal y la democracia. Participación y control en el Gran Buenos Aires*, Buenos Aires: CEDES.

Geller, Lucio (1993) 'Cambio tecnológico, trabajo y empleo: industria manufacturera del Gran Santiago, 1988–1990'. Santiago: PREALC.

Glynn, A., A. Hughes, A. Lipietz, and A. Singh (1990) 'The Rise and Fall of the Golden Age', in Stephen Marglin and Juliet Schor (eds), *The Golden Age of Capitalism: Re-interpreting the Post-War Experience*, Oxford: Clarendon Press.

Gordon, Sara (1993). 'La política social y el programa nacional de solidaridad', *Revista Mexicana de Sociologia*, 54(2) (April).

Goulet, Denis (1989) 'Participation in Development: New Avenues', *World Development*, 17(2).

Green, Duncan (1995) *Silent Revolution: The Rise of Market Economics in Latin America*, London: Cassell.

Greenberg, James (1989) *Blood Ties: Life and Violence in Rural Mexico*, Tucson: University of Arizona Press.

Griesgaber, Jo Marie and Bernhard Gunter (eds) (1996) *Development: New Paradigms and Principles for the Twenty-first Century*, London: Pluto Press.

Griffin, Keith (1995) 'Global Prospects for Development and Human Security', *Canadian Journal of Development Studies*, XVI(3).

Griffin, Keith and John Knight (1989) 'Human development in the 1980s and Beyond', *Journal of Development Planning*, No. 19: 9–40.

Griffin, Keith and Rahman Khan (1992) *Globalization and the Developing World*, Geneva: UNRISD.

Guerra Rodriguez, Carlos (1994) 'Democracia y cuidadana: en busca de la equidad o de nuevos recursos?' *Revista Mexicana de Sociologia*, No. 3 (July–September).

Guerrero de Lizardi, Carlos and Alejandro Valle (1995) 'Salario, participación del salario en el producto y productividad, in De la Garza, L. A. and Enrique Nieto (eds), *Distribución del ingreso y política sociales*, Vol. I, México: ed. Juan Pablo.

Guimaraes, R. (1989) Desarrollo con equidad: ¿un nuevo cuento de hadas para los años de noventa?' LC/R. 755, Santiago de Chile: CEPAL.

Hardoy, Jorge and Alejandro Portes (eds) (1984) *Ciudades y sistemas urbanos*, Buenos Aires: CLACSO.

Harvey, David (1989) *The Condition of Postmodernity: an Enquiry into the Origins of Cultural Change*, Oxford and Cambridge, Mass.: Blackwell.

Henriquez, Helia and I. Reca (1994) 'La mujer en el trabajo: la nueva puesta en escena de un tema antiguo', *Economia y trabajo en Chile 1993–1994*, Cuarto Informe Anual, Santiago de Chile: Programa de Economía del Trabajo (PET).

Hernandez Laos, Enrique (1992) *Crecimiento económico y pobreza en México*, Mexico DF: CIIH, UNAM.

Hernandez, Luis (1992) 'La UNORCA: doce tesis sobre el nuevo liderazgo campesino en Mexico, in J. Moguel Botey and L. Hernandez (eds), *Autonomia y nuevos sujetos sociales en el desarrollo rural*, Mexico.

Herrera, Gonzalo (1995) 'Tendencias del cambio tecnológico en la industria Chilena', *Economía y Trabajo en Chile 1994–1995*, Santiago: Programa de Economía del Trabajo (PET).

Hobsbawm, Eric (1994) *The Age of Extremes: A History of the World*, New York: Pantheon.

Hoogvelt, Ankie (1984) *The Third World in Global Development*, London: Macmillan Press.

Hunt, Diana (1989) *Economic Theories of Development: An Analysis of Competing Paradigms*, Hertfordshire: Harvester Wheatsheaf.

Hunter, Allen (1995) 'Los nuevos ovimientos sociales y la revolución',*Nueva Sociedad*, 136: 3–4.

Infante, Ricardo and Victor Tokman (1994) 'Monitoring Poverty and Employment Trends: an Index for the Social Debt, in Ralph van der Hoeven and Richard Anker (eds), *Poverty Monitoring: an International Concern*, New York: St. Martin's Press.

Instituto del Tercer Mundo (1993) *Third World Guide 91/92*, Montevideo: Instituto del Tercer Mundo.

Instituto del Tercer Mundo (1996) *The World: A Third World Guide 1995/96*, Montevideo, ITM.

Inter-American Development Bank (IDB) (1990, 1991) *Economic and Social Progress in Latin America*, Washington, DF: IDB.

International Commission on Peace and Food (chaired by M.S. Swaminathan) (1994) *Uncommon Opportunities: An Agenda for Peace and Equitable Development*, London: Zed Books.

International Labour Organisation [ILO] (1996) *World Employment 1996*, Geneva: ILO.

Ito, Takatoshi (1997) 'What Can Developing Countries learn from East Asia's Economic Growth?' in Boris Pleskovic and Joseph Stiglitz (eds), Annual World bank on Development Economics, Washington, DC: The World Bank.
Jacobi, Pedro (1985) *Movimentos sociais urbanos e a crise: da explosao a participacao popular autonoma*, São Paulo: FESP.
Jameson, F. (1991) *Postmodernism, or, The Cultural Logic of Late Capitalism*, London: Verso.
Jazairy, Idriss, Mohiuddin Alamgir, and Theresa Panuccio (1992) *The State of World Rural Poverty*, London: Intermediate Technology Publications (for the International Fund for Agricultural Development).
Jelin, Elizabeth (1990) *Women and Social Change in Latin America*, London: Zed Books.
Johansen Frida (1993) *Poverty Reduction in East Asia: The Silent Revolution*, World Bank Discussion paper No. 203, Washington, DC.
Kapstein, Ethan (1996) 'Workers and the World Economy', *Foreign Affairs*, 75 (3) (May–June).
Khan, Azizur Rahman (1993) *Structural Adjustment and Income Distribution: Issues and Experience*, Geneva: International Labour Office.
Kliksberg, Bernardo (1993) *Pobreza: Un Tema Impostergable: Nuevas Respuestas a Nivel Mundial*, Mexico, DF: Fondo de Cultura Economica.
Knight, Alan (1988) 'Debt Bondage in Latin America' in L.J. Archer (ed.), *Slavery and Other Forms of Unfree Labour*, London/New York: Routledge.
Korten, David (1995) *When Corporations Rule the World*, (ed.) W. Hartford, CT: Kumarian Press.
Krischke, P. (1990) 'Social Movements and Political Participation: Contributions of Grassroots Democracy', *Canadian Journal of Development Studies*, 11(1).
La Botz, Dan (1994) *Chiapas and Beyond: Mexico's Crisis and the Fight for Democracy*, Boulder, CO: Westview Press.
La Botz, Dan (1995) *Democracy in Mexico: Peasant Rebellion and Political Reform*, Boston: South End Press.
Laclau, Ernesto (1989) 'Politics and the Limits of Modernity', in A. Ross (ed.), *Universal Abandon? The Politics of Postmodernism*, Edinburgh University Press.
Laclau, Ernesto (1990) *New Reflections on the Revolution of our Time*, London: Verso.
Laclau, Ernesto (1995) 'El nuevo progresismo', *El Caminante* No. 1, Buenos Aires.
Laclau, Ernesto and Chantal Mouffe (1987) 'Post-Marxist without Apologies', *New Left Review*, 166: 79–106.
Laclau, Ernesto and Chantal Mouffle (1985) *Hegemony and Socialist Strategy*, London: Verso.
Laurell, Ana Cristina (1994) 'Pronasol o la pobreza de los programas contra la pobreza', *Nueva Sociedad*, 135.
Lechner, Norbert (1992) 'El debate sobre el Estado y Mercado', *Nueva Sociedad*, 121 (Sep–Oct): 80–89.
Leiva, Fernando (1996) 'Flexible Labor Markets, Poverty and Social Disintegration in Chile, 1990–1994', unpublished manuscript, CETES, Santiago de Chile, March.

Leiva, Fernando and James Petras, with Henry Veltmeyer (1994/1997) *Democracy and Poverty in Chile*, Boulder, CO: Westview Press.
Leiva, Fernando and Rafael Agacino (1994) 'Mercado de trab'jo flexible, pobreza y desintegración social en Chile, 1990–1994', Santiago: Universidad ARCIS.
Lerner, Bertha (1996) *Los debates en política social, desigualdad y pobreza*, Fideicomiso-Banco Internacional/UNAM.
Levitt, Kari (1990) 'Debt, Adjustment and Development: Looking to the 1990s', *Economic and Political Weekly*, July 21: 1585–1594.
Lipietz, Alain (1982) 'Towards Global Fordism', *New Left Review*, 132 (March–April).
Lipietz, Alain (1987) *Mirages and Miracles: The Crisis in Global Fordism*, London: Verso.
Lustig, Nora (ed.) (1995) *Coping with Austerity: Poverty and Inequality in Latin America*. Washington, DC: The Brookings Institution.
Lyotard, J. F. (1987) *The Postmodern Condition: A Report on Knowledge*, Manchester University Press.
Machado, A., L. C. Castilolo, and I. Suarez (1993) *Democracia con campesinos, Campesinos sin democracia*, Bogota, CO: Ministerio de Agricultura, Fondo DRI, IILCA / Universidad del Valle.
Maddison, Angus (1995) *Monitoring the World Economy, 1820–1992*, Paris: OECD Development Centre.
Marcos, Jaime (1993) *Cooperación y conflicto entre municipio y comunidad: el caso de Tantara (Huancavelica)*, Tesis de Maestria, Lima: PUC.
Marcos, Jaime (1994). 'Disolución de comunidades campesinos y dinámica municipio-comunidad', *Debate Agrario*, No. 19, Lima: CEDES.
Marcos, Jaime (1996) 'Las comunidades campesinas en el proceso de regionalizacion del Perú, *Nueva Sociedad*, 142 (April–May).
Marglin, Stephen and Juliet Schor (eds) (1990) *The Golden Age of Capitalism: Reinterpreting the Postwar Experience*, Oxford: Clarendon Press.
Marini, Ruy Mauro (1981) *Dialéctica de la dependencia*, Mexico DF: Era.
Martin, Hans-Peter and Harald Schumann (1997) *The Global Trap*, London: Zed Press.
Max-Neef, Manfred, Antonio Elizalde and Martin Hopenhayen (1965) 'Desarrollo a Escala Humana: una opcion para el futuro', *Development Dialogue*, special issue (CEPAUR / Dag Hammarskjold Foundation).
McMichael, Philip (1996) *Development and Change: A Global Perspective*, Thousand Oaks, CA: Pine Gorge Press.
Meier, Gerald and Dudley Seers (eds) (1984) *Pioneers in Development*, New York: Oxford University Press (for the World Bank).
Meiksins Wood, Ellen (1995) 'What is the "Postmodern" Agenda? An Introduction', *Monthly Review*, 47(3) (July–August).
Meillasoux, Claude (1978) *Mujeres graneros y capital*, Mexico DF: Editorial Siglo XXI.
Mejía Piñeros, Maria Consuelo and Sergio Sarmiento Silva (1987) *La lucha indígena: un reto a la ortodoxia*, Mexico.
Meller, Patricio (1991) 'IMF and World Bank Roles in the Latin American Foreign Debt Problem', in Patricio Meller (ed.), *The Latin American Development Debate*, Boulder, CO: Westview Press.

Mercado, Alfonso (1990) 'La adquisición de máquinas-herramientas de control numérico en América latina', in Gerard Boom and Alfonso Mercado (eds), (1990) *Automatización flexible en la industria*, Mexico: ed. Limusa Noriega.
MIDEPLAN, Departamento de Planificación y estudios Sociales (1994) *Participación Laboral, estructura de empleo e ingresos*, Santiago de Chile: MIDEPLAN.
Moises, Jose and Lucio Kowarick *et al.* (1981) *Cidade, povo e poder*, São Paulo: CEDEC-Paz e Terra.
Molina, Natacha (1986) 'Movimiento de mujeres en Chile', in Fernando Calderon and Jose Reyna (eds), *La irrupción encubierta*, Mexico, DF: IIH-UNAM.
Montalbano, William (1991) 'A Global Pursuit of Happiness', *Los Angeles Times*, 1 October.
Montesinos, Mario and Roberto Góchez (1995) 'Salarios y productividad', *ECA* 564 (October).
Moore, David (1995) 'The Crisis in Development Discourse and the Concepts of Sustainability, Equity and Participation: A Way Out of the Impasse?' in David Moore and Gerald Schmitz (eds), *Debating Development Discourses: Institutional and Popular Perspectives*, London: Macmillan Press.
Morales, Josefina (1992) 'La reestructuración industrial', in J. Morales *et al.* (eds), *La reestructuración industrial en México: cinco aspectos fundamentales*, Mexico DF: Editorial Nuestro Tiempo.
Morley, Samuel (1995) 'Structural Adjustment and Determinants of Poverty in Latin America', in Nora Lustig (ed.), *Coping with Austerity: Poverty and Inequality in Latin America*, Washington, D.C.: The Brookings Institution.
MST, Dirección Nacional (1991) *Como Organizar a la Masa*, São Paulo: MST.
Munck, R. (1994) Workers, Structural Adjustment and *Concertacion Social* in latin America', *Latin American Perpectives*, 21(3).
Muro, Victor y Canto Chac, Manuel (eds) (1991) *El estudio de los movimientos sociales. Teoria y método*, Mexico: El Colegio de Michoacan-UAM-Xochimilco.
Nelson, Paul (1995) *The World Bank and NGOs: The Limits of Apolitical Development*, London: Macmillan.
Nugent, Daniel (1995) 'Northern Intellectuals and the EZLN', *Monthly Review*, 47(3) (July–August).
O'Connor, James (1973) *The Fiscal Crisis of the State*, New York: St. Martin's Press.
OECD (1994) *Monthly Statistics of Foreign Trade*, Series A, Paris: Organisation of Economic Cooperation and Development
OECD (1994) *The OECD Jobs Study: Facts, Analysis, Strategies*, Paris: OECD.
Olave, Patricia (1994) 'Reestructuración productiva bajo el nuevo patrón exportador', in Juan Arancibia Córdova (ed.), *América latina en los ochenta: reestructuración y pespectivas*, Mexico DF: IIEC-UNAM.
Olivera, Luis *et al.* (1991) 'Municipios: desarrollo local y participación', *Serie Cuadernos*, 16, DESCO, Lima.
Ominami, Carlos (ed.) (1986) *La tercera revolución industrial, impactos internacionales, el actual viraje tecnológico*, Mexico: RIAL-Anuario-Grupo, ed., Latinoamericano.
Oppenheimer, Andrés (1996) *México: en la frontera del caos*, México DF: Vergara Editores.

Palorames, Laura and Leonard Mertens (1993) 'Empresa y trabajador ante la automatización programable', in Leonel Corona (ed.), *Mexico ante las nuevas tecnológias*, Mexico, DF: CIIH-UNAM.

Patel, Surendra (1992) 'In Tribute to the Golden Age of the South's Development', *World Development*, 20(5).

Patel, Surendra (1994) 'East Asia's Spectacular Development: Its Lessons for Others', UNCP, *Asia-Pacific Development Journal*, 1(1) (June).

Patel, Surendra (1995) *Technological Transformation*, Vol. 5: *The Historic Process*, Aldeshot: Avebury.

Petras, James (1990) 'Retreat of the Intellectuals', *Economic and Political Weekly*, September 22.

Petras, James (1991). 'Latin America: Poverty of Democracy or Democracy of Poverty', *Economic and Political Weekly*, XXVI (30), July 27.

Petras, James (1996) 'Latin America: The Left Strikes Back', in James Petras, *The Left Strikes Back*, Boulder, CO: Westview Press.

Petras, James and Fernando Leiva (1986) 'Chile's Poor in the Struggle for Democracy', *Latin American Pespectives*, 13(4).

Petras, James and Howard Brill (1985) 'The Tyranny of Globalism', in James Petras *et al.*, *Latin America: Bankers, Generals and the Struggle for Social Justice*, Totowa, NJ: Rowman and littlefield.

Petras, James and Howard Brill (1988) 'Latin America's Transnational Capitalists and the Debt: A Class-Analysis Perspective', *Development and Change*, 19(2): 179–201.

Petras, James and Morris Morley (1990) *US Hegemony Under Siege: Class, Politics and Development in Latin America*, London: Verso.

Petras, James and Soñia Arellano-Lopez (1997) 'Non-Government Organisations and Poverty Alleviation in Bolivia', in Henry Veltmeyer and James Petras (eds), *Neoliberalism and Class Conflict in Latin America*, London: Macmillan/New York: St.Martin's Press.

Petras, James and Steve Vieux (1992) 'Myths and Realities: Latin America's Free Markets', *Monthly Review*, 22(4).

Petras, James and Steve Vieux (1994) 'The Transition to Authoritarian Electoral Regimes in Latin America', *Latin American Perspectives*, 21(4): 5–20.

Petras, James and Henry Veltmeyer (1995) 'La Recuperación Económica en America Latina: El Míto y la Realidad', *Nueva Sociedad*, No. 137.

Pior, Michael and Charles Sabel (1984) *The Second Industrial Divide*, NY: Basic Books.

Prates, Susana and Silvia Rodriguez (1988) *Las movimientos sociales de mujeres en la transición a la democracia*, Montevideo: CIESU.

PREALC (1988) *La evolución del mercado laboral entre 1980 y 1987*, Santiago, Chile: ILO-PREALC/328.

PREALC (1993) *PREALC Informe*, Santiago, Chile: ILO-PREALC.

Prieto, Mercedes (1985) *Notas sobre el movimiento de mujeres en el Ecuador*, Quito: CERLAC.

Rahman, Anisur (1991) 'Towards an Alternative Development Paradigm', *IFDA Dossier*, No. 81.

Rahman, Anisur (1993) *People's Self-Development: Perspectives on Participatory Action Research*, Zed Books.

Razeto, L. (1985) *Economía de solidaridad y mercado democratico*, Santiago de Chile: PET.
Restrepo, Luis Alberto (1989) 'Los movimientos sociales, la democracia y el socialismo', Sociedad Civil y Cultura Democratica-Mensajes y Paradojas, Santiago de Chile: CEPAUR: 13–42.
Roberts, Martin (1994) 'Revolt of the Other Mexico', *New Stateman and Society*, January 7: 11.
Robinson, William (1996) 'Globalization: Nine Theses on our Epoch', *Montelibre Monthly*, March/April.
Rosenbluth, Guillermo (1994) 'Informalidad y pobreza en América Latina', *Revista de CEPAL*, 52 (April): 57–78.
Ross, Robert J.S. and Kent C. Trachte (1990) *Global Capitalism: The New Leviathan*, Albany, NY: State University of New York Press.
Rudolph, James (1992) *Peru: The Evolution of a Crisis*, Wesport, CT: Praeger.
Rufino dos Santos, Joel (1985) *O movimento negro e a crise brasileira*, San Paulo: FESP.
Rus, Jan (1995) 'Local Adaptation to Global Change. The Reordering of Native Society in Highland Chiapas', *European Review of Latin American Studies*, 58 (June).
Sachs, Ignacy (1995) 'Searching for New Development Strategies: Challenges of the Social Summit', *Economic and Political Weekly*, July 8.
Sachs, Wolfgang (1992) *The Development Dictionary: A Guide to Knowledge as Power*, London: Zed Books.
Saffioti, Meileth and Vera Ferrante (1985) *Formas de participacao da muljer em movimentos sociais*, San Paulo: FESP.
Sagasti, Francisco and Gregorio Arevalo (1992) 'América Latina en el nuevo orden mundial fracturado: perspectivas y estrategias', *Comercio Exterior* (Mexico), 42(12) (December).
Salop, Joanne (1992) 'Reducing Poverty: Spreading the Word', *Finance & Development*, 29(4) (December).
Sanfuentes, Alejandro (1987) 'Effects of the Adjustment Policies on the Agriculture and Forestry Sector, *CEPAL Review*, No. 3 (December).
Schryer, Frans (1990) *Ethnicity and Class Conflict in Rural Mexico*, Princeton University Press.
Schuldt, Jurgen (1995) *Repensando el Desarrollo: Hacia una Concepción Alternativa para los Paises Andinos*, Quito: Centro Andino de Acción Popular-CAAP.
Schuurman, Frans J. (ed.) (1993) *Beyond the Impasse: New Directions in Development Theory*, Zed Books.
Schwartz, Rami (1994) *El Ocaso de la Clase Media*, Mexico DF: Grupo Editorial Planeta.
Scott, James (1976) *The Moral Economy of the Peasant*, New Haven and London: Yale University Press.
Scott, James (1985) *Weapons of the Weak: Everyday Forms of Peasant Resistance*, New Haven: Yale University Press.
Scott, James (1990) *Domination and the Arts of Resistance*, New Haven: Yale University Press.
SEDESOL (1993) *Solidarity in National Development*, Mexico DF: SEDESOL.
SEDESOL (1996) *Regiones prioritarias*, Mexico, DF: SEDESOL.

Slater, D. (1994) 'Power and Social Movements in the Other Occident: Latin America in an International Context', *Latin American Perspectives*, 21(2).

Slater, David (1985) *New Social Movements and the State in Latin America*, Amsterdam: CEDLA.

Smith, Gavin (1991) *Livelihood and Resistance: Peasants and the Politics of Land in Peru*, Oxford and Berkeley: University of California Press.

Sondereguer, Maria (1985) *El Movimiento de derechos humanos en Argentina (1976–83)*, Buenos Aires: CEDES.

Sotelo Valencia, Adria (1995) 'La reestructuración del trabajo y el capital en América latina', in Ruy Mauro Marini and Márgara Millán (eds), *La teoría social Latinoamericana: cuestiones contemporáneas*, Vol. IV, Mexico DF: Ediciones El Caballito/UNAM.

South Centre (1996) *Liberalization and Globalization: Drawing Conclusions for Development*, Geneva: South Centre.

South Centre (1997) *South Letter*, 3–4, (29).

Stahl, Karin (1996) 'Anti-Poverty Programs: Making Structural Adjustment More Palatable', *NACLA Report on the Americas*, XXIX(6) (May/June).

Stedile, Joao Pedro and Sergio Frei (1993) *A Luta pela Terra no Brasil*, São Paulo: ed. Pagina Alberta Ltda.

Stepan, Alfred (1988) 'Caminos hacia la redemocratización: consideraciones teóricas y analísis comparativos', *Transiciones desde un gobierno autoritario*, vol. 3, Buenos Aires: Paidós.

Stiefel, M. and M. Wolfe (1994) 'A Voice for the Excluded: Popular Participation', in *Development: Utopia or Necessity?* Geneva: UNRISD/London: Zed Books.

Strange, Susan (1994) *States and Markets*, London and New York: Pinter.

Sunkel, Osvaldo (1991a) 'Del desarrollo hacia adentro al desarrollo de adentro', *Revista Mexicana de Sociología*, No. 1: 3–42.

Sunkel, Osvaldo (1991b) *Desarrollo Desde Dentro*, Mexico: Fondo de Cultura Economica.

Taylor, Lance (1988) *Varieties of Stabilization Experience*, Oxford: Clarendon Press.

Tironi, Eugenio and Ricardo Lagos (1989) 'Ajuste estructural, actores sociales y estado: cinco hipoteses', *CEPAL Review*, Santiago de Chile.

Tironi, Eugenio and Ricardo Lagos (1991) 'The Social Actors and Structural Adjustment', *CEPAL Review*, No. 44 (August).

Touraine, Alain (1984) *Le retour de L'acteur*, Paris: Fayard.

Touraine, Alain (1989) *América Latina. Política y sociedad*, Madrid: Espasa.

Tovar, Teresa (1987) 'Barrio, ciudad, democracia y politica', in Eduardo Ballon (ed.), *Movimientos sociales y democracia: la fundación de un nueyo orden*, Lima: DESCO.

Toye, John (1987) *Dilemmas of Development: Reflections on the Counter-Revolution in Development Theory and Policy*, Oxford: Basil Blackwell.

Trejos, Rafael A. (ed.) (1992) *Ajuste Macro-economico y Pobreza Rural en America Latina*,. San Jose: Instituto Interamericano de Cooperación para la Agricultura (ILCA).

UNCTAD, Division of Transnational Corporations (1994) *World Investment Report 1994: Transnational Corporations, Employment and the Workplace*, New York and Geneva: UN.

UNCTAD, Secretariat to the VIIIth Conference (1990) *Analytical Report*, New York: UNCTAD Conference secretariat.

UNDP (1991) *La Economia Popular en América Latina: Una Alternativa para el Desarrollo*. Bogota.
UNDP (1992, 1996) *Human Development Report*, New York: Oxford University Press.
UNICEF (1987) *The Invisible Adjustment: Poor Women and the Economic Crisis*, Santiago, Chile: Alfa Beta Impresores.
UNICEF (1988) *Participación comunitaria y cambio social en Colombia*, Bogotá: DNP.
UNIDO (UN Industrial Development Organization) (1991, 1992, 1996) *Industry and Development Global Report*, Vienna: UNIDO.
United Nations (1996) *Estudio Económico y Social Mundial 1996: Tendencias y Políticas en la Economia Mundial*, New York: UN.
United Nations, Dept. of Economic and Social Development (1993) *1992 International Trade Statistics Yearbook* (E/F. 94.XVII.3, Vol. 1), New York: UN.
United States DOC. (1993) *Final 1993 Merchandize Trade Tables* [Internet], Available: Internet-Economic Bulletin Board (UMich): Foreign Trade, Final 1993 Merchandize Trade Tables, December.
United States, Dept. of Commerce - Bureau of Economic Analysis (1999) *International Transactions, International Accounts Data*, Washington, DF: US Dept. of Commerce, BEA.
United States, Dept. of Commerce - Bureau of Economic Analysis (1994) *US International Transactions: European Communities: Balance on Merchandize Trade. Balance on Merchandize Trade* CD-ROM), Available: National Trade Data Bank-US Dept. of Commerce, BEA, June 29.
United States-International Trade Administration (1993) *US Total Trade Balances with Individual Countries, 1980–93*, [Internet], Available: Internet-National Trade Data Bank: US Foreign Trade Highlights.
UNRISD (1995) *States of Disarray: The Social Effects of Globalization*, Geneva: UNRISD.
Uphoff, N. (1993) 'Grassroots Organizations and NGOs in Rural Development: Opportunities with Diminishing States and Expanding Markets', *World Development*, 21: 607–22.
US Department of Commerce (1989/1991) *Trends in International Direct Investment*, Sep.–July.
Van Cott, Donna Lee (ed.) (1994) *Indigenous Peoples and Democracy in Latin America*, New York: St. Martin's Press.
Veltmeyer, Henry (1978) 'Marx's Two Methods of Social Analysis', *Sociological Inquiry*, 48(3).
Veltmeyer, Henry (1983) 'Surplus Labour and Class Formation on the Latin American Periphery', in Ron Chilcote and Dale Johnston (eds), *Theories of Development*, Beverly Hills, CA: Sage Publications.
Veltmeyer, Henry (1993) 'Liberalisation and Structural Adjustment in Latin America: In Search of an Alternative', *Economic and Political Weekly*, XXVIII(38), September 25.
Veltmeyer, Henry (1996) *La búsqueda de un desarrollo alternativo*, Working Paper, Maestria en Ciencia Política, Universidad Autónoma de Zacatecas.
Veltmeyer, Henry (1997a) 'Decentralisation as the Institutional basis for Partricipatory development: The Latin American Perspective', *Canadian Journal of Development Studies*, XXVIII(2).

Veltmeyer, Henry (1997b) 'Latin America and the New World Order', *Canadian Review of Sociology*, 22(2).
Veltmeyer, Henry (1997c) 'The World Bank's Report on Labour: A Capitalist Manifesto', *Transition*, January 26.
Veltmeyer, Henry (1997d) 'Decentralisation as the Institutional Basis for Participatory Development: The Latin American Perspective', *Canadian Journal of Development Studies*, 18, 2.
Veltmeyer, Henry, James Petras and Steve Vieux (1997). *Neoliberalism and Class Conflict in Latin America*, (London: Macmillan Press/New York: St. Martin's Press).
Vergara, Pilar (1990) *Políticas hacia la extrema pobreza en Chile, 1973–1988*, Santiago de Chile: FLACSO.
Vergara, Pilar (1996) 'In Pursuit of "Growth with Equity"', in *NACLA Report on the Americas*, XXIX(6).
Vieira, Pedro Antonio (1994) *Luchas obreras, control de la fuerza de trabajo y automatizacion de los medios de trabajo*, Doctoral Thesis, Economics Faculty, UNAM, Mexico.
Virtuoso, Jose (1996) 'Cotidianidad politica y descentralizacion', *Nueva Sociedad*, 142 (April–May).
Vives, Cristian (1985) *El Pueblo Mapuche: elementos para comprenderlo como movimiento social*, Santiago de Chile: ILET (Mimeo).
Vuskovic, Pedro (1993) *Pobreza y Disegualdad en America Latina*, Mexico, DF: CIIH, UNAM.
Walton, John and David Seddon (1994) *Free Markets and Food Riots: The Politics of Global Adjustment*, Oxford: Blackwell.
Watkins, Kevin (1995) *Oxfam Poverty Report*, Oxford: Oxfam.
Waylen, G. (1993) 'Women's Movements and Democratisation in Latin America', *Third World Quarterly*, 14(3).
Wilber, Charles and Jameson Kenneth (1989) 'Paradigms of Economic Development and Beyond', in C. Wilber (ed.), *Political Economy of Development and Underdevelopment*, 4th edn. New York: Random House.
Williamson, J. (ed.) (1990) *Latin American Adjustment. How Much Has Happened?* Washington, DC: Institute for International Economics.
Wolfe, Marshall (1984) 'La participación: una vision desde arriba', *Revista de CEPAL*, No. 23, Santiago de Chile: CEPAL.
Wolfe, Marshall (1988) 'Los actores sociales y las opciones de desarrollo', *Revista de CEPAL*, No. 36, (August).
Wolfe, Marshall (1991) 'Los multiples facetas de la participación', *Revista Pensamento Iberoamericano*, No. 19, Madrid: ICI-CEPAL.
Wolfe, Marshall (1996) *Elusive Development*, London: Zed Press.
Woodward, David (1992) *Debt, Adjustment and Poverty in Developing Countries*, London: Pinter Publishers/Save the Children.
World Bank (1988, 1990, 1993) *World Development Report*, Oxford: Oxford University Press.
World Bank (1991) *Development Strategies: World Development Report 1991*, Oxford University Press.
World Bank (1993) *Latin America and the Caribbean: A Decade After the Debt Crisis*, Washington DC: World Bank.

World Bank (1994) *The World Bank and Participation*, Washington: World Bank, Operations Policy Department, September.

World Bank (1995) *Workers in an Integrating World*, Oxford: Oxford University Press.

World Commission on Culture and Development (1995) *Our Creative Diversity*, Paris: UNESCO.

Zambrano, Angel (1987) 'Asociaciones de vecinos y procesos de democratización', in Luis Gomez Calcagno (ed.), *Los movimientos sociales: democracia emergente en el sistema politico venezolano*, Caracas: CENDES.

Zamora, Ruben (1995) 'Foreword', in Fred Rosen and Deidre (eds), *Free Trade and Economic Restructuring in Latin America*, New York: Monthly Review Press.

Index

accumulation, 1, 2, 4, 7, 8, 11, 14, 16, 18, 19, 21, 45, 53, 54, 55, 56, 57, 59, 66, 96, 98, 107, 114, 116, 129, 146
Africa, 10, 12, 21, 23, 26, 27, 46, 61, 63
Aglietta, M., 10, 146
Alfonsin, R., 78, 82
Alimir, O., 53
Argentina, 6, 22, 24, 25, 47, 49, 50, 52, 53, 54, 56, 64, 78, 80, 82, 84, 85, 86, 89, 95, 119, 123, 125
Asia, 2, 4, 7, 11, 14, 17, 21, 22, 26, 27, 42, 43, 44, 46, 49, 50, 61, 129
Asian, 2, 14, 42, 44, 50
austerity, 23, 66, 78, 79, 81, 82, 83, 85, 86, 87, 89, 91, 106, 108, 116, 123

banks, 6, 14, 34, 96
Barnet, R., 2, 146
Barrig, M., 107
Belaunde, President, 78
Bell, D., 102
Benjamin, T., 111, 114
Bienefeld, M., 11, 13
Bolivia, 29, 30, 31, 50, 54, 56, 67, 69, 70, 71, 73, 80, 81, 85, 87, 90, 91, 116, 118, 119, 123, 132, 133, 141
Botz, D., 114
bourgeoisie, 24, 137, 138, 142
Brass, 106
Brazil, 6, 47, 49, 50, 51, 53, 54, 56, 64, 78, 79, 80, 81, 82, 85, 88, 89, 90, 91, 95, 96, 116, 117, 118, 119, 123, 124, 125, 132, 141
Bretton Woods, 5, 61
Brill, H., 10
Bucaram, A., 123
Burt, J.-M., 33

Caldera, R., 85, 87, 89, 90, 124, 125
Calderon, F., 108, 110
Candia, J.M., 127

capital accumulation, 1, 2, 4, 11, 16, 21, 45, 53, 55, 56, 57, 59, 66, 107, 129
capital flows, 6, 23
Cardenas, C., 125
Cavallo, D., 82
Cavanagh, J., 2
Central America, 31, 119
CEPAL, 41, 49, 54, 56, 61, 73, 74, 75
Chiapas, 20, 89, 99, 100, 111, 112, 114, 115, 117, 118, 119, 120, 130, 133, 135, 136, 138, 139
Chile, 22, 23, 29, 35, 41, 43, 47, 49, 50, 51, 52, 53, 54, 55, 56, 63, 67, 124, 125
China, 50
Chossudovsky, M., 14
Civic Alliance, 131
civil society, 19, 41, 44, 61, 63, 67, 70, 71, 72, 84, 100, 107, 120, 121, 122, 129, 130, 135, 136, 139, 140, 141, 143
class, 1, 2, 4, 5, 8, 11, 12, 18, 19, 20, 21, 22, 23, 24, 25, 27, 29, 30, 32, 34, 41, 42, 43, 44, 53, 57, 66, 67, 70, 71, 73, 74, 77, 79, 81, 83, 85, 87, 89, 90, 91, 92, 93, 94, 95, 97, 98, 99, 100, 101, 102, 103, 104, 105, 107, 108, 109, 110, 111, 112, 113, 115, 116, 118, 120, 121, 122, 124, 126, 127, 128, 129, 132, 134, 137, 138, 140, 141, 143
Collor, F., 80, 81, 82
Colombia, 49, 51, 52, 54, 56, 67, 117, 124, 133
comparative advantage, 23
CONAIE, 118
Cordova, D., 86
Cornelis, L., 25
Council on Foreign Relations, 16
crisis, 3, 4, 5, 7, 13, 17, 22, 23, 44, 61, 63, 64, 65, 66, 67, 79, 89, 90, 93, 94, 95, 97, 102, 106, 117, 121, 127, 129, 130, 142, 146
currency, 6, 23, 66, 79, 106, 126

Index

de la Cruz, 110
de la Madrid, 78, 89
debt, 6, 7, 22, 23, 24, 34, 44, 55, 63, 64, 65, 78, 79, 80, 82, 83, 90, 95, 96, 97, 105, 106, 117
decentralization, 8, 15, 19, 28, 30, 32, 65, 66, 67, 68, 69, 70
democracy, 15, 16, 61, 63, 68, 70, 71, 75, 94, 100, 101, 107, 109, 111, 115, 121, 122, 127, 135, 136, 137, 138, 139, 140, 146
democratic, 4, 15, 16, 44, 49, 66, 68, 72, 73, 75, 90, 102, 106, 118, 124, 125, 129, 138, 139, 140, 143, 144
dependency, 22, 97, 102
dependency theory, 37
deregulation, 6, 10, 23, 63, 66, 81, 96, 97, 106
development, 1, 2, 3, 4, 5, 6, 7, 9, 10, 11, 12, 13, 16, 17, 18, 19, 20, 21, 22, 28, 29, 30, 31, 35, 36, 37, 38, 39, 40, 41, 42, 43, 44, 48, 49, 51, 52, 54, 56, 57, 58, 59, 60, 61, 62, 63, 65, 66, 67, 69, 70, 71, 72, 73, 74, 75, 78, 80, 83, 85, 94, 95, 96, 101, 102, 104, 105, 111, 122, 128, 129, 130, 131, 142, 143, 144, 146
Development Dialogue, 37
division of labour, 4, 6, 7, 144

ECLAC, 29, 32, 38, 41, 42, 43, 44, 61, 65, 72, 142, 143
Ecuador, 54, 67, 68, 73, 117, 118, 119, 123, 133
El Barzon, 25
El Salvador, 47, 50, 54, 117, 118, 133
electoral process, 19, 20, 92, 93, 118, 133, 142
electoral processes, 19, 92
employment, 4, 8, 14, 24, 25, 26, 27, 29, 35, 40, 45, 47, 48, 51, 52, 53, 55, 56, 58, 62, 65, 66, 74, 78, 79, 81, 82, 83, 84, 86, 87, 88, 91, 96, 117, 127
Europe, 4, 9, 11, 14, 57, 104
EZLN, 99, 100, 112, 115, 120, 132, 134, 135, 136, 137, 138, 139, 140, 141

FDI, 7
Federal Reserve Board, 5
Fernandez, R., 86
FMLN, 118
Foncodes, 33
Forbes 400, 26
Fordist, 4
foreign direct investment, 7
foreign exchange, 6
FOSIS, 29, 35, 36
free market, 15, 21, 23, 50, 61, 64, 78, 80, 81, 83, 84, 85, 90, 91, 92, 93
Frente Amplio, 124
Fuentes, L.A., 32
Fujimori, President A., 33, 80, 83, 84, 85, 86, 90, 125
FUSADES, 53

G-7, 2, 16
Garcia, A., 78, 79
GATT, 9, 10
General Agreement on Tariffs and Trade, 9
globalism, 3, 10
globalization, 1, 2, 3, 10, 11, 12, 13, 15, 16, 17, 18, 19, 39, 142, 144
Golden Age, 5, 61
Gortieri, C., 33, 69
Goulet, D., 38
governance, 16, 102
grassroots, 30, 31, 63, 73, 122
Green, D., 95
Greenberg, J., 112, 114
Griffin, K., 1, 11, 13, 146
growth, 1, 4, 5, 6, 7, 8, 10, 13, 14, 15, 17, 18, 21, 22, 26, 32, 40, 42, 43, 46, 49, 50, 52, 59, 61, 62, 64, 66, 78, 81, 82, 84, 86, 92, 94, 96, 97, 101, 129, 130, 146
Guatemala, 73, 138

Hammarskjöld, D., 37, 128
Harvard Business Review, 6
hegemony, 5, 94, 108
Heritage Foundation, 9
Hobsbawm, E., 117, 133
Honduran Fund of Social Investment, 32

Index

Honduras, 32, 33
Hunter, A., 108

IADB, 22
IDB, 11, 28, 33, 65, 68, 143
IFIs, 2, 6, 11
ILO, 9
IMF, 2, 9, 11, 16, 22, 23, 26, 28, 29, 44, 63, 65, 66, 78, 79, 81, 82, 83, 87, 88, 89, 92, 125, 143
imperialism, 2, 3, 12, 15, 20, 102, 137, 144, 146
indigenous, 30, 34, 36, 37, 39, 68, 70, 71, 73, 99, 100, 101, 108, 109, 111, 112, 113, 114, 115, 117, 118, 119, 120, 121, 127, 133, 134, 135, 136, 137, 138, 139, 140, 141
industrialization, 2, 5, 38, 42, 146
International Labour Organization, 8
International Monetary Fund, 2, 12
International Trade Organization, 9
investments, 6, 7, 54, 69, 95, 96
ISI, 42

Jamaica, 63
Japan, 5, 14
Jazairy, I., 56
Jelin, E., 108
jobs, 8, 17, 45, 46, 78, 81, 86, 89

Kapstein, E., 16
Keynes, J.M., 11
Khan, R., 14, 146
Knight, A., 106
Korten, D., 38
Kurtzman, J., 6

labour, 4, 6, 7, 8, 9, 10, 16, 17, 18, 19, 22, 23, 24, 25, 27, 33, 45, 46, 47, 48, 49, 50, 51, 52, 53, 55, 56, 57, 58, 59, 64, 66, 78, 80, 82, 86, 87, 92, 95, 96, 97, 98, 102, 105, 107, 109, 112, 114, 117, 125, 127, 144
LaCalle, L., 80
Laclau, E., 109
Latin America, 3, 7, 8, 13, 15, 17, 19, 22, 23, 26, 27, 28, 31, 41, 42, 45, 46, 47, 48, 50, 52, 53, 54, 55, 56, 57, 58, 60, 61, 63, 64, 65, 66, 67, 74, 75, 77, 80, 89, 91, 96, 99, 100, 101, 104, 105, 106, 108, 111, 115, 117, 120, 121, 123, 126, 127, 128, 136, 137, 141
LDCs, 26
liberal democracy, 15, 16, 107
liberalization, 1, 6, 10, 15, 23, 47, 66, 95
Lipietz, A., 10, 146
Lira, E.A., 34
loans, 6, 7, 14, 78, 79, 82, 83, 84
Lozada, G., 87, 90

MAI, 9
maquilladora, 47
Marcos, F., 27, 115, 118, 121, 135, 136, 138, 140
Marx, K., 4, 24, 37, 56, 57, 59, 100, 102, 103, 104, 105, 107, 108, 110, 113, 114, 118, 120, 128, 129, 134, 136, 137, 146
MDCs, 26
means of production, 9, 17, 23, 63, 74, 105, 112, 114, 117, 120
Menem, C., 80, 82, 83, 84, 85, 86, 87, 89, 90, 125
Mercosur, 96
Mexico, 6, 25, 28, 29, 30, 31, 33, 35, 47, 49, 50, 51, 52, 53, 54, 56, 58, 59, 67, 68, 69, 73, 78, 80, 84, 85, 89, 90, 99, 100, 111, 114, 115, 117, 123, 125, 126, 130, 131, 133, 134, 135, 136, 138, 139, 141
military, 15, 22, 23, 36, 63, 66, 77, 78, 82, 83, 84, 89, 92, 94, 106, 108, 126, 127, 129, 135, 136, 138
Mills, C. Wright, 102
modernization, 2, 5, 23, 38, 85, 93, 102, 146
Montesino, 54
Movement of Landless Workers, 116
Movement of Women in Struggle, 25
Multilateral Agreement on Investment, 9
multinationals, 97, 98, 125

NAFTA, 96, 115, 125
nationalism, 5, 125
neoclassical, 21

Index

neoconservative, 60, 63, 66, 127
neoliberal, 12, 15, 16, 19, 20, 22, 23, 25, 26, 27, 28, 29, 31, 32, 34, 38, 39, 41, 42, 43, 44, 53, 60, 63, 64, 69, 75, 77, 78, 79, 80, 81, 82, 83, 84, 85, 86, 87, 88, 89, 90, 91, 92, 93, 94, 95, 96, 97, 98, 99, 101, 102, 110, 115, 116, 117, 118, 119, 120, 121, 122, 123, 124, 125, 126, 129, 130, 131, 132, 133, 134, 138, 141, 142, 143
New Economic Order, 19
New Social Movements, 99
New World Order, 9
NGOs, 28, 30, 31, 36, 39, 63, 64, 72, 118, 122, 128, 130, 131, 134
NIDOL, 6, 7
North America, 11, 14, 104, 115, 125
NSP, 29, 31, 35, 66
NWO, 9

OECD, 7, 9, 26, 27, 45

Paraguay, 90, 91, 116, 117, 118, 119, 133, 141
participation, 15, 16, 28, 29, 30, 31, 32, 34, 38, 39, 40, 41, 44, 49, 52, 60, 61, 62, 63, 65, 66, 67, 68, 70, 71, 72, 73, 75, 109, 122, 129, 130, 142
participatory, 19, 38, 49, 60, 62, 63, 66, 71, 72, 73, 75, 103, 123, 124
Patel, S., 4, 5
Perez, 80, 87
Peru, 33, 35, 47, 50, 51, 52, 53, 54, 56, 64, 73, 78, 80, 83, 84, 85, 112, 119, 125
Petbon, T., 125
Petras, J., 10, 121, 136
political economy, 5, 21, 103, 146
Popular Participation Law, 31, 70, 71
Portillo, L., 28
postmodern, 20, 100, 101, 102, 104, 105, 106, 107, 108, 110, 111, 112, 113, 116, 120, 127, 132
poverty, 14, 27, 28, 29, 31, 32, 34, 35, 36, 43, 47, 58, 62, 64, 65, 80, 81, 83, 84, 85, 86, 87, 89, 90, 91, 114, 128, 139, 144
PREALC, 45, 143

privatization, 7, 10, 23, 47, 80, 81, 82, 87, 88, 89, 93, 98, 123
Procampo, 34
productive transformation, 8, 38, 42, 44, 45, 47, 48, 49, 56, 58, 59, 75
productivity, 4, 5, 7, 25, 34, 45, 49, 50, 51, 52, 55, 56, 57, 61, 87, 96
proletariat, 17, 25, 108, 114, 137

resistance, 2, 13, 16, 18, 20, 25, 28, 41, 64, 87, 95, 99, 101, 106, 108, 109, 111, 112, 116, 118, 121, 122, 123, 125, 129, 132, 136, 142
Robinson, W., 8, 16
Rosenbluth, G., 53
Rousseau, J.-J., 101

Sachs, I., 27, 38, 40
Salinas, C., 33, 69, 80, 89, 138
Samper, E., 124, 125
Sanchez de Losada, 85
Sanguinetti, J., 78
Santos, M. dos, 108
SAP, 15, 22, 23, 24, 26, 28, 49, 63, 64, 66, 77, 78, 85, 88, 94, 95, 97, 98, 106, 130
Sarney, J., 78, 79
Schuldt, J., 38
Smith, A., 22, 74, 112, 113
social justice, 31, 38, 40, 100, 101, 108, 115, 121, 137, 138, 140, 146
social liberalism, 29, 30, 38, 65, 122, 142
social movements, 20, 71, 85, 91, 99, 100, 101, 104, 105, 107, 108, 109, 110, 111, 116, 120, 121, 122, 124, 127, 128, 129, 132, 134, 142, 143
solidarity, 29, 30, 71, 130
Sondereguer, M., 108
South Commission, 9
South Korea, 2, 7, 22, 50
speculative, 6, 7, 18, 55, 84, 96, 97
stagnation, 23, 65, 71, 80, 88, 106, 126
Stroessner, A., 91
structural adjustment, 9, 13, 17, 22, 23, 26, 27, 28, 30, 31, 33, 42, 46, 47, 49, 60, 63, 64, 65, 66, 77, 78, 79, 99, 102, 129

subsidies, 23, 25, 66, 81, 83, 86, 125
Sunkel, O., 38, 75
surplus labour, 9, 17, 26, 57, 58, 114

tariffs, 9, 82, 95
Third World, 4, 61
TNCs, 2, 6, 7, 11, 14, 40, 138
Touraine, A., 120
trade, 1, 5, 6, 9, 10, 14, 23, 24, 42, 58, 63, 80, 82, 85, 87, 88, 89, 95, 97, 98, 141
transformation, 2, 8, 26, 37, 38, 42, 44, 45, 47, 48, 49, 56, 58, 59, 63, 71, 75, 99, 102, 105, 107, 109, 112, 113, 140, 141
transnational, 1, 2, 6, 12, 19, 24, 125
Trilateral Commission, 2

UNCTAD, 6, 7, 9, 146
UNDP, 2, 10, 12, 14, 30, 32, 38, 44, 72, 129, 143, 146
UNICEF, 30, 38, 129, 143
UNIDO, 12, 14, 30, 146
United Nations, 5, 19, 30, 35, 143
UNRISD, 63, 72
Uruguay, 10, 22, 54, 56, 78, 80, 119, 123
Uruguay Round, 10

USA, 5, 6, 8, 9, 14, 15, 16, 27, 35, 44, 51, 58, 106, 115, 131, 137

Vargas Llosa, 83
Venezuela, 47, 52, 53, 54, 56, 64, 80, 85, 87, 89, 95, 123, 124, 125

wages, 5, 8, 13, 14, 18, 22, 25, 27, 33, 35, 45, 47, 48, 49, 51, 52, 53, 54, 56, 57, 58, 59, 64, 81, 82, 83, 87, 89, 97, 112
WEF, 2
welfare, 1, 4, 11, 23, 29, 32, 43, 62, 78, 83, 91, 95, 129
women, 28, 29, 39, 62, 65, 107, 109, 119, 127
World Bank, 2, 9, 11, 12, 15, 16, 22, 23, 26, 28, 30, 31, 32, 44, 45, 46, 47, 48, 49, 50, 51, 55, 56, 57, 58, 59, 61, 65, 66, 68, 69, 72, 73, 74, 75, 78, 79, 82, 83, 106, 128, 129, 130
World Economic Forum, 2
World Trade Organization, 9
WTO, 9

Zamora, R., 80, 81, 88, 126
Zapatista, 20, 89, 90, 115, 120, 121, 125, 134, 135, 137, 138, 139, 140
Zedillo, E., 31, 85, 89